Goddess Shift

Women Leading for a Change

edited by
Stephanie Marohn

www.GoddessShift.com

Elite Books, Santa Rosa, CA 95404, www.EliteBooksOnline.com

Library of Congress Cataloging-in-Publication Data

Goddess shift : women leading for a change / edited by Stephanie Marohn. — 1st ed.
p. cm.
ISBN: 978-1-60070-067-5
1. Women—Case studies. 2. Leadership in women—Case studies. 3. Self-realization in women—Case studies.
HQ1155.G63 2010
305.42092'2—dc22

2009051986

Cover design by Victoria Valentine
Typeset by Karin A. Kinsey

Printed in USA by Bang Printing
First Edition

10 9 8 7 6 5 4 3 2 1

CONTENTS

Part V: Speaking Truth to Power

Part VI: The New Marketplace

Part VII: Visionary Medicine

Part VIII: Living Goddess Wisdom

Stephanie Marohn is the author of eight books, including *Audacious Aging* (the previous anthology in the Elite Books series), *The Natural Medicine Guide to Autism*, and *The Natural Medicine Guide to Bipolar Disorder*, as well as more than fifty magazine and newspaper articles. Her work has also been included in poetry, prayer, and travel-writing anthologies. In addition to her writing, she runs Angel Editing Services, specializing in books on body-mind-spirit topics. She is also the guardian of the Animal Messenger Sanctuary, a safe haven for farm animals, and has a practice in Healing Touch for Animals.

♪ Introduction ♪

The River She Is Flowing
Stephanie Marohn

I was in my twenties when I read *When God Was a Woman,* by
Merlin Stone.* It was life changing for me, as it was for many
other women in the 1970s when it was published. I remember
turning the pages in amazement as I read that there had been a
time before the patriarchy that was angering me so when women
were honored and the divine was the Goddess. It raised fresh anger in me that this information was kept from us. If children had
been taught this history throughout time, the world would look
quite different. Instead of the devaluation of women around the
world that I found so painful to contemplate, there might actually
be reverence for both the feminine and the masculine.

How thrilled I am then, thirty years later, to see this reverence
flowing through the human race and to watch us returning to balance! As a species, we are in the midst of a remarkable shift from
division to oneness, from exploitation of nature and each other to
reverence for our planet and all beings on it, from self-interest to
responsibility. We are moving from the head to the heart, from the
Age of Power to the Age of Compassion. The return of women to
the world table makes this shift possible.

---

*   I tried to find Merlin Stone to ask her to contribute a chapter to this book but was unable
to locate her. Merlin, if you are reading this, my deepest thanks to you.

In order to return to the table, we have had to step out of victimhood into goddesshood, find the Goddess within, that is, empower ourselves, recover our voices, and return to honoring ourselves as women. To my joy, I see that girls and young women of the future may not have to go through this process because they will have grown up in a world that honors girls, boys, women, men, and indeed all beings.

Goddess Shift: Women Leading for a Change is a celebration of our new community, the vision of a more just and loving world. Gathered in this book are some of our living goddesses who have much to say about what women bring to leadership, how women can empower themselves, and how women are creating change in all walks of life.

Part I of the book looks at the shift that carries the hope for the survival of the human race and the planet. Part II reveals our roots in the sacred feminine and details this ancient history that is still unknown to many. Part III explores the Goddess within and how women can connect to their inner knowing and strength. The chapters in Part IV are by women who have forged their own paths, staying true to who they are. In Part V, we hear from women inside the institutions of politics and religion. Part VI explores how women leaders are changing business and the professional world. In Part VII, we see how women are transforming the field of medicine. Part VIII gives us life wisdom from some of the most famous women in the world.

May this book send flowing through you the celebration of life that is the Goddess!

Part I:
The Shift

Photo credit: Richard Carter

Riane Eisler, PhD, is the only woman among twenty great thinkers including Hegel, Marx, and Toynbee selected for inclusion in *Macrohistory and Macrohistorians* in recognition of the lasting importance of her work as a cultural historian and evolutionary theorist. She is also included in the award-winning book *Great Peacemakers,* as one of twenty leaders for world peace, along with Mahatma Gandhi, Mother Teresa, and Martin Luther King. Among her numerous writings is the bestselling *The Chalice and The Blade: Our History, Our Future.* Desmond Tutu hailed her latest book, *The Real Wealth of Nations: Creating a Caring Economics,* as "a template for the better world we have been so urgently seeking."
www.rianeeisler.com, www.partnershipway.org

CHAPTER ONE

The Way of Partnership

Riane Eisler

Our search for a better world is urgent because what we are seeing now is an unsustainable system reaching its logical end. I don't identify that system by any of the conventional categories—religious or secular, northern or southern, eastern or western, capitalist or socialist—because those categories don't describe the core configuration of what we need to leave behind nor the core configuration of the kind of social system, family system, educational system, religious system, and economic system that we need to build. My research has identified the core configurations of these two underlying human possibilities, and we have today an urgent necessity to shift from the domination system, which is what we've been primarily living under, to a partnership system. By partnership, I don't just mean working together. I mean a system that really works for people and for the planet.

In prehistory, there was a reverse transformation, from the partnership to the domination system, which I tell about in *The Chalice and the Blade*. That earlier transformation was from cultures that were oriented more to the partnership. They were more egalitarian, they were less violent, and they did not rank one half of humanity over the other half. There was a much more equal partnership between the two halves of humanity: women and men. The chalice and the blade are two symbols of power. The blade is an appropriate symbol for a domination system: the power to dominate, to control, to destroy, to take life. But there's another power, the chalice, which is the power to give life, to nurture life, to illuminate life. Archaeological evidence and myths that have survived show us that this was the power that was venerated in these earlier societies before the shift to a domination system.

The shift did not just occur in Old Europe. It happened worldwide. After *The Chalice and the Blade* was published in China, for example, a group of scholars at the Chinese Academy of Social Sciences wrote a book called *The Chalice and the Blade in Chinese Culture*. They showed that the shift occurred in Asia as well. In fact, the shift occurred in all the major early cradles of civilization, including Africa and South America. We not only have archaeological data pointing in that direction, but also stories. Every society has stories of this earlier time. For example, the *Tao Te Ching*, the classic work by Lao Tzu, written around 600 BC, tells us that there was a time—and it's very specific about it in terms of gender relations—before the yin, or feminine principle, was ranked under the yang, or male principle. It specifically says it was a time when the wisdom of the Mother was still honored and it was a period that was more peaceful and more equitable. You find these stories everywhere.

Despite the archaeological evidence, there is a big ideological struggle about whether there ever was or ever can be—which is the implication here—anything other than the domination system. That system is one of top-down authoritarian control in *both* the family and the state, a system that ranks one half of humanity over the other, and subordinates anything, whether it resides in a woman or a man, that is stereotypically considered soft or feminine, such as caring, nonviolence, and caregiving. This results in a high level of violence and abuse, because how else do you maintain these rankings of domination, be it men over women, men over men, religion over religion, race over race, or humans over nature? The conquest of nature that people used to celebrate is, of course, all part of the domination system.

Again, there are stories that tell us of the shift, such as the Babylonian story of how a new god called Marduk, a very violent god, creates the world by dismembering the body of the Mother Goddess, of Tiamat. Obviously, that's a shift and a metaphor for what was actually happening.

Disequilibrium Then and Now

One theory for why the shift occurred is ridiculous. It says it happened when men finally figured out that males have a role in reproduction. Though they saw animals mating and then having offspring, they couldn't figure it out, the story says, and when they did, they were so brutish that they immediately turned and subordinated women. That's a dominator story.

The story that I think makes the most sense and has the most support, both in terms of the archaeological evidence and in terms of what we know about climate changes preceding and during this period of the shift, which was not a short period, is that in the more arid areas, as the climate became drier and drier and there was more desertification and more scarcity, the domination system began. After a while, as the climate changes got worse, these people invaded, in incursion after incursion, the more fertile areas where a partnership-oriented system existed, where the life-giving powers of woman and of Mother Earth were honored.

I'm not saying these partnership societies were perfect. It's odd, though, that people accept all kinds of horrible things in domination systems as just the way things are, but when there's an alternative and it isn't perfect, it's dismissed. Instead, we perpetuate the domination system as the way humans are by nature. We teach this to children. Look at the so-called caveman cartoon, the famous one where one hand is holding a club or weapon and the other hand is dragging a woman by the hair. People think nothing of showing that to little children whose critical mental faculties have yet to be formed. We know from neuroscience that they don't form until much later. So the notion that that's how it has always been, and by implication that's how it has to be, is inflicted on us from an early age. That's why stories of origin are important, and especially so now because we need to effectuate the shift from domination systems to partnership systems if we are to survive.

We need to learn the lessons of history and change our policies and our practices, toward nature's life-sustaining activities and away from the devaluation we inherited from earlier more domination-oriented times of the caring for life, of the life-sustaining activities stereotypically relegated to women and to sissy men, men who aren't *real* men. We've got to recognize that we inherited a gender system of values that has not only been terrible for girls and women worldwide, but has negatively affected us all. In devaluing what in domination systems is stereotypically associated with women and the feminine, we devalue the very qualities that make us human: a caring consciousness. This is not an issue of women against men. It's an issue of freeing both women and men from the straightjacket of these dominator gender stereotypes.

Disequilibrium impels the shift. In prehistory, the disequilibrium was brought about by climate change and subsequent incursions of nomadic tribes. In areas where there was drought and farming was no longer possible, herding became the primary technology. These nomadic people then overran the settled people. Our shift today started hundreds of years ago with the shift from an agrarian technology to an industrial technology. That destabilized a lot of things. The destabilization accelerated further with the shift from the industrial to the postindustrial society. Our current disequilibrium opens the door for understanding that what people used to accept as just the way things are, doesn't have to be that way. There is a natural human wish for more caring connection, for more peace, for a more fulfilling existence—which means not just meeting everyone's material needs, which we really need to figure out how to do, but also our emotional and spiritual needs—so that our great human capacity for caring, for empathy, for creativity can be freed.

We cannot build a more balanced system on an imbalanced foundation, which is the devaluation not only of women but also of anything stereotypically considered feminine, such as caring for people, caring for a clean environment. There is a connection between the devaluation of women and the destruction of the environment. I sometimes say this as a joke, but women would never have created nuclear waste with no idea of where to put it. It's not because women are better than men, but because we've been taught to accept the notion that someone, namely a woman, will come and clean up men's messes. It's all interconnected, and what my work does is connects the dots. One of our important projects at the Center for Partnership Studies is the Spiritual Alliance to Stop Intimate Violence because as long as we don't stop traditions of domination and violence against women and children, as long as children learn that it's okay to use violence to impose your will on others, we can't seriously speak of a peaceful world.

When we look around at the world, we see that we've created so much of it, both for good and for ill. We've created the bad parts: the mix of high technology and an ethos of conquest and domination, including conquest of nature. But we've also created incredible marvels: art, music, beautiful architecture, and wonderful social inventions, not just economic and material ones. We are partners in our own evolution, and now is the time when we need to create the social system that will support rather than inhibit our enormous biological capacity for caring, for consciousness, for empathy—all qualities that we so need now.

Partnership Resurgence

All through recorded history, which has been largely dominator history, there have been partnership resurgences. In *The*

Chalice and the Blade, for example, I talk about the early Christian movement as a partnership resurgence. After all, what was Jesus teaching? If you look at it from a gender perspective, in terms of the engendered values, he was teaching stereotypically feminine values of caring, of empathy, and of nonviolence, certainly not the way *real* men are supposed to behave in dominator systems. In modern history, the eighteenth-century Rights of Man movement (though it was only for men, and men of a property elite at that), the movement for the rights of women, and the abolitionist movement were all challenges to traditions of domination. The Rights of Man movement challenged the hallowed tradition of the so-called divinely ordained right of kings to rule over their "subjects." The women's movement challenged the so-called divinely ordained right of men to rule over the women and children in the "castle," a military metaphor, the castle of their home. The abolitionists and then the civil rights movement later challenged the so-called divinely ordained right of one race to subordinate, oppress, and even enslave another. The environmental movement challenges the once-hallowed conquest of nature. The peace movement challenges the domination model of war. All of these are partnership resurgences.

Caring Economics

Another movement is required to shift our economic system from the dominator to the partnership model. The real wealth of our nation and of the world is not financial. We need economic measurements, economic rules, and economic practices that give visibility and value to the most important human work: the work of caring for people, beginning in early childhood; and the work of caring for nature. This need seems obvious, but we have to go much deeper to get there. Just putting "caring" and "economics" in the same sentence causes people to do a double take. This is largely due to the devaluation of the feminine, so caring is commonly regarded as economically inefficient.

In my book *The Real Wealth of Nations: Creating a Caring Economics,* I provide evidence after evidence that giving visibility and value to the work of caring and caregiving is much more economically efficient. For example, in the market economy, the companies that appear regularly on the Working Mothers or the Fortune 500 best companies to work for—that is, companies that have more caring policies—have a much higher return to investors. It makes sense. When people get good health care, good childcare, flex time, and paid parental leave, they work hard because they want that company to succeed. There are companies that are maintaining these even in the midst of the massive budget cuts we are seeing. They are the companies that are going to make it.

It can't just be companies, however. We need government policies that support this work. Take health care. The American car manufacturers that went bankrupt were at a tremendous competitive disadvantage with those nations that have national health care. You would think that they would agitate for that, but we have become so brainwashed, about socialism and this notion of "the nanny state"—again, devaluing the feminine, the caring. We need to move beyond socialism and capitalism to what I call partnerism, to a caring economics.

Sweden, Finland, and Norway have been tremendously successful in making this change. At the beginning of the twentieth century, these nations were so poor that people fleeing famine populated American states, for example, Minnesota. Today, because these Nordic nations invested more in caring and caregiving, they are invariably in the highest ranks of both the United Nations Human Development Report and the World's Economic Forum's Global Competitiveness Report. It is not coincidental that these nations are also nations that moved more to the partnership side. They have more democracy, not only in the state, but also in the family, as contrasted to the authoritarian, top-down family structure of dominator regimes. And women have much higher status; consider that approximately 40 percent of their national legislators are female.

Today we're talking about a triple bottom line, which includes people and nature, not just financial profit. What my work shows is that the three are inextricably interconnected. Policymakers, especially during the last thirty years of regression to the domination side, have taken the position that there is always enough money for weapons, war, prisons, and the military but no money for the stereotypically feminine activities and programs—caring for people, health care, and childcare.

We need to understand that these are values. Once we become aware of the values that stem from a domination system, we can change them. We can change the ridiculous situation of professions that don't entail caregiving earning much higher pay than caregiving professions. We think nothing of paying plumbers $50 to $100 an hour, but the person to whom we entrust our children, not our pipes, gets only $10 an hour and no benefits. That makes no sense. The government needs to invest in this high-quality human capital that economists keep telling us we need for the postindustrial knowledge information economy. That means investing in high-quality childcare, in parenting education, in stipends for parents, in paid parental leave, and in social security credits, like Norway has, for the first seven years of caring for a child. These things all make a lot more economic as well as human sense.

I believe that to get people to change you can't just exhort them to be nice. You have to show them that it will benefit them and then they will work to change the economic measurements, the economic rules, and the economic practices.

Transformative Leadership

We can all be leaders in this shift, not only to a different economic system but to what underlies economics, which are cultural values. I'm now teaching online for a master's and doctoral program in transformative leadership at the California Institute of Integral Studies. Transformative leaders are people who understand the difference between a domination system and a partnership system and that we have to look at factors not considered in the conventional left-right, capitalist-socialist, or East-West conversation. We have to consider the construction of the primary human relations between women and men and parents and children, because they have such systemic effects. Transformative leaders are grounded in the interventions that will produce a cascade of systemic effects for cultural transformation. For example, one of my students, a minister, is applying what she has learned in creating ceremonies at her church for children to learn about the shift from domination to partnership. Another student, a corporate executive, is working on changing his corporate culture in a partnership direction. You apply it wherever you happen to be, but you also apply it politically, which is extremely important. We need to change the political and the economic conversation.

I'm passionate about the shift from domination to partnership, not only as a scholar, a writer, and a teacher, but also as a mother and grandmother deeply concerned about the future that our children and grandchildren will inherit. I invite people to join the partnership movement. Whether you're working on the environment or against rape or against discrimination, it's all the same thing—a partnership movement. All of us can share in the excitement of being agents of transformation, of being transformative leaders.

Jean Shinoda Bolen, MD, is a psychiatrist, Jungian analyst, clinical professor of psychiatry at the University of California–San Francisco, and internationally known speaker who draws from spiritual, feminist, Jungian, medical, and personal wellsprings of experience. She is a Distinguished Life Fellow of the American Psychiatric Association and the recipient of numerous other professional honors and awards. Among the many books she has authored are *Goddesses in Everywoman*, *The Millionth Circle*, and *Urgent Message from Mother*. She is featured in the Academy Award–winning antinuclear documentary *Women—For America, For the World*, and the first of the Canadian Film Board's *Women and Spirituality* trilogy, *Goddess Remembered*. www.jeanshinodabolen.com, www.5wcw.org

CHAPTER TWO

Gather the Women

Jean Shinoda Bolen

This is an amazing and very good time to be a woman. The human race is growing up, potentially, from just taking from the planet to taking responsibility for the planet. And the major focus or the major potential for us getting through this transition well has to do with women stepping up and bringing what we know, feel, and perceive into the conversation to shift consciousness for humanity.

Women are vital to this because women are the empathic gender. Not every woman fits the description when you describe the differences between the genders, but overall, women are the empathic gender. Women have the ability to reduce stress by talking about the situation and learning from each other or from others. In relating, the level of oxytocin, the maternal bonding hormone, goes up and stress goes down, which facilitates dialogue. Men as a gender respond to stress with fight-or-flight. In fight-or-flight, which is enhanced by testosterone and is an adrenaline reaction, stress begets competition, the need to have power over. And "power over" is the problem. To talk about the return of the feminine in any form is to say, "Time for patriarchy to recede because patriarchy has reached a certain pinnacle and is now bringing an end to the planet as we know it."

Women are biologically set up to step forward with what is needed right now, which is a different response to the great change and stress in the world today. The emphasis of the women's movement on the need to empower women and provide a voice has taken root in a great many women. In fact, one of the things that is delightful about being a third-phase aged woman now is that we are numerous and, given our numbers and what we learned from our involvement in the women's movement, the possibility of being an influence is very great. There are times of transition when individuals acting together do make a difference. This was true in the historical shift from the Dark Ages to the Renaissance, for example. It is like a teeter-totter in which people at the center can tip it in either direction. I think women influenced by the women's movement are that critical group that can shift things away from the brink.

The Grail Carriers

The story of the grail, which could heal the wounded fisher king and restore the wasteland, was a story that didn't work a thousand years ago. Now we get it. The wounded fisher king is a symbol of patriarchy and as long as that patriarchy rules, the kingdom is psychologically and spiritually a wasteland, and our planet could literally turn into a wasteland. The healing element is the sacred feminine brought by individual women out of the unconscious into the world. This is the return of the goddess, the concern for life, the interdependence of life, and the empowerment of the feminine. Every woman who brings this into the culture is a grail carrier. We could call this shift the return of the sacred feminine or, as I once described it, the "Age of the Daughter."

The Great Mother is archetypal so she is in our psyche. Anything that humanity has experienced deeply over the millennia is represented in the collective unconscious or morphic field of the human race. When we turn inward, we invite connection with something that has been suppressed, welcoming it back into the psyche. Reconnecting with the Great Mother is an awareness that God or divinity was once revered as a great goddess that brought us into the world. In Greek mythology, Gaia was "out of which everything was born," which is true. All life on this planet has come out of the body of Gaia, or the planet. The Gaia hypothesis, which is that there is an ongoing life to this planet and new forms evolve, shows us that there is a homeostasis that occurs and we are part of it. We are not separate from her.

I think one of the major shifts in the evolution of humanity began when we saw the image of Earth from outer space in 1968, just as the women's movement was emerging. To see Mother, separate from us, was highly significant. Not only did we see that she is beautiful, but against the void of space, we saw that she's all we have. If something happens to her, if we ignite nuclear winter, the beauty, this gorgeous planet of which we are so fortunate to be part, will be gone, as we know it. I think that this was a new consciousness that came into humanity's collective psyche.

The return of the sacred feminine, the age of the daughter, is evolutionary; that is, it's part of the human species' story. We have now the possibility of living up to our name: *Homo sapiens sapiens* (*sapiens* means wisdom). The quality of wisdom we need comes from the feminine in both men and women. It has to do with recognizing interdependency and being able to work collaboratively for the common good. It is a capacity to listen and to be empathic and to not use power to dominate.

Our current remarkably symbolic president, Barack Obama, is married to a strong, grounded woman, and this pair represents the shift that we are in the midst of, because it's a shift in which patriarchy ends by the bringing of the best in the masculine and feminine together in a conscious partnership or relationship. Obama is not "a father's son." There is a difference in archetype between "a father's son" and "a mother's son."

Fathers' sons are brought up with the values of patriarchy and seek to extend the authority of the family name, the tribe, the nation, or the fraternity. Fathers' sons together act in a competitive, testosterone-driven risk-taking way and lose empathy and actually a quality of thinking. There's some good research on this. The answer to the question "What were they thinking?" is that they weren't. They were caught up in the frenzy of alpha-male competitiveness and the inflation that power brings.

Mothers' sons respect and know that the contribution of their mother—the personal mother or maternal figure that helped them grow into manhood, the Great Mother, the feminine—is something of great value. This is what men who are in relationship with the feminine bring into culture. They understand that the competitive drive, which is a masculine trait, needs to be balanced by the empathic wisdom of the feminine through mother, wife, and friends.

Worldwide Circle

The shift is happening in pockets all over the world. When I wrote *The Millionth Circle: How to Change Ourselves and the World— The Essential Guide to Women's Circles* in 1999, it was on the edge of being an idea whose time had come. The idea behind the millionth circle concept is the allegorical story of the hundredth monkey and the principle that when a critical number of any species learn, perceive, or do something different, it reaches a tipping point and that which was resisted or not known becomes the new norm. The hundredth monkey, like the millionth circle, is a metaphoric number, rather than an actual number. It refers to the number, whatever it might be, that when reached becomes the tipping point.

Having lived through the women's movement of the 1970s, I knew the power of circles. The movement began with and was carried forward by groups of women in consciousness raising groups, supporting each other to tell the truth and encouraging each other to do whatever it was that would help to bring equality to their lives and to the world. The seventies became the decade of the women's movement and brought with it evolutionary social change. The grass roots—ordinary women learning together, raising consciousness, moving out from our groups to change what-ever we individually took on as our assignment—changed the world. That's how the hundredth monkey phenomenon works, how the millionth circle works.

The circles this time have a spiritual center, which is a return to what we as human beings naturally have: a natural affinity for the numinous. We've been worshipping since people started painting in caves forty thousand years ago. Spirituality and religion are two different things. Spirituality is an innate element in our spiritual-psychological makeup as human beings. And then we have religion. The three major religions were founded in a highly patriarchal tribal time. They grow out of what we would psychologically call a hugely dysfunctional family setting.

The circles forming today are outside of that patriarchal setting where obedience to authority is the rule. The third wave of the women's movement, as I see it, is to bring peace to the world. The first wave was political, to get the vote. The second wave was the further empowerment movement of the 1970s. The third wave, the one we are in now, is the spiritual wave. Spirituality can move consciousness forward in a different way from empowerment.

The Millionth Circle led to the formation of the Millionth Circle Initiative, which I didn't form but was invited to be part of. It came out of a workshop at the World Parliament of Religions in South Africa. The Millionth Circle Initiative is the idea of seeding circles (mostly of women, but of men and women too) with a spiritual or sacred center until the critical mass shifts and ends patriarchy and we come into balance. As a result of the initiative, there is now a millionth circle movement quietly moving through the grass roots and a World Day of Circles of Compassion in Geneva on the United Nations calendar.

It is often a series of synchronicities that lead up to the creation of an idea, a book, or a movement. One of the things that affected me through synchronistic connection was the phrase "gather the women." Words sometimes touch others deeply. These three words touched me deeply and I wrote *Urgent Message from Mother: Gather the Women, Save the World.* I really got it that gathering the women is what we need to do. The book supports the intention of another grassroots organization, Gather the Women, which advocates forming circles all over the world.

It was a natural step from the Millionth Circle Initiative to becoming an advocate for a fifth women's world conference. The fourth of these UN-sponsored conferences was held in Beijing in 1995, and more than forty thousand women attended. There, Hillary Clinton spoke the iconic line "Women's rights are human rights and human rights are women's rights," which still isn't true even now in so many parts of the world.

If we bring women's wisdom, empathy, and voice into humanity's consciousness now, the transition zone we're in could go positive. We can do this by empowering women through circles with a spiritual center and accelerating the whole movement by convening a UN-sponsored fifth world conference on women. United Nations sponsorship makes it a goal for 192 member states and allows for attendance by women from third world countries that otherwise wouldn't give the women visas or support. We need to raise consciousness about what is happening to women around the world and also make known the existing United Nations resolutions that, if implemented, would go far toward restoring balance to the world. For example, UN security resolution 1325, which is referred to as the Women's Peace and Security Resolution, acknowledges that women as a gender have something to bring to the peace process table. Small countries have acted on this, but it hasn't happened in the Middle East where the people that determine the fate of the Middle East and therefore perhaps of the planet are all competing alpha males.

This is also true in many African countries. The stellar exception is Liberia where grassroots Muslim and Christian women, who prayed together and demonstrated together for peace, brought the warlords who were Muslim and the tyrant who was Christian to the peace table and followed through. Liberia is now the least corrupt of African countries and the only one with a woman president. In Rwanda, after the horrible eight hundred thousand murders, mostly Hutus murdering Tutsis, but also vice versa, it was women who created a peaceful transition. Now in their elected democracy, there are more women in their equivalent of parliament than any other country in the world.

Coming together is powerful, and the Internet has enlarged our ability to influence one another and influence the world. With one to two hundred thousand people attending, with satellite broadcasts bringing in the whole world, the fifth women's world conference will be a major influence on both world culture and consciousness.

The Goddess and the Third Wave

All of my books are about individuals having meaning to pursue. In *Urgent Message from Mother,* I urge a whole generation of women to step up to make a difference, but I always recognize that it depends on whether it's meaningful to you, whether it's fun for you, and whether it's motivated by something deep within you, and motivated by love. In *Goddesses in Everywoman,* which was published in 1984, I wrote that we have different goddesses or archetypal patterns in us, and that if we can embody them, if we can grow into them, and have them be a part of us, not take us over but be a part of us, then we live from our depths.

My involvement as an activist and my depth work as a Jungian analyst came together in this book. Gloria Steinem wrote the introduction, which happened because I had been the voice of reaction against the American Psychiatric Association after the referendum to not support the ERA passed. The next annual meeting after that referendum was to be in San Francisco, which is my home area. Motivation to speak up and protest comes from an inner voice that says, "Silence is consent," which led me to become an activist and to make a connection with Gloria Steinem.

As a Jungian analyst, I realized how woefully wrong the Freudian view of women was. Carl Jung's archetypal realm of listening to dreams and the collective unconscious made sense to me. His view of women had also been affected by being a part of the nineteenth- and twentieth-century patriarchal view of women, but it was a much kinder view. Still, it too had limitations. At the time of writing the book, I was developing what I came to call a "binocular" perspective of women's psychology. In my practice, in my friends, and in myself, I could see the archetypal patterns that affected women from within. I could also see and feel the powerful effect of expectations or stereotypes on women.

So I came up with this book that sees us as needing to raise our consciousness about two separate powerful effects that shape who we are: the archetypes in us and the stereotypes that act on us. I could not have written the book had I been born at a different time; ten years earlier, ten years later, I probably wouldn't have written that book. There was something about being at a time, again, of transition, and stepping up to the plate. That's how *Goddesses in Everywoman* came about.

I wrote about the archetypes that were represented by the classical Greek goddesses and how there is diversity and complexity among us and within each of us. I used the Greek goddesses because they lived under patriarchy and responded in their various ways because of the kind of pattern, or archetype, each one was. It was a nonpathological way of understanding their strengths and their vulnerabilities. It was the timing and the message that made *Goddesses in Everywoman* a bestseller in the 1980s, and the book is still quite alive and well now.

I wrote *Goddesses in Older Women: Archetypes for Women Over Fifty* when I was old enough to write it. In that book, I used some ancient goddesses from other cultures because the Greek goddess-es didn't have, for example, a goddess of compassion like Kwan Yin; or the power of an outraged goddess like Kali, whom I called "the enough is enough" archetype; or a goddess of healing laughter, like Baubo once was.

Knowing our goddess heritage is important because it gives us our lineage. Learning that people once worshipped divinity as the Great Mother and that women are made in her image affirms the feminine and women, which patriarchy has demeaned and deval-ued. At this time of historical shift, it matters that there are moth-ers' sons, grail-carrying daughters, and a grassroots circle move-ment, all of which can together bring about an evolutionary shift.

Barbara Marx Hubbard, regarded as Buckminster Fuller's philosophical heir, is a social innovator, speaker, author, educator, and leader in the new worldview of conscious evolution. In 1990, she cofounded the Foundation for Conscious Evolution, with a global educational curriculum focused on developing the next stage of human evolution. She is the producer and narrator of an award-winning, ongoing DVD series entitled *Humanity Ascending: A New Way Through Together.* Among her books are *The Hunger of Eve: One Woman's Odyssey Toward the Future* and *Conscious Evolution: Awakening Our Social Potential.* www.barbaramarx hubbard.com; sign up for her free newsletter at www.evolvingnow.com

CHAPTER THREE

The Evolutionary Woman
Barbara Marx Hubbard

I view the rise of women as an evolutionary event. There have been great women in the past, but we've never had the planetary conditions that we have now. The key condition is we have realized that we're hitting a limit to population growth: One more doubling of the population and we will all be destroyed.

No matter what the culture in which women have found themselves, whether the goddess culture or the patriarchy or everything in between, it has been the evolutionary reality that we were reproducing the species. People had five to ten children and died young. Then suddenly, in the 1960s, it became obvious that if women continue to reproduce at the maximum, we will destroy all life. So not only did we have the women's movement, the cultural change, the social change, and the space program, but we also had this evolutionary factor that we were not to reproduce up to maximum.

I think what has happened is that, at the very deep psychic and even hormonal level, women's creativity and yearning to express life purpose and unique talent had to come forward. I call that yearning the rise of the feminine cocreator. This is beyond any specific desire to be equal to men or to be able to win in the existing world. It's comparable to the passion of birth. When you're pregnant with a child, you're yearning for that child. It feels to me, as a woman who is now eighty and has had five children, that what happened in our generation is that women were turned on to life's purpose as an evolutionary phenomenon and they had to break through the patriarchal culture. In the 1950s, when I got married, we had to break through the idea that women did not have a major identity beyond wife and mother. We had to break through the glass ceiling of many of the existing systems.

Giving Birth to the Authentic Feminine Self

The evolutionary crisis we're facing is not only about the population. The economic system, the political system, the environmental system, and the energy system are not sustainable. So women are literally shifting internally to the impulse to give birth to the authentic feminine self—its expression, its work, and its contribution to the human family. This is an obvious evolutionary reality. In addition, women are living longer lives. We used to feel old at fifty, and menopause used to be a sense of aging and somehow losing our attractiveness or meaning. Now what's happening is that a woman over fifty is a young woman, and during the period of life when we are no longer producing eggs and reproducing, we are producing the authentic feminine self. We're giving birth to the self in the world.

As someone who has been through this whole thing, I experienced the cultural impact of the 1950s when I was a wife and mother and totally accepted that that was my main work, even though I'd been to Bryn Mawr, had a degree in political science, and wanted to go to Washington DC and get a job. Instead I got married, got pregnant, had a baby, and then another baby, and another. I had a sense of duty that I was here to reproduce and take care of my husband. When I got really depressed in my late twenties with all these children that I deeply loved, it became obvious to me that something was missing. Then I read Betty Friedan's *The Feminine Mystique* and saw it wasn't missing for me alone, that it was widespread, particularly among educated women in the United States, where we had the freedom but didn't have the identity, the image, or the greater purpose.

In my depression, I began to reach out and I discovered Abraham Maslow and his well-known book *Toward a Psychology of Being*. Maslow was studying well people rather than sick people. And the characteristic of wellness, which he called self-actualizing, was that beneficent, self-actualizing, joyful people have one thing in common: chosen work they find intrinsically self-rewarding as a service to at least one other. So here's the key: If you are not vocationally driven to be a mother and you are a mother, the mothering is not the full expression of who you are. For many women, who are having fewer children by choice, or no children, or chosen children, the energy that is in the woman's body and psyche, capable of transformation, of unconditional love of the unknown child, is rising in feminine creativity.

After reading Maslow's book, I called him up, told him that his book had saved my life, and asked to take him to lunch. I had to step out of my role; I had to do something. And he accepted my invitation. At the lunch, I told him that I had the sense of something great coming, that there was a potential for the future. I wasn't sure what it was, but I somehow had to have a part in it. I had had one brush with my local Freudian analyst because I was depressed, and his diagnosis was that I was neurotic. The Freudian analysis of somebody with five children who thinks there's a lot more, that she hasn't fulfilled herself yet, is that she is sick. It wasn't that at all. It was growth potential.

So I said to Maslow, "I just felt I was neurotic, but when I read your book, I knew that there was within me a life force, that far from being sick, it was the best thing about me. And I want you to know that I intend to find as many people as I can who have a sense of what's emerging, what's creative, so that nobody has to be as stuck as I was and thinking there is nothing to be done but reproduction and trying to make everybody comfortable."

Maslow was very taken with me and said, "I'm going to give you the most precious things that I have, which is the people I have met, who have in them this flame of expectation, this sense of emergence." He gave me a list of three hundred people that he had collected over his lifetime. He called them the Eupsychian Network, *eu psyche,* for "good soul." This was before the human potential movement.

I wrote to all of them and asked them what they thought. That launched me as an evolutionary seeker.

Pioneers of Earth

At that time, there was the Soviet-American conflict and the security program was called mutually assured destruction, with fifty thousand nuclear weapons pointed at fifty thousand nuclear weapons. It was obvious to me that this security program called MAD was mad. It's so interesting that women had the cultural imprint of wife and mother only, and the men who were advocating and putting the human species at the threshold of total holocaust were called pragmatic. This was considered normal. Many years later, in the harmonic convergence of 1987, the Voice of America called me and this sort of snobby woman said, "Well, don't you think it's weird, Barbara, that people would be going to mountaintops and humming on this day?" And I said, "You know, I don't really. I think what's really weird is to get up every morning and drive to the places where they make bombs to destroy the world. That's weird."

So I jumped into the evolutionary movement rather than the feminist movement. The environmental crises and social crises that were becoming apparent in the sixties, along with viewing Earth from space in the Apollo program, led me to realize that we were emerging as a cocreative universal species. I felt like I was one of these emerging humans. This transcended being equal to men because I could see that men couldn't do this. So I skipped that middle movement, feminism, but I'm grateful to it. I had a slightly different part of the pattern to work on. I think it's all necessary. The great movements of civil rights, peace, women, consciousness—all were absolutely vital.

I don't fully understand why, but these hugely important movements didn't pick up on the evolutionary movement. The cultural, popular arc veered toward existentialism, theatre of the absurd, the pointing out of the degradation of humans. The people who inspired me, like Teilhard de Chardin, Abraham Maslow, Buckminster Fuller, and Jonas Salk, had a vision of what was emerging, but that vision was not picked up in the popular arc. Science fiction writers like Jean Roddenberry, Ray Bradbury, and Arthur Clarke moved us in the direction of something new happening, but it was in the fiction realm. I began to be a pioneer in how the emerging human potential, the emerging technological potential, and the idea of social cooperation and synergy could be the new movement on Earth.

I think it didn't happen back then because we didn't have a sufficiently obvious crisis. Now, collective awareness of crises for the survival of our species is changing everything. Global warming, the extinction of species, and the pressure that the population and the pollution are putting on the biological life support system transcend anything we've ever faced as a species. All the movements for change have brought us to an awareness, but a new movement has to be born now, *is* being born. It's a movement that I think of as global social synergy. It's a movement that requires us to stand for, map, connect, and communicate what's working in the world and begin to cultivate synergistic convergence of that which is emergent, because we cannot solve these terrible crises in a linear manner and there's not enough time.

My experience is that women have an intuition, a guidance, and an innate ability to go beyond the win-lose structures of male society into the win-win-win, synergistic, whole-system approach to the world. With women living longer, having fewer children, and having more energy, more creativity, and more vitality to express their life purpose, they are in a way the pioneers of Earth now.

The reason is that the structure of male-dominated civilization, which has been going on for five or six thousand years, has topped out. It has created all this power, but it cannot handle the complexities it has created. The structure of society is wrong for the challenges we're facing. It's all structured on separation, whether it be global corporations structured on competition, organized religion structured on divisions from other religions, or academe structured on separate disciplines. It's very hard to get a university to look at the conscious evolution of humanity as a whole. There's no field or discipline.

As the old structures that have been male-dominated and run by men are failing, there is an opening for the approach of seeing the system as a whole. It isn't just women who will do it, but women have an innate sense of the whole and when they find their life purpose within it, there's a passion and a lovingness that transcends the purely competitive win-lose structures created by men. I'm a great lover of men and the people who inspired me in my earlier life in the sixties were men. It's really interesting now, though, the men are coming to me as a woman who has seen that our crisis is a birth of a cocreative humanity. The best of men that I know are coming to the best of women, asking to be our partner.

Women have a guidance system of which men are desperately in need. In the deepest sense, that guidance system is the incarnation of the process of creation. This is my word for the evolutionary aspect of God. If you look at the fourteen billion years from the big bang to the present, and you look at the turn from energy, matter, life, animal life, human life, and now our human life trying to come together as a whole, you see a pattern of a rise of consciousness and freedom to a more synergistic order. Of cells to multicells, to animals, humans, and now to us becoming a highly complex system. That pattern, which is subjectively as well as objectively discovered (it's inside you and me), toward greater consciousness, greater freedom, and greater connectivity is actually innately feminine. It's more feminine in its nature and it's also, if you want to put gender on it, anima-animus. The animus part is the thrust to create. The anima is this whole process of connectivity and oneness.

What I've noticed in myself as a woman, the feminine cocreator type, is that I have made an internal synthesis between the creator aspect of the divine, the creator God, and the connecting, loving aspect of the creation that has traditionally been more feminine. So the cocreative woman is the synthesis right there, and she has also the passion of giving birth to the expression of her own authentic self, which goes back to Maslow's self-actualization.

The challenge for men in giving birth to their own creativity is that there is such a tradition of male dominance in that. It is very hard not to fall into that social structure. You can see what happens to someone like Barack Obama who is naturally a whole man, meaning that he has the feminine and the masculine well integrated. The system that he is at the top of is totally dominated by oppositional tactics. Win-lose all the way. When a win-win-win person is in the midst of a win-lose, oppositional structure, there's only so much he can do. The structure is based on separation and winning over one another.

The feminine cocreator that has the greatest opportunity right now is not embedded in the existing structure. The opportunities are more at the pioneer level. We have pioneers like, for example, Jean Houston, who's doing trainings all over the world in human creativity and leadership; Hazel Henderson who has ethical marketplace; Riane Eisler, with all her work on partnership and the feminine (see chapter 1). These are extraordinary women. These are not women in existing hierarchical structures. I am in awe of and admire women who can work in those structures, but they don't have a lot of flexibility. So the women and men that I look to as the leaders and pioneers are going out in front of the existing system.

My term for this type of person is a pioneering soul. Now a pioneering soul, a woman or man, is motivated from within by the impulse of evolution, the impulse of creation, and has a yearning to self-express her or his life purpose and to connect with others to cocreate. Pioneering souls tend to move toward cosmic consciousness, a more universal consciousness, rather than any dogma or existing path, but they all are spiritually motivated.

Conscious Evolution

So what we have are conscious evolution and a new spirituality. Conscious evolution means the evolution of evolution from unconscious to conscious choice. In a sense, we are the face of evolution. This is how it looks when you get to be human. When you get to see you could destroy your life support systems, this is how it looks, this is how it feels. The field of conscious evolution, which I am working to establish as an academic discipline, is one that identifies what's emergent in every field and connects it.

The new spirituality, which I call evolutionary spirituality, is inward, forward, and backward. The inward aspect is traditional; you go into the one, the source of creation, or whatever you call God. Backward means cosmogenesis; you have learned that the universe was created, is evolving, and is evolving now, that you—your atoms, molecules, genes, cells—are a resume of the whole story of creation. So inward is you are one with source and backward is you are an expression of the whole fourteen billion years of universal evolution in your body-mind. The forward part is that you are a participant in the story of evolution, you are a cocreator, your creative expression is that core of the spiral localized as you. When you find a life purpose that really touches your soul, as I've found a life purpose in communication, when you find out whatever it is that is self-rewarding and that is of service to others, you become a cocreator. When you are a cocreator, you are incarnating the divine as your own expression of creativity.

My view is that it takes time for the human species to overcome its illusion of separateness. We have a reptilian brain, a mammalian brain, and an early neocortex. We're very young as a species. We grew up in a world of kill or be killed, although nature selects for the more cooperative groups; nature has a tendency to select for that which is synergistic. Survival was extremely demanding. Evidently, evolution produced competition as well as cocreation, but now we have a different situation. In a planetary system that is now integrating itself into a whole facing common global threats, if a competitive desire for one culture to live over another continues as it has in the past, we won't survive. If we continue to grow into separate but warring states, with the degree of power we have to pollute our entire biosphere, we won't survive. That's why we have to behave differently, and that's why we *are* beginning to behave differently.

I refer to this period in human evolution as late transition. The pretransition would be human history, the last forty thousand years, in which human beings gained self-reflective consciousness and civilization itself. I think the transition began in 1945 when we dropped the bombs on Japan. Suddenly, this same species had the power to destroy, could destroy the world. So the transition from 1945 to 2009 has been learning how to use our new power, mainly science and technology, to create a sustainable, evolvable world, or not. If we don't, we can kill ourselves. And 1945 to 2009 involved a rapid learning process for a species that never had to learn this before.

Now we're in late transition. According to what scientists tell us, we don't have a lot of time to change our behavior. The timing factor here trumps any kind of linear projects. If in five or ten years we're going to have global warming, the rise of the seas, not enough food, and mass die-off, that means it's not business as usual here. And if it's not business as usual, what is it? That's where

I'm proposing massive synergistic convergence of what's working, massive communication of how to match needs with resources to achieve common goals, and massive synergistic activity using the Internet and local processes. This is my global curriculum, as I call it.

This curriculum recognizes that the whole woman, the universal woman, the evolutionary woman, the feminine cocreator is vital to the survival and evolution of our whole species.

Jane Fonda is an actor, writer, fitness maven (the Jane Fonda Workout), and lifetime activist. Her acting career spans nearly five decades, from *Tall Story* (1960) to *Georgia Rule* (2007), with many hit movies in between, including *Cat Ballou, Coming Home, Nine to Five,* and *On Golden Pond.* She is the recipient of two Academy Awards, myriad Golden Globes, and other acting accolades. She is dedicated to numerous causes, among them the empowerment of youth (see www.janefondacenter.emory.edu).

CHAPTER FOUR

Reuniting the Head, the Heart, and the Body

Jane Fonda

It was while I was laughing when I first saw Eve Ensler (see chapter 10) perform *The Vagina Monologues* that my feminism slipped out of my head and took up residence in my body, where it has lived ever since…embodied at last.

Up until then I had been a feminist in the sense that I supported women. I brought gender issues into my movie roles. I helped women make their bodies strong. I read all the books. I thought I had it in my heart and my body. I didn't. I didn't. I didn't. It was too scary. It was like stepping off a cliff without knowing if there was a trampoline down below to catch me. It meant rearranging my cellular structure. It meant doing life differently. And I was too scared. Women have internalized patriarchy's tokens in various ways but, for me, I silenced my true authentic voice all my life to keep a man. God forbid I should be without a man! Preferably an alpha male. Because without that, what would validate me?

And I needed to try to be perfect because I knew that if I wasn't, I would never be loved. My sense of imperfection became focused on my body. I hated my body. It started around the beginning of adolescence. Before then I had been too busy climbing trees and wrestling with boys to worry about being perfect.

What was more important than perfect was strong and brave. But then suddenly the wrestling became about sex and being popular and being right and good and perfect and fitting in. And then I became an actress in an image-focused profession. And, being competitive, I said, "Well, damn. If I'm supposed to be perfect, I'll show them." Which, of course, pitted me against other women and against myself.

Carl Jung said perfection is for the gods. Completeness is what we mortals must strive for. Perfection is the curse of patriarchy. It makes us hate ourselves. And you can't be embodied if you hate your body. So one of the things we have to do is help our girls to get angry. Angry. Not at their own bodies, but at the paradigm that does this to us, to all of us. Let us usher perfection to the door and learn that good enough is good enough.

There's a theory of behavioral change called social inoculation. It means politicizing the problem. Let me tell you a story that explains this. In one of the ghettos of Chicago, young boys weren't going to school anymore. And community organizers found out they didn't have the "right" Nike Air Jordan shoes. So the organizers did something differently. They invited all the boys going to school into the community center and they took a Nike Air Jordan shoe and they dissected it. They cut off one layer of the rubber and they said, "See this? This is not a god. This was made in Korea. People were paid slave wages to make this, robbing your mothers and fathers of jobs." And he cut off another slice. And so it went. Deconstructing the Nike Air Jordan sneaker so the body would understand the false god that they had been worshipping. We need to name the problem so that our girls can say, "It's not me and we're going to get mad."

We also have to stop looking over our shoulder to see who is the expert with the plan. We're the experts, if we allow ourselves to listen to what Marion Woodman calls our feminine consciousness. But this has been muted in a lot of us by the power-centered male belief center called patriarchy. I don't like that word. It's so rhetorical. It makes people's eyes glaze over. It did for me. The first time I ever heard Gloria Steinem use it back in the 1970s, I thought, "Oh, my God, what that means is men are bad and we have to replace patriarchy with matriarchy." Of course, given the way women are different from men, maybe a dose of matriarchy wouldn't be bad, maybe balancing things out. My favorite ex-husband, Ted Turner—maybe some of you saw him say it on Charlie Rose: "Men, we had our chance and we blew it—we have to turn it over to women now."

But I've come to see that it's not about replacing one -archy with another. It's about changing the social construct to one where power is not the chief operating principle.

There's this dual journey that we're on. There's the inner journey, this New Age stuff, and the other journey. Let's talk about governments first. Governments normally work within the power paradigm and governments play a central role in making us who we are. An empathic government encourages a caring people. A government that operates from a "might makes right" place creates a nation of bullies, envied by the rest of the world for its things, but hated for its lack of goodness.

I first noticed this phenomenon of government when, many years ago, I was making a movie in a little town in Norway and there was a party scene. It was Ibsen's *A Doll House*. It took three days to shoot and I had a lot of chance to spend time with the local people and I kept thinking, "There's something very different about these people. What can it be?" And as I began to talk to them, I realized it's because they felt seen by their government. They felt valued. They mattered. Pregnant women got free milk. There was maternity leave. All the things that made women's and men's lives easier were addressed by their government.

I never told these stories in a context like this, but now I'm going to tell you two stories.

I went to Hanoi in 1972, in July. I was there while my government was bombing the country that had received me as a guest. I was in a lot of air raids. I was taken into a lot of air-raid shelters. Every time I would go into a shelter, the Vietnamese people would look at me and ask the interpreter—probably they thought I was Russian—who was this white woman? And when the interpreter would say American, they would get all excited and they would smile at me.

And I would search their eyes for anger. I wanted to see anger. It would have made it easier if I could have seen what I know would have been in *my* eyes if I were them. But I never did. Ever. One day I had been taken several hours south of Hanoi to visit what had been the textile capital of North Vietnam that was razed to the ground and we were in the car and suddenly the driver and my interpreter said, "Quick, get out!" All along the road there are these manholes that hold one person and you jump in them and you pull kind of a straw lid over to protect you from shrapnel if there's a raid. I was running down the street to get into one of these holes and suddenly I was grabbed from behind by a young girl. She was clearly a schoolgirl because she had a bunch of books tied with a rubber belt hanging over her shoulder and she grabbed me by the hand and ran with me in front of this peasant hut. And she pulled the straw thatch off the top of the hole and jumped in and pulled me in after her. These are small holes. These are meant for one small Vietnamese person. She and I got in the hole and she pulled the lid over and the bombs started dropping and causing the ground to shake and I'm thinking, "This is not happening. I'm going to wake up. I'm not in a bomb hole with a Vietnamese girl whom I don't know." I could feel her breath on my cheek. I could feel her eyelash on my cheek. It was so small that we were crammed together.

Pretty soon the bombing stopped. It turned out it was not that close. She crawled out and I got out and I started to cry and I just said to her, "I'm so sorry. I'm so sorry. I'm so sorry." And she started to talk to me in Vietnamese. And the translator came over.

She must have been fourteen or fifteen. And she looked me straight in the eye and she said, "Don't be sorry for us. We know why we're fighting. It's you who don't know."

Well, it couldn't have been staged. It was impossible for it to have been staged. This young girl says to me, "It's you—you have to cry for your own people because we know why we're fighting." And I'm thinking, "This must be a country of saints or something. Nobody gets angry."

Several days later I was asked to go see a production of a play by a traveling troupe of Vietnamese actresses. It was Arthur Miller's play *All My Sons*. They want me, as an American, to critique it to say if the capitalists are really the way they look. (Two-toned saddle shoes and a polka-dot tie, and I was like, OK, that will work!) It's a story about a factory owner who makes parts for bombers during the Second World War. He finds out that his factory is making faulty parts for the bombers, which could cause an airplane crash, but he doesn't say anything because he doesn't want to lose his government contract. One of his sons is a pilot and dies in an airplane crash. The other son accuses, attacks his father for putting greed and self-interest ahead of what was right. Well, I watched the play and I kept thinking, "Why are they doing this? There's a war going on. Why are they performing *All My Sons* in North Vietnam?" I asked the director and he said, "We are a small country. We cannot afford to hate you. We have to teach our people there are good Americans and there are bad Americans, so that they will not hate Americans because, one day when this war ends, we will have to be friends."

When you come back home from a thing like that and people talk about the enemy, you think, "Wait a minute. Will we ever have a government here that will go to such sophisticated lengths to help our people not hate a country that is bombing them?"

Anyway, this is what I mean by the role of a government. It wasn't an accident that people didn't look at me during a war with hatred in their eyes. Their government taught them to love and to separate good from evil. That, to me, is a lesson I will never ever forget.

So there's a dual journey to be taken. There's an inner journey and an outer journey and there's no conceptual model for the vision that we're working for. There's no road map for the politics of love. It's never happened.

Women have never yet had a chance in all of history to make a revolution. But if we're going to lead, we have to become the change that we seek. We have to incubate it in our bodies and embody it. The teachers, healers, and activists with the most impact are always people who embody their politics.

I'm going to tell you another story. I had been living in France for eight years from 1962 to 1970 and I decided to leave my—not my favorite ex-husband, but my first ex-husband—and come home to be an activist. And I realized that in order to do that properly, I had to get to know this country of mine again. And I decided that I was going to drive across the country for two months. It was during the spring of 1970. As I was driving, Nixon invaded Cambodia. Four students were killed at Kent State, two at Jackson State, 35,000 National Guard were called out in sixteen states and a third of the nation's campuses closed down. I was arrested five times. But when I think back over those difficult two months, none of that is what I remember.

I remember a woman who was on the staff of a GI coffeehouse in Texas near Fort Hood. Her name was Terry Davis. And the moment I was in her presence, I sensed something different. It wasn't something I had been missing because I didn't know it existed. But I felt different in her presence. Because she moved from a place of love. She saw me not as a movie star, but as a whole me that I didn't even know existed yet.

She was interested in why I had become an activist and what I was doing to get involved in the movement. We were planning an upcoming demonstration and she asked my opinion. And she included me in all the decisions to make sure I was comfortable.

This was very new for me. I was thirty-one years old. I had made *Barbarella*. I was famous. But this was new to me. I saw the same sensitivity and compassion in the way she dealt with the GIs from Fort Hood at the coffeehouse. Unlike others in the peace movement at that time, she didn't judge the young men who were on their way to Vietnam. She knew most of them were from poor rural or inner city situations and had no good alternatives.

It was my first time experiencing a woman's leadership and it was palpable, like sinking into a warm tub after a cold winter. It was also my first time experiencing someone who embodied her politics, who tried to model in her everyday life the sort of society that she was fighting for. She fought not only against the government that was waging the war and depriving soldiers of their basic rights, she also fought against the sexism, the power struggles, and judgmentalism within the movement itself. During that difficult two-month trip, it was this time spent with Terry that stands out most strongly. A harbinger of the new world beyond -isms and -archy that I could envision because of her. She was in her power.

What we're seeing now is the balance so out of kilter, so barnacled with the wrong kind of power and lust. But right beneath the surface, a great tectonic shift is taking place.

I'll tell you why I know it. Have you ever been to Yellowstone National Park? Yellowstone is the place in the world, next to Siberia, where the earth's crust is the thinnest, where the molten interior of the earth pops out. Old Faithful is the most well-known example of this. But if you walk through the park, you can see steam rising above the trees and over here mud bubbling up from cracks and crevices in the crust.

I've traveled all over the world and I've seen the steam. And I've seen the mud bubbling up. And it's women and men all over the world that are starting to come through those cracks and crevices. It's an army of love and that's what we have to be. We have to ripen the time and turn that steam and those bubbles into a volcano. So let's be a volcano.

Part II:
Our Goddess Heritage

Joan Marler and Marija Gimbutas

Joan Marler, MA, worked closely with archaeologist Marija Gimbutas as her personal editor and authorized biographer. She is the editor of *The Civilization of the Goddess* (1991) by Marija Gimbutas and *From the Realm of the Ancestors: An Anthology in Honor of Marija Gimbutas* (1997). Joan has taught courses in archaeomythology at Sonoma State University, New College of California, and the California Institute of Integral Studies in San Francisco where she is a member of the adjunct faculty. She is the founder and executive director of the Institute of Archaeomythology (www.archaeo-mythology.org), an international, interdisciplinary organization dedicated to fostering an archaeomythological approach to cultural research.

CHAPTER FIVE

The Life and Legacy of Marija Gimbutas

Joan Marler

Every woman carries within her an unbroken lineage of mothers and daughters reaching back to the most ancient human communities. The imbalance of leadership roles between women and men at this time in human history is not a reflection of an innate inferiority of women that has been with us from the dawn of time, but of deeply engrained patterns of enculturation. Every woman who has tenaciously developed her potential and has risen above societal restrictions has done so in spite of external as well as internalized (learned) limitations. We are indebted to a long lineage of courageous women, known and unknown, who have dared to be themselves, to press beyond expected boundaries to model new ways of being.

One such woman, whose life's work has profound significance at this time in human history, is the Lithuanian/American archaeologist Marija Gimbutas. I first learned about this remarkable scholar from the mythologist Joseph Campbell who said that if he had known of her research earlier, he would have written some of his own work quite differently. When I heard these words, I knew that I had to meet her and to study her work.

At that time, I was producing radio programs in the humanities at KPFA FM in Berkeley, California. In 1987 I set up an interview with Marija Gimbutas for my hour-long show *Voices of Vision*. That session led to a close and fruitful collaboration that continued until her death seven years later. Since I had also worked as an editor, she asked me to edit some of her articles and eventually to work with her on her magnum opus, *The Civilization of the Goddess: The World of Old Europe* (1991), which was published as a sister volume to *The Language of the Goddess: Unearthing the Hidden Symbols of Western Civilization* (1989).

Marija Gimbutas devoted her entire life to the cultivation of a multidisciplinary encyclopedic scholarship, often in the midst of enormous challenges. She trusted her own vision, and encouraged each one of us to trust ourselves as well. "Don't be sheep!" she often said. "Do what you want to do. It's very important to be mobilized, to have determination to do what is meaningful. If you feel a need to do something, you must do it!"[1] Only then will it be possible to bring forth a new world.

War and Study

Marija Birute Alseikaite (1921–1994) was born and raised in Vilnius, Lithuania, in a family of scholars. She inherited a complex stream of cultural, intellectual, and spiritual influences, and from her earliest years, her parents (both physicians) repeatedly stressed the necessity to become thoroughly educated and to contribute to the development of culture.

Lithuania was one of the last European countries to be Christianized and many ancient traditions survived into the twentieth century. The rivers, forests, and hills were still considered sacred: "The earth was kissed and prayers were said every morning, every evening," and in the countryside, people continued their traditional ways: "The old women used sickles and sang while they worked. The songs were very authentic, very ancient.... I fell in love with what is ancient because it was a deep communication and oneness with Earth. I was completely captivated. This was the beginning of my interest in folklore."

Marija was eighteen when World War II began. In 1940, when the Soviet Union first occupied Lithuania, members of her family and friends were killed or deported to Siberia. Although the Lithuanian Uprising pushed out the Soviet troops in 1941, the German occupation soon followed. In the midst of this chaos, Marija married her fiancé, Jurgis Gimbutas, then managed to complete her master's degree in archaeology with secondary studies in folklore and philology at the University of Vilnius in 1942.

Over the next year, while living with a new infant under the pressures of occupation, she published eleven articles on the Balts and prehistoric burial rituals in Lithuania. "That clearly kept me sane," she recalled. "I had something like a double life. I was happy doing my work; that was why I existed. Life just twisted me like a little plant, but my life was continuous in one direction."[2]

In 1944, while the Soviet front was advancing on Lithuania for the second time, Marija and Jurgis fled with their baby daughter to Austria with thousands of other refugees. Despite the wartime conditions, she worked intensively on her dissertation, and when peace was declared in 1945, she enrolled in Tübingen University (in the French occupation zone) to complete her doctorate in archaeology (1946) with emphases in ethnology and the history of religion. Their second daughter was born the following year, and in 1949 the family emigrated to the United States.

Soon after arriving in America as a refugee, Marija presented herself at Harvard. Due to her excellent credentials and knowledge of most Eastern and Western European languages, she was invited to work as a researcher (eventually becoming a Research Fellow) at Harvard's Peabody Museum, and to produce texts on European prehistory. "I had such a strong determination that I started right away to do research," she said. "For three years, I wasn't given any money. I felt like a drowning person." Her book, *The Prehistory of Eastern Europe,* published by Harvard in 1956, summarized the full range of archaeological research on post-Paleolithic cultures from the Baltic to the Caucasus (in all languages up to 1955), making this material available to Western scholars for the first time. This text was followed by volumes on *The Balts* (1963), *Bronze Age Cultures in Central and Eastern Europe* (1965), and *The Slavs* (1971).

In 1963 she accepted a position as professor of European archaeology at University of California, Los Angeles, where she was described as "the one person who was, even then, revolutionizing the study of East European archaeology...[bringing together] archaeology, linguistics, philology, and the study of non-material cultural antiquities."[3]

By that time, Marija Gimbutas was known as a world-class scholar of the European Bronze Age, a period typified by male dominance, territorial aggression, and the burials of warriors with bronze weapons. After extensive travel and research in Eastern Europe as an exchange scholar, it became clear to her that the earlier Neolithic farming cultures of Southeast Europe (approximately 6500–3500 BC) were very different from the Bronze Age societies that replaced them and she was determined to understand why.

The Goddess of Old Europe

From 1967 to 1980, Marija Gimbutas was project director of five major excavations of Neolithic culture sites in Greece, Macedonia, and Italy. These early sites—and hundreds of Neolithic settlements throughout Southeast Europe—were stable, long-lived agrarian communities that produced well-constructed houses, elegant sculptural and ceramic art, and persistent ritual traditions. The richness of the cultural materials and the prevalence of female imagery so captivated her that she devoted the rest of her life to an in-depth study of the symbolism of these "Old European" societies.[4] In order to adequately investigate the symbols, beliefs, and rituals of Neolithic peoples, she developed an interdisciplinary methodology called "archaeomythology."

The Gods and Goddesses of Old Europe (1974) was the first in a series of publications in which she investigated Old European symbolism. Although most of the sculptural images presented in this book are female, the publisher refused to allow her to put "Goddesses" first in the title, deeming it "improper." When the book was republished in 1982, however, it bore her intended title, *The Goddesses and Gods of Old Europe.*

The survival of the first farmers in Southeast Europe depended on their cultivation of a sensitively tuned relationship with the cycles of the natural world. These communities not only survived, but also thrived, creating sustainable societies that lasted many hundreds of years. At the center of their survival was their ritual life and the transmission of ancestral knowledge and wisdom that guided their communities; and at the center of their ritual life was the profusion of female images. In Marija's view, this broad range of female imagery expressed essential metaphoric concepts of the sacred source of life, which she called Goddess.

"Goddess" does not refer to a female version of the transcendent monotheistic God. In *The Language of the Goddess,* Marija defines "Goddess," in all her manifestations, as "a symbol of the unity of all life in Nature.... Hence the holistic and mythopoeic perception of the sacredness and mystery of all there is on Earth."[5] Marija understood that this cosmogonic Goddess—who is One and Many—is ultimately the entire natural world, teeming with the continual cycles of new life coming into being, maturing, dying, and regenerating. To imagine the source of life as female creates a primal intimacy with what is otherwise infinitely vast.

In Marija's view, Old European symbols, burial patterns, and domestic ritual practices reflect a sacred cosmology and the centrality of women's activities within a mother-kinship system. She refused to use the term "matriarchy," which has typically implied a society dominated by women, in the same way that men dominate women in patriarchy.[6] In *The Civilization of the Goddess,* she points out that, while women were respected and honored, the sexes were more or less on equal footing. "The burial rites and settlement patterns reflect a matrilineal structure, whereas the distribution of wealth in graves speaks for an economic egalitarianism."[7]

The scholarship of Marija Gimbutas provides nothing less than a reinterpretation of the origin story of European civilization. The commonly prevailing story, which justifies male dominance, warfare, and the subjugation of women, has been used as the basic template for who we are and what we are capable of manifesting. While the Bronze Age societies did indeed express those patterns, the more ancient, Neolithic societies of Old Europe were long-lived, primarily peaceful, mature, and egalitarian. She writes:

> I reject the assumption that civilization refers only to androcratic warrior societies. The generative basis of any civilization lies in its degree of artistic creation, aesthetic achievements, nonmaterial values, and freedom which make life meaningful and enjoyable for all its citizens, as well as a balance of powers between the sexes. Neolithic Europe was not a time 'before civilization'.... It was, instead, a true civilization in the best meaning of the word.[8]

The Neolithic cultures of Old Europe can now be recognized as the earliest foundation of European civilization. This understanding has the potential to "affect our vision of the past as well as our sense of potential for the present and future."[9] In *The Civilization of the Goddess* Marija writes, "We must refocus our collective memory. The necessity for this has never been greater as we discover that the path of 'progress' is extinguishing the very conditions for life on earth."[10]

A Message from the Ancestors

Shortly after Marija died, in 1994, I had a vivid dream in which she told me she is now in the realm of the ancestors. She spoke in a fierce voice, saying, "YOU MUST REMEMBER US!" I was shaken awake with the distinct feeling that this dream was not only for me.

Marija Gimbutas reminds us that our human lineage, and our very survival, is inseparable from the life of our Mother, the Earth, and that our earliest ancestors lived this reality.

We are all ancestors in training, moving inevitably toward the ancestral realm. At this precious moment—while we are privileged to be alive—may we embrace the courage to step forward into our powers, as women of our time, to remember our most ancient birthright in order to model responsibility, wisdom, and wholeness for the younger generations and for those yet to come.

Notes

1. All quotations from Marija Gimbutas, unless otherwise noted, are from interviews conducted by Joan Marler between 1987 and 1993.
2. Joan Marler (ed), *From the Realm of the Ancestors: An Anthology in Honor of Marija Gimbutas* (Manchester, CT: Knowledge, Ideas and Trends, 1997), 11.
3. Recollection by Dr. Jaan Puhvel, Memorial Service for Marija Gimbutas, Fowler Museum of Cultural History, UCLA, March 3, 1994.
4. Marija Gimbutas coined the term "Old Europe" to refer to the Neolithic farming communities found throughout Southeast Europe and beyond, before the Indo-Europeanization of the continent.
5. Marija Gimbutas, *The Language of the Goddess* (San Francisco, CA: Harper & Row, 1989), 321.
6. The term "matriarchy" is being redefined by a number of contemporary scholars to represent the concept of balanced societies with "women at the center"—very similar to Marija Gimbutas's interpretation of Old European societies. See, e.g., Peggy Reeves Sanday, *Women at the Center: Life in a Modern Matriarchy* (Ithaca, NY: Cornell University Press, 2002).
7. Marija Gimbutas, *The Civilization of the Goddess* (San Francisco, CA: HarperSanFrancisco, 1991), 324.
8. *Ibid.,* viii.
9. *Ibid.,* vii.
10. *Ibid.*

Elaine Pagels, PhD, professor of religion at Princeton University, Mac-Arthur fellow, and bestselling author, is well known for her writing on the Gnostic Gospels, the texts of the Nag Hammadi Library, ancient scrolls unearthed in Egypt in 1945. *The Gnostic Gospels* (1979), which arose from her work with the scrolls begun during doctoral studies at Harvard, revealed to the public for the first time gospels that had been banned from inclusion in the New Testament as well as other sacred text. The book was a bestseller, won numerous awards, and was cited by the Modern Library as one of the hundred best books of the twentieth century. Her other books include *Adam, Eve, and the Serpent* and *Beyond Belief: The Secret Gospel of Thomas.*

CHAPTER SIX

What Happened to God the Mother?

Elaine Pagels

Jesus said, "If you bring forth what is within you, what you bring forth will save you. If you do not bring forth what is within you, what you do not bring forth will destroy you."

When I first read these words in the Gospel of Thomas, one of fifty-two texts in the Nag Hammadi Library, I thought, "It's not necessary to *believe* that; I just know it's true." What the Gospel of Thomas suggests is that we can find spiritual resources within. The authors of these texts are often called "Gnostics," for the Greek term *gnosis,* usually translated as "knowledge," but better as "insight." Those who used the term this way were saying that when we know ourselves, at the deepest level, we come to know God, as the source of our being. The Gnostic Gospels, written in the early centuries after the death of Jesus, actually offer not only a different view of spiritual knowledge, but also of Jesus and his teachings, of women, and of divinity itself. The banning of these texts as heretical by early church fathers who called themselves orthodox Christians shaped the collection we now call the New Testament, and was much involved in the practices and beliefs of Christianity.

Since some leaders called the Gnostics "heretics," much was left out when they were banned—and that's what I write about—no wonder it's controversial!

Just when *The Gnostic Gospels* was published, I actually dreamed that the book was bright purple! When I woke up, I realized that I felt the book was going to be seen as pornographic, in a way, because it was so revealing—and the content had so long been forbidden.

When the book came out, it was sharply attacked in the *New York Times,* on the front page of the *Book Review.* The reviewer said that books like the Gospel of Thomas were "rubbish when they were written, and still rubbish!" I was taken aback because he was a scholar who otherwise had respected and liked me—but what he said wasn't a surprise. Nobody had ever actually read these texts—they were discovered hidden in an ancient jar, buried in Egypt, in 1945, and first published in 1977—and said anything like what I was saying in this book: that the gospels of the New Testament were not the only gospels, that the inclusion of some gospels and the exclusion of others from the Bible was a decision based on the social and political situation of the time, and that the ideas the gospel authors presented were completely intertwined with social and historical circumstances, as well as politics.

Scholars studying the gnostic texts at that time thought, "Well, these heretics simply have crazy ideas." They think of God dualistically—and sometimes speak of God as "mother"—referring to the holy spirit, or wisdom—both feminine words in Hebrew. But what I realized is that if people think of God only as "king," "lord, "father"—only in masculine terms—this often means that only men are in charge. So *The Gnostic Gospels* suggests that what people called "history of ideas" is not something up there in the stratosphere—it plays out right here in the social world of human beings. Talking about religion in terms of social history was new and startling to many people, and created a lot of controversy, but many historians have come to see it that way since then.

My thinking on this actually started at a conference on women at Barnard College where I had just started to teach. Being asked to give a talk on women in the early Christian church, at first I laughed and said what I'd learned at Harvard—"We don't have any evidence about that!" But then I thought, "Wait a minute, these texts I work on are full of feminine imagery for God—and full of suggestions that women tend to like heresy—and were taking "masculine" roles in these groups that upset certain Christian bishops. So after thinking about that, I gave a talk called "What Happened to God the Mother?" in one of the early feminist conferences in the seventies. When I was showing what we found in some of these secret texts—stories about the God who says, "I am God and there is no other God beside me," and his mother, Life (the name is Eve!), speaks forth from the heavens above, and says to her son, this arrogant and ignorant creator, "Do not tell lies, Sabaoth"—about two thousand women cracked up laughing! That showed me how deeply connected our language and concepts are with our social reality.

Many of the gnostic texts—the Gospel of Thomas, the Gospel of Mary, *Trimorphic Protennoia,* the Secret Book of John, and *Thunder, Perfect Mind,* among others—speak of God in feminine as well as masculine terms, and "heretics" were also accused by their opponents for the fact that among them women participated with men in worship, teaching, and leadership.

I discovered, too, that in texts like the Secret Revelation of John, the original trinity was imagined as Father, Mother, and Son—and that suddenly made sense: Who else would you expect to find with "father" and "son"? In this secret book, Jesus says, "John, I am the one who is with you always; I am the Father; I am the Mother; and I am the Son." As I mentioned, in Hebrew and Syriac, the holy spirit, as well as "wisdom" and "life" were gendered—and feminine—words—easy, then, to imagine as feminine presences. But when you translate *Ruah,* the feminine Hebrew word for "spirit," into the Greek word *pneuma,* it becomes neuter—or masculine, in

Latin *(spiritus).* So when these terms were translated, people imagined instead a "holy spirit" that has no gender—a kind of disembodied "spirit"—and the image of the divine "mother" was lost. Yet since Jesus spoke Aramaic and perhaps Hebrew, when he spoke of "spirit," the term would have a feminine connotation—as it does in Jewish mysticism, in which terms like *Shekinah* ("divine presence") and *Ruah* (spirit) occur. We also find that in the Gospel of Mary, another ancient gospel unknown until the nineteenth century, when part of it was discovered, Mary Magdalene is seen as a disciple, and the one Jesus especially loved; and here she tells the other disciples, "The Son of Man is within you. Follow after him! Those who see him will find him."

In the *Thunder, Perfect Mind,* a divine feminine power speaks the revelation of wholeness. "Thunder" is a feminine word in Greek. The word "perfect" would be better translated *"complete mind"*—for this revelatory poem is written in paradox, suggesting that the complete mind includes very different aspects of feminine experience:

> *I am the first and the last*
> *I am the honored one and the scorned one*
> *I am the whore and the holy one...*
> *I am knowledge and ignorance...*
> *I am strength and I am fear*

The *Trimorphic Protennoia* ("Triple-formed Primal Thought") also suggests that the feminine aspect of the divine is the one immanent in the world, and in ourselves, while the transcendent aspect of God is imagined as masculine. This idea, common in Jewish mystical teaching, does, certainly, reflect an ancient—sexist—view that envisions men as "higher" than women; these texts, too, reflect the social world in which they were written. Yet sources like this do encourage people to speak of gender metaphorically and, when using anthropomorphic language for the divine, at least to use both genders!

What we often find in these secret texts are modes of perception and experience traditionally associated with women—that is, imagination and intuition. And every one of these texts was called "heretical," and left out of the New Testament canon—along with the suggestion we find here frequently that Mary Magdalene was not only one of Jesus' most trusted disciples, but, some say, his foremost disciple. She also appears as his "companion," whom he loves, but here, too, she is seen as a manifestation of divine wisdom and spirit, only figuratively, not literally, his lover and wife—suggestions that we don't find in the New Testament. In most of the Christian groups that prevailed, women were banned from taking the roles of teacher, healer, priest, or prophet. From 200 CE, we have little evidence for women taking such roles in orthodox churches; so we can see that the exclusion of the gnostic texts from the Christian canon has had serious repercussions for women ever since. With the recovery and translation of the Nag Hammadi Library, we have the opportunity to hear the voices of the "heretics" for the first time—and discover much that was left out of Christian history.

Although I don't surf the Web looking for conservative Christians, I've been told that I've been demonized often; I do know of some Christian leaders, both Roman Catholic and Protestant, who've said that I'm just out to attack and destroy Christianity. That, of course, isn't true; I love Christian traditions—but it's a love that includes deep ambivalence. While fascinated by Christian tradition, I could never swallow it whole—nor, I think, should anyone—it would be quite indigestible. Many people think either you accept what you were taught as a child, or else reject the whole thing. I think that could deprive us of a lot: of recognizing a spiritual dimension in our culture, or even in our own lives, although many of us find a spiritual dimension elsewhere—in nature, in each other, in other traditions like Buddhism.

I was brought up to think religion was obsolete, but at thirteen, I went to an Evangelical rally, and fell right in—was "born again"!

My parents were upset, having been Protestant by background but not religious (my father had given up Christianity for Darwin, and became a biologist). He thought of the Bible as a bunch of ancient folktales—which in a way it is. But I've found some of these stories to be absolutely extraordinary; they can open up aspects of experience that we might otherwise miss: This can be a revelation of the power of poetic, emotionally charged spiritual language— the poetry of the spirit. What Marianne Moore said of poetry, that it is "imaginary gardens with real toads in them," is how I sometimes think of religion—imaginary gardens, but with some real, and surprising, presences in them, as my experience suggests.

For a while I loved going to the Evangelical church, until I found it was too confining. After one of my closest friends was killed in a car accident at the age of sixteen, and church members told me he was in hell because he was Jewish, and not "born again," I quit that kind of church—it no longer made any sense to me.

But the experience I'd had there left me very much interested in finding out what had been so powerful about it: What is religion, anyway? How does it appeal to people? Now I'd say that some of us seem to need the sense of a spiritual dimension in life—I do. Yet that need doesn't necessarily lead us to religion—many people explore it in music, poetry, science, and other ways besides an explicitly religious one. I love seeing how poets, painters, filmmakers, and artists pick up some of the ideas, images, and stories that are part of religious tradition and reinterpret them, play with them, speak through them.

Sometimes I go to a local church here; after I wrote the book *Beyond Belief,* I realized that when I'd mentioned going to church, in each case it was the music that I loved most. I have found I am enormously susceptible to almost any kind of religious service— whether it's a bat mitzah or bar mitzvah, or the dances of the Hopi, or the cathedral of Notre Dame—or the mountains that I love in Colorado.

What's clearly out of date, though, is the view that Christianity is the "only true religion"—even for many people who are Christian. People engaged in spiritual exploration today draw from many traditions, just as we come to love art, music, and poetry, from all parts of the world.

I'm glad, too, that situations for women have changed so much—from the time when I first applied to graduate school—at Harvard, as it turned out—and was told that the committee had declined to accept me because I was a woman, and "women always quit." Today the graduate schools are filled with women, as are the professional schools—now, of course, the presidents of universities like Harvard and Princeton, where I teach, are women!

And our views of religion and spirituality are much more open as well. What used to be called "heresy"—choosing what accords with one's own experience and insight—is now, many of us recognize, essential for coming to know who we are, and learning to speak with our own voices. I'm amazed and grateful for the opportunities available for women now; and as for myself, feel amazingly lucky to have found work that I love to do and love to share with other people.

Zsuzsanna "Z" Budapest is a Hungarian-born writer, Dianic high priestess, and foremother of the women's spirituality movement. Z's books include *The Holy Book of Women's Mysteries* and *The Goddess in the Office*. In 1975, Z was arrested in Los Angeles on the charge of fortune telling, after reading Tarot cards to an undercover policewoman, which made her the last person arrested and tried for witchcraft in the United States. She was convicted and spent nine years in appeals, maintaining that Tarot reading is a form of women spiritually counseling women in the context of their religion. Her ultimate acquittal resulted in the law against fortune telling being struck from California law. www.zbudapest.com

CHAPTER SEVEN

Bringing Back the Mysteries
Zsuzsanna Budapest

When I was a baby, my grandmother Ilona stole me away from my house to be christened because my father had no such intentions. He said, "Let her grow up and she will choose her own religion."

This was a very radical statement in 1940. Babies usually got christened very soon after birth, and I was already three months old. Grandma Ilona worried about my immortal soul. Father was away with the military; by the time he came home, I was christened. He just turned around and went right back he was so angry.

Grandmother was a devoted Hungarian. In my country, being a Hungarian is almost a separate religion by itself. She chose me a wonderful historical name: Emese. Emese was a chieftain, and she dreamt up our country. She is regarded as the Mother of the Magyars (Hungarians). She saw us in her dream—Magyars streaming out like a river from her lap in all directions. She saw us taking back the land that Attila the Hun (a very close family) once lived on but that was now settled by Slavic nations. On this night, when Emese had this wet dream about Attila the Hun, she conceived a magical child, Almos. It was he, when grown enough to lead, who started the migration west with all the Magyars, seeking the land that had silky grasses for the horses, clear lakes and rivers, and plenty of wildlife.

So I was going to bear her name, Emese. But there was a terrible mistake. The priest said "Emese" doesn't appear to be in the Bible; it isn't even a Christian name. He stopped the christening and told my grandmother to choose another name.

Mother suggested Zsuzsanna. This name was sort of in the Bible, the story about the beautiful Susanna and three old men leering at her when she was bathing. Mother created ceramic pieces around this story of Susanna. The priest accepted this name, so I became Zsuzsanna Emese.

When I was a year old, the grown-ups planned a very special Christmas for the "child." My aunt Titi taught me a short little greeting that I was supposed to deliver in front of all my relatives. My first public appearance!

The angelic bell was rung and the door opened to the miracle of the Christmas tree ablaze with lit candles. Underneath the many presents, there was a very good-looking yellow teddy bear. I recall feeling that there was far too much fire going on. Were the grown-ups sure about this?

I recited my little verse, and even before we could sing the traditional "Menybol az Angyal" ("Angels from Heaven") song, the Christmas tree simply went up in a huge flame. My first Christmas tree burned down to the floor.

I was snatched away, but before they got to me I grabbed that yellow teddy.

Then came World War II. My family never again gathered for Christmas like that first time. Grandmother Ilona died of hunger. Grandfather refused to come down to the bunkers, shrapnel hit him in the thigh, and he later died of bone cancer. Mother and father divorced three years after their wedding. Titi taught me a new prayer. Of course it was once again to the blessed Virgin.

I rather liked the blessed Virgin. She had beautiful white-blue outfits and wore a crown of stars. Humbly she cast her eyes down, and folded her delicate hands in prayer. Yet the prayer she said was mighty: *"Where humans cannot help each other, your power could still dismiss the pain and tragedy."*

This was my only prayer, the one that I could say flawlessly.

The hardships of living in the basement on top of the coal pile we used in the winter were simply awful. We had to live with the earlier residents of the underground—the rats and mice. We all had lice in our hair and most everybody had diarrhea. Mother bound me to her belly with a big scarf. She warmed me with her own body. In these trying times, we all held together.

The Russians were coming. They said they were the liberators, and they searched for alcohol. They even drank perfume for its alcohol content. But after that, they came into our bunkers searching for women to "peel potatoes." This was their way of gathering local women to be raped. All wars sooner or later turn on women for rape.

Mother hid underneath my mattress.

I was now a toddler, feeling increasingly important. I had to defend my mother, ailing grandma, and Titi.

Then it happened. A soldier came to our door with his bayonet, started poking about underneath the mattresses. Before he could poke my mom, I jumped up and, with hands stretched out to the Great Above, I prayed my prayer, asking the Virgin to do her miracle.

The soldier was surprised. A little two-year-old girl praying to the Goddess to make him go away. Unnerved, he turned around and left us alone. My family was stunned by my brave act.

I felt like somebody else had done this, not me. It felt as though an entity had stepped in and taken over. I received a lot of grateful kisses, and I felt elevated from my toddler status to that of a brave toddler Amazon.

People from neighboring bunkers wanted me to defend them as well. They asked my mom if I could pray for them, too, defend the entire sixth floor, which now lived on coals beneath our building. My folks didn't think so, but I was on duty. I don't recall how often I repeated my brave toddler feat, standing in front of the bunker with arms outstretched, authentically praying my little heart out to the Virgin Mother.

My womenfolk did escape the rapes. Russians have a tender spot for little children. I was lucky to be a child when I confronted them.

I think these experiences were definitely the budding high priestess's first manifestations. Defending women felt like a natural act for me. My belief in the power of the Virgin Goddess was now unshakable.

In time, mythology taught me about many more Goddesses, names of old—Diana, Hecate, Artemis, Persephone, Hera, even Themis of social consciousness. In the United States, I learned of Our Lady of Guadalupe who was also a defender of women and children.

Eventually, my understanding of this power became fused with a feminist education. Male gods, nearly all old men with personality disorders, appeared to be murderous and revengeful, jealous and possessive, and insecure. Most of the male god religions (Christianity, Islam, Judaism, and their derivatives) were born within forty miles of each other. Desert religions. Scarcity informed. An eye for an eye—which leaves everybody blind. No matter what their names or culture of origin, male gods were a backlash to the earlier gentle Goddess. There may be many differences amongst the male god religions, but they warmly agreed on one point: women must be controlled. Women must be subservient to males because when god is male all men are gods.

Fast forward to my awakening as a woman via feminism. When I was thirty years old, I moved to Los Angeles. Exotic flowers in backyards, jasmine-scented air, nightingales singing all night, the ocean lapping gently at the shores—I felt I belonged in California.

Feminism to me was a life-stimulating movement. In order to create ourselves as women today, we had to learn about the women who went before us. We had heard few of their names before. We had to create women's studies in order to dig them up and learn what they have done for us.

The suffragists in particular amazed me.

My grandmother was a suffragist. Ilona, the Virgin worshipper, created schools for girls to learn to make a living.

Suffragist Matilda Joslyn Gage wrote *Woman, Church, and State* to explain how oppression emanated from male god religions. She was banned by the pope, which was something she had dreamt about, so when it happened, she was deeply satisfied.

Elizabeth Cady Stanton, with ten other sisters, rewrote the Bible. *The Woman's Bible* is still in print.

Victoria Woodhull, who ran for president even before women got the vote, was into séances, and communion with spirits.

Unlike in the suffragist movement, there was no spiritual activity in modern feminism. I wrote articles about how revolutions must have spiritual roots, how in order to resource ourselves we had to have some cosmology, and festivals celebrating nature and our lives. When I first said the word "witchcraft," there was a pregnant pause.

Then the objections came: "Yeah, that's all we need, to be called witches! It's bad enough now they call us all dykes."

My response to this was, "So? What's the worst they can do to us? Witchcraft is an honorable spirituality with female roots, wise women died for it, and there is enough left of the tradition that we can rebuild our own version."

That has become my feminism. I have blended feminism with witchcraft. My small group, the Susan B. Anthony Coven Number One, was the first political witches' group. We practiced our craft in circles under the full moon, we created songs, and we created Goddess celebrations in accord with the seasons. From thirty to two hundred women showed up at Sabbaths, always new faces amongst the familiar ones. We learned to bless each other with power, and we learned to hex the rapists, murderers, and serial killers with power as well. We matched these spells with accompanying women to police stations and bearing witness to police behavior. There began to be convictions, whereas before rapists went free most of the time. Our group was involved in a wide spectrum of political activities, from childcare to war protests, and sparked the formation of many other Goddess circles.

My soul felt it was my job to bring back Goddess rituals and customs, and remake those we can do better in modern times. With this in mind, I wrote *The Feminist Book of Light and Shadows,* which went into reprint immediately. That book has now nourished women spiritually for thirty-five years, under the title *The Holy Book of Women's Mysteries.*

Goddess spirituality gives us all equality. There is a celebration every six weeks, or more often if you add the full moon observances as well. Aligning ourselves with the Universe gives us a cosmic sense. The spirit in which we regard ourselves has changed for the better because of the influx of Goddess spirituality.

I have no idea how many women practice Goddess worship. It is good so. We should never be centralized. Let it be like wildflowers, everywhere and uncountable.

B. Raven Lee, PhD, LCSW, DCEP, a Jungian psychotherapist, Tibetan Buddhist meditation instructor, shamanic healer, and founder of Integrative Wisdom Path, has nearly thirty years of clinical experience. In her private practice in Pasadena, California, she integrates interpersonal neurobiology, clinical hypnotherapy, Reiki, energy, and dreamwork, specializing in mind-body healing, spirituality, trauma, and soul fragmentation. In addition, she presents workshops on dreams, energy healing, transformation of consciousness, and the Sacred Feminine, and leads a Celtic Dharma pilgrimage to southern France each fall. She also co-leads "The Way of the Mystic Shaman" training program. www.integrativewisdompath.com

CHAPTER EIGHT

Embodying the Sacred Feminine and Magdalene Wisdom

B. Raven Lee

> *For I am the first and the last.*
> *I am the honored one and the scorned one.*
> *I am the whore and the holy one.*
> *I am the wife and the virgin...*
> *For I am knowledge and ignorance.*
> *I am shame and boldness,*
> *I am shameless; I am ashamed.*
> *I am strength and I am fear.*
> *I am war and peace.*
> *Give heed to me.*
> *I am the one who is disgraced and the great one.*
>
> —from "The Thunder, Perfect Mind,"
> the Nag Hammadi Library

Seeing me now, it is difficult to imagine the shy, insecure young woman that I once was. Born and raised as a Catholic in Hong Kong, I was taught well to be a dutiful Chinese daughter, deferring to authorities and silencing my own voice. A crisis in 1985 awakened me from this illusion, and I was propelled on a spiritual odyssey, which has taken me on a labyrinthine path from Jung to

Taoism, Shamanism, Buddhism, and finally to the ancient religion of Tibet known as Bön. I also immersed myself in the study of energy, quantum physics, and neurobiology. It was not easy to stay connected to my inner voice and trust the visions that guided me. There were times of doubts and confusion, but I kept surrendering to this mysterious "Calling" in my soul. It was not a path of certainty, practicality, or logic, but one of Sacred Feminine wisdom. Having found refuge in Bön Buddhism, I settled into a decade of teachings and practice, after which my journey took another interesting turn.

In March 2007, I received an e-mail from Rene, whose friend connected us as he thought we shared mutual interests. "Would you like to come to southern France to present at a conference on Tibetan Healing practices?" he wrote from his home base in Nepal, having moved there years ago from Belgium. In the course of a series of convoluted, disorganized messages from him, the conference turned into a solo presentation. Inclined to say no to traveling across the continent at the request of this stranger, I was nonetheless intrigued by his passion for Celtic Dharma. "There is a connection between the Celtic tradition, the Holy Grail, and Tibetan Buddhism," he told me.

As a Jungian therapist, I had studied Celtic symbolism and the Grail legend and its archetypes. Hearing that they are related to Tibetan Buddhism captured my attention. I needed more information to make the leap, however, so I sought guidance in a shamanic journey. In a trance state, I flew out of my body and landed in front of an arched doorway set into the side of a mountain. I knocked on the door and asked for permission to cross the threshold. I could smell a strong, musty, yet sweet scent. It was dark inside and, as my eyes adjusted, I saw that I was in a cave. A circle of men appeared. I glimpsed strange insignia on the front of their clothing, which looked ancient and sacred. In the center of the circle was a stream of golden light in which stood a female figure. I asked for her name. She spoke only one word, "Trust!" This was reason enough for me to make the trip. As soon as I got this answer, I was back in my body, which was vibrating and filled with bliss.

In October 2007, four of my meditation students accompanied me to southern France. None of us knew how it would unfold. I arrived a day earlier and there at the airport, smiling at me, was Rene, long hair flowing, dressed in a purple Tibetan silk shirt, which seemed to me later to be the only garment he owned. Over dinner that evening, Rene showed me a book of local power places. As I flipped the pages while relishing my steamed mussels and salad niçoise, I suddenly froze when I saw a picture of the arched doorway. "Is there a cave behind this door?" I asked.

Rene nodded, amused by the sudden change in my demeanor. "This is the cave of Saint Tropheme, who is also known as Lazarus," he said. "Mary Magdalene's brother."

All at once, a golden light appeared, and I knew beyond a doubt that the figure I had seen was none other than Mary Magdalene, whom I had only known as the penitent prostitute healed by Jesus.

The others arrived soon after, and the message of the Feminine wisdom began immediately when one of the participants misplaced her medication. Her initial anxiety was met by an outpouring of love and support, which transformed her frenzy into laughter and joy.

We began the pilgrimage the next day with a meditation in a small village where an iron statue of the Black Madonna resides, three stories high. The love that we had all felt the previous evening emerged again, and I sensed a vibration coursing throughout my body and an opening of the earth beneath my feet. I felt as if I were on fire, engulfed by an inexplicable joy that spilled into my dreams that night. Carried by this profound energy, we left Nice the following day and headed west to visit the sacred sites of Mary Magdalene. According to legend, she fled Jerusalem for Egypt and then later sailed to southern France, where she spent the rest of her days in meditation at the Cave of Sainte-Baume, near Aix-en-Provence.

Each day we deepened our journey until we came to an obscure village in a mountainous region. As I stood inside an ancient church, I experienced entering a portal to another dimension, and a feminine energy came repeatedly with messages and guidance. I was drawn to sit on a bench where I looked up and saw a small arched window carved into the walls. Through it, I could see a faint white image along the side of a mountain. As I stared into that white spot, a pulsating energy entered my forehead, shot through the back of my head, and straight out another window into the fields beyond. I was in a powerful meditative state filled with white light, and I heard a voice that whispered, "Remember! You are to be the beacon for the Feminine." This was the same message I had received in a dream two decades earlier, and then in 1996 at Agung Temple in Bali.

"That is the cave of Saint Tropheme," said Rene, affirming my experience, as if he understood my connection to the Sacred Feminine and Mary Magdalene. He proceeded to explain that the land we were standing on was part of a mandala known as the Isle of Crystal, or Caer Sidi, which was a sacred archaeological site of the Celts, Cathars, and Knights Templar. "It was an ancient seat of rituals and initiation for healing and divination practices," he told me, "which descended originally from the Black Sea and the Sino-Asian Steppe, and continued into early Roman times, encompassing the Holy Grail legend."

Rene was giving me information far too complicated for me to digest. He added that beginning in the 1970s, Tibetan monasteries were built on Celtic power places in France and the United Kingdom. By 1985, Tibetan lamas, including Rene's teacher, recognized that this mandala site where we stood could be a portal to the Celtic Annwn (the land of ancestors, or the Tibetan Shambhala) if approached with the right "keys," which Rene had been researching for three decades. "You must have a strong karmic connection to this place," he said, smiling mysteriously.

Returning to Los Angeles with visions and messages, I dove into reading *The Gospel of Mary Magdalene* (translated and with commentary by Jean-Yves Leloup; Inner Traditions, 2002), which contains the teachings she received directly from Jesus. Discovered in an antique shop in Egypt in 1896, the parchments of this gospel are housed in the National Museum of Berlin. Authorities estimate that the original, written in Sahidic Coptic language, dates from around 150 CE. Portions of the gospel of Mary Magdalene were also found with the Gnostic Gospels unearthed in Egypt in 1945 in the find that became known as the Nag Hammadi Library. I was surprised to discover that Mary Magdalene was revered in early Christianity, until 591 CE, when Pope Gregory pronounced her a prostitute, though there was no evidence to support this claim. Even more astounding, the Catholic Church did not retract this false proclamation until 1969. This significant piece of Christian history has been relatively unknown, however, and her teachings were not only effectively obscured, but also unrecognized by the church.

Though I had left the institution of Catholicism, I retained a strong connection to the essence of Christ consciousness and the Blessed Mother. I had not been drawn to Mary Magdalene, however, even when *The Da Vinci Code* became so popular. But here I was, making a detour from my Buddhist readings to immerse myself in the study of ancient Christianity and Gnosticism, and reading everything I could about "the exiled bride." Though popular fiction had revived interest in Mary Magdalene, it focused on whether she was Jesus' consort and whether she carried the lineage of his royal blood in her womb. Few addressed the wisdom of her teachings, and the fact that she was Jesus' closest disciple, the one who first saw Jesus alive at the tomb. Far from being a repentant sinner, Mary Magdalene was the apostle of the apostles, the leader of Christ's disciples.

Hearing her messages resounding in my heart, I opened her gospel teachings, and as I read the first few lines, I immediately understood the subtle esoteric meanings, which were strikingly similar to those found in Tibetan Buddhism, especially Dzögchen, the highest, innermost teachings. Throughout the thin volume, Jesus repeated these words to Mary Magdalene, *"Those who have ears, let them hear."* These were new teachings given to Magdalene, and were meant only for those who have cultivated a subtle perception, a special kind of understanding regarding the interrelatedness of all existence, and direct knowing that is all-embracing. *"All that is born, all that is created, all the elements of nature are interwoven and united with each other.... Everything returns to its roots.... Attachment to matter gives rise to passion against nature.... There is no sin. It is you who makes sin exist, when you act according to the habits of your corrupted nature. This is where sin lies."*

The message is that everything in life is impermanent, interdependent, and what causes suffering is our attachment to matter. The Greek for "sin" means "to miss the mark." Jesus was teaching that sin arises from identifying with our attachment, from separating the self from the other, which misses the mark of our true nature. This ignorance of our essence and the wisdom of impermanence generates illusion and attachment to matter, resulting in suffering. The essential teachings of Christ echo the central tenet of Buddhism, known as the Four Noble Truths. The gospel continued to describe a path out of suffering through developing *nous,* an intermediate realm between the physical and spiritual. This place of the imaginal is where the subject and object become interdependent and, from the seamless sense of reality, visionary knowledge can spontaneously arise. The portal to *nous* is through the feminine awareness.

The reawakening of the Sacred Feminine is being ignited in our collective consciousness, which has been dominated by patriarchal values and fed by a climate of consumerism, exploitation, greed, and aggressive takeovers. The effect of the imbalance is now being felt globally. Mary Magdalene, who has been denounced, suppressed, and vilified, symbolizes the return of the Sacred

Feminine wisdom to its rightful place. She is calling us, especially women, to honor our bodies and the earth as sacred vessels to birth *gnosis,* a direct knowing of our true nature. The cultivation of this special form of conscious attention and wisdom, as her gospel teaches, is through stillness, silence, and breath. Through this entering of the inner world, the Magdalene wisdom teaches us to honor collaboration, harmony with all, including the environment, and to become compassionate guardians of our universe.

As we move toward embodying these sacred messages, I am reminded of one word that kept coming to me during the first pilgrimage to France. I was sitting on a grassy knoll facing the cave of Saint Tropheme, settling into my breath and stillness. I felt a gentle breeze caress my face and then "Unity" floated like a mantra into my senses. It spoke of a union between East and West, spirit and nature, and the feminine and masculine principles.

In recognizing how far I have traveled from the fearful, suppressed woman I once was, I am in awe of the transformation of which we are all capable and which gives faith to the power of change. Globally, we are on the edge of a precipice, and this crisis can serve as an awakening to the purpose and meaning of our lives. Through cultivating the Sacred Feminine mind, which can balance the masculine energy in cocreating a new partnership for the future, we can come together to journey into our inner Isle of Crystal, and bring this message of balance and compassionate wisdom to others.

Photo credit: Bert Meijer

Starhawk is a lifelong activist, a pioneer in the revival of earth-based spirituality and Goddess religion, and the author of *The Spiral Dance: A Rebirth of the Ancient Religion of the Great Goddess*, *The Fifth Sacred Thing*, and *The Earth Path: Grounding Your Spirit in the Rhythms of Nature*, among numerous other books including a children's picture book, *The Last Wild Witch*. She consulted on and contributed to the acclaimed *Women's Spirituality* film trilogy by the National Film Board of Canada. Director Donna Read and Starhawk subsequently formed their own film company, Belili Productions. Their 2004 documentary, *Signs Out of Time*, is about archaeologist Marija Gimbutas (see chapter 5) and is narrated by Olympia Dukakis (see chapter 40). www.starhawk.org, www.reclaiming.org, www.EarthActivistTraining.org

CHAPTER NINE

Rooting Spirit in Nature
Starhawk

We're at a time of huge cultural change. Our environmental situation alone is calling us to make enormous changes to cope with climate change and keep it to a level that will continue to make civilization possible and won't doom our descendents to being wandering bands of root gatherers up around the Arctic Circle. We must transform our technology, our economy, and our energy systems, and we must do it all very quickly, within the next couple of decades. This is the time crunch. This is when we can no longer do that thing we do as humans of procrastinating and putting off making changes.

We need to make a shift in consciousness that is related to the whole question of women and women's roles. The shift is away from looking at the world as a set of isolated objects to seeing the world as a set of relationships. And women, of course, are relational beings; we see the world that way.

I call the shift the Return of the Goddess or the Great Transformation. The environmental crisis now is a very strong driver of this shift, but the shift began many decades ago back in the late sixties and seventies as women woke up and said, "Wait a minute, we've been working on civil rights and we've been working for the rights of all kinds of oppressed people and, you know what, we're actually oppressed too, we ought to do something about that and not just accept it as a condition of our being." That insight prepared the ground for where we are today. Of course, there is still a long way to go.

Some of us feminists from the seventies don't get a lot of credit these days, but I believe we deserve credit for some enormous changes that have happened. I tell the story of my Goddess daughter. When she was about nine, her dad and I were talking politics and we mentioned Barbara Boxer. She said, "Who's Barbara Boxer?" and I said, "She's our senator." She looked up at me, with this look of wonder and delight on her face, and she said, "We have a Senate?"—like in *Star Wars*. After her dad and I stopped laughing, I explained to her about the Senate and the House of Representatives, and that Barbara Boxer is our senator, Diane Feinstein is our other senator, and Nancy Pelosi is our representative. She thought for a moment and then asked, "Hmm, do they all have to be girls?" Her experience of life at age nine is so completely different from mine at age nine when it never occurred to me that women could be senators or representatives or presidents or in any position of power, responsibility, and authority in our culture.

My mother was a professional woman, though. She had to be because my father died when I was five, so she raised my brother and me. She was a social worker, which is a traditional woman's career, but she loved her work. She was fascinated with human beings and how we thought, how our minds and our emotions work, and she shared that with me from the time I was very young. I credit her with being a great role model, who showed me that a woman's focus doesn't have to be wife and mother only, that there are many other things a woman can do. In my work that focuses on relationships, I again credit her with being a model for this, because that was her whole view of the world, her whole interest was in human beings, our relationships with one another. She was particularly an expert in loss and grief and how that affected people, coming very much out of her own experience as a widow.

My mom came from an Orthodox Jewish family, but she and my father were both of a generation that rebelled. My mother, in some sense, rebelled rationally. I don't think she believed in the religion of her childhood. She practiced it sporadically. When she'd decide that it was important to have a cultural identity, she'd light the candles on Friday night and then it would sort of peter out when she got busy with other things. I went to Sunday school and Hebrew school when I was in high school, not because she forced me to, but because I was interested. I think her real spirituality was an understanding of the profound gifts that grief can give to us if we honor that process. If we allow it to go forward and don't try to suppress it or rush through it, but let it have its way, grief is a profoundly deepening process that leads to deeper compassion and ultimately to creativity and resolution.

Loss and grief are profoundly at the heart of spirituality and religion because that is how we often cope with the experience of loss, death, and grief. We turn to grapple with those big questions: Why are we here and what is life about? What happens after we die? Do we continue to exist in some form? Is there some consciousness that continues after death? Those are the questions that spirituality poses, and because my father died when I was so young, they've always been present for me.

The Mother Earth Transition Team

These questions have informed my work in the Goddess movement and in political activist movements. Now I'm doing a lot of work with Reclaiming, which is a network of many different communities around the United States, Europe, and other parts of the world that share a commitment to an earth-based spirituality and are also engaged with social issues and political questions. Reclaiming runs classes, workshops, trainings, and public rituals, as well as Witch camps, which are weeklong intensives to learn some of the basics of the Wiccan spiritual practices and tradition and also to work on both personal healing and community building. The global justice movement, in which I'm also involved, and Reclaiming overlap to some extent, but they also have large areas that are quite different from one another. There are many people in Reclaiming, for example, who are more focused on spirituality and ritual rather than the political aspect of the network, and there are plenty of people in the global justice movement who don't want to have anything to do with spirituality. Wherever we find it and whatever form it takes, it's important for all of us working to change the world to have some kind of community of support that we can go to for renewal of our spirits during this difficult work.

I'm also very involved in the permaculture movement. Permaculture is a system of environmental design that teaches us how we can meet our basic human needs such as food, clothing, and shelter in ways that regenerate the environment around us. To me, it's the practical application of the spiritual idea that the earth is sacred, and it's also the positive vision of not only how do we want to change the world, but what do we want to change it toward, how do we want it to work once we've changed it. I also teach workshops called Earth Activist Trainings, which combine training in permaculture with a focus on activism and organizing and a grounding in spirituality. Besides intensives and short trainings, Earth Activist Training also has an ongoing project working with a group called Hunters Point Family in the inner city in San Francisco to train youth in sustainability and develop green jobs and businesses.

The global permaculture movement has a whole curriculum that teaches how to care for a piece of the earth, whether a garden, a ranch, a city, or an entire region. It looks at the issues of how water comes into your site and goes out again, and how you can catch it, store it, transport it, and clean it; how to develop energy sources that are renewable, local, and benign; how you can take toxic ground and bring it back to life, heal it, remove the poisons, and make it fertile again; and how you can develop systems that can provide food, clothing, and shelter for people, using biological resources instead of fossil fuel. These systems work like a forest works—they take care of themselves, nurture themselves, and provide for themselves.

I love combining permaculture skills with the spirituality that's rooted in the earth, so you're not just thinking and praying about the earth, but you're actually saying how do I take this piece of ground and bring it back to life again? You're not just digging around and planting your garden, but you also understand that your garden embodies a set of relationships with beings that have a consciousness and a life of their own. When you honor those interconnections, open your ears and listen to that communication, not only does everything grow better, but you are fed on a spiritual level as well as a physical.

I like to think of all the people working on the transition that's required if Earth is going to survive as the Mother Earth Transition Team. We must make the shift to renewable alternative energy, the shift to local food supplies, growing food locally and organically, building our soil because our soil can be a tremendous store of carbon if we treat it right. It actually requires all the things that we ought to do anyway to make the world healthier and function better, and improve our lives on this planet. This includes ending the tremendous disparity we have in this world between the rich and the poor, the haves and the have-nots. We need to understand that, just as a forest doesn't grow well if half the trees are starving and a few of the trees have all the nutrients, we as a global human community can't survive now unless we distribute the true wealth that is around and make sure that everybody has enough. Unless we take care of everybody's health, none of us are truly healthy.

That's the basis of global justice and it's also the basis of Goddess morality, because Goddess spirituality says, "Thou art Goddess." We are all part of this living being, this living body that is the Earth. So just as you are not going to feel well if you have a left foot in which gangrene has been festering, we as human beings can't be whole unless all of us are whole and all of us are healthy.

Things have shifted enormously in the last few years in terms of people's awareness and consciousness. This is especially true in the United States, where we've come out of a place of complete denial about climate change. For a while, I think people went into a sort of shock of despair and apathy. Now I see people getting activated and motivated to do positive things. For example, there's a whole movement called the Transition Town movement, which was started by British permaculturist Rob Hopkins. It's a movement that encourages ordinary people to organize their neighborhoods, towns, and villages to make a plan for moving into a lower energy use future, using the resources they have to create the resources they need. The movement has taken off and is spreading in the United States.

We've got to push the government to do certain things that need to be done at the federal level, such as renovating the whole electricity grid to be able to accept renewables and alternatives and act as a smart grid to monitor and reduce energy usage. That's just something we can't do in our own backyards, but there are many things that we can do such as developing local food-growing systems. Right now, the average piece of food that you put on your plate travels fifteen hundred miles before it gets to you. That's a tremendous burden of fossil fuels in transport and has an impact we don't even know how to measure on the vitality and the healing properties of the food. Growing food organically is just as important. Food that is grown by conventional techniques uses, again, tremendous amounts of fossil fuels in pesticides, herbicides, and fertilizers that are made from petroleum products, all of which are destructive to the soil and to the environment.

Shifting to organic and local, and not just sustainable but really regenerative agricultural practices that build soil, not only gives us healthier foods that don't have to travel so far, but links us in a very deep relational way back into the earth, back into what we put into our bodies, back into a sense of community. Even Western ranchers, who you might think would be the last people to get on board, are getting excited about new kinds of grazing management techniques that instead of destroying the land actually regenerate the land, build soil very quickly, pull carbon out of the atmosphere and sequester it in the soil, and actually produce more meat and better quality meat for those who eat meat than conventional ranching techniques do.

Those who want to make changes in their habits, don't necessarily know how. Even among Neopagans who believe nature is sacred, you will find a certain percentage of people who believe that in theory but in practice are working at jobs where they get up in the morning and drive to work or take the subway, are in a windowless office all day, and come home to be on the computer half the night. They don't have much real contact with nature. I wrote *The Earth Path: Grounding Your Spirit in the Rhythms of Nature* as a way to take people back to the basics of our spiritual tradition, learning to connect with the elements of air, fire, water, and earth, seeing and understanding the Goddess as Gaia, as Mother Earth herself, as the planet that is a living being, a living organism of which we're all part. The book goes through the four elements and has suggestions for observing nature, for developing a spiritual practice of regularly putting yourself in contact with nature, and also for practical things we can do around each of those elements to help heal the earth.

Pagan, Witch, Goddess

Newsweek and the *Washington Post* recently invited me to be one of the panelists on a website devoted to spirituality and religion, called *On Faith*. The panelists include Christians, Jews, Muslims, Hindus, Buddhists, and atheists. Each week they ask a question and we respond if we have time to, want to, feel moved to, and then people can go there and make comments. There are no other Witches or Pagans. As far as I can tell, there are no

Native Americans or other indigenous spirituality represented. I give my perspective on Paganism. It's a good opportunity to educate people who maybe wouldn't otherwise run across these ideas on what it really means to be Pagan. They asked the question, for example, about how your religious tradition responds to torture. I wrote a piece about how as Witches we identify very strongly with the women and men who were murdered during the Burning Times, the sixteenth and seventeenth centuries, as heretics by both the Catholic and the Protestant churches, and tortured in horrific ways. So we have a very strong spiritual aversion to any form of torture and coercion.

To me, a Pagan is somebody who sees the earth as sacred, who draws spiritual sustenance from relationship with that sacred being who is the earth, and who seeks spiritual community with which to express that connection. The terms "Pagan," "Goddess spirituality," and "Witch" are not synonymous. "Pagan" is broader because there are some Pagans who identify with the Goddess tradition, but there are others who might believe that nature is sacred but not want to personify it as the Goddess. There are many indigenous cultures and traditions that could be considered Pagan but don't necessarily identify themselves as in the Goddess tradition. In the Goddess tradition, there are Witches and Wiccans who strongly identify with the pre-Christian religious traditions of Europe and the Middle East that were focused on the Goddess. And there are many other kinds of Goddess worshippers who come from other places or other cultures or just have a different take on it. We are all part of earth-based spirituality, just as within the Christian religion there are different denominations.

When I wrote *The Spiral Dance: A Rebirth of the Ancient Religion of the Great Goddess,* which has been in print continuously since its publication in 1979, I was trying to write the book that I wished I had had when I started my spiritual search. I think *The Spiral Dance* did a couple of things. One is it let women know there was a way to look at the world and a way to look at spirituality that didn't need to be cast in male terms, didn't have to be focused on male deities, and didn't have to be led, directed, and controlled by men, which in the 1970s was a radical idea. Second, it let women know that there was a history, a long and ancient history, of religions and spiritual traditions that saw the sacred in female form and envisioned it that way. Third, it let people know that you can still practice that spirituality today and you can do it in a way that honors your own creativity, encourages you to be your own spiritual authority and not put yourself under somebody else's control, and encourages people to form community and groups of support with which to explore ritual and ceremony and create the rituals that we need today. These new rituals might draw on some of the ancient roots but might be very different from the kinds of rituals that the tradition practiced back in 5000 BC.

It's tremendously empowering to women to know about this history. When I show *Signs Out of Time,* the documentary my friend Donna Read and I made on the life of archaeologist Marija Gimbutas who uncovered much of this information (see chapter 5), what I hear over and over from the young women who see it is "I didn't know this. Why didn't anyone ever tell me this?"

Knowing that the Goddess tradition existed in the past shifts your perception of what's possible today. And there are key insights from the Goddess that can help us meet the challenges of today. The first is to value and trust relationships. Wealth is not about things; it's about relationships. The second is to take root in the Earth and give yourself time to connect with nature and let nature nurture you. The third insight is that everything is a cycle: birth, growth, death, and regeneration. All of it is part of the cycle. We can't honor just one part of the cycle without understanding the rest. When we do, we understand that one thing's waste becomes another thing's food, that there is no waste, that everything is potentially meant to nurture something else. Even the death of something, the death of a leaf, nurtures the soil and that ultimately nurtures the tree. The message in this for us now is that we may be losing things that we have cared about or invested in or trusted in, but if we let them go and let them compost, they may nurture other things and may actually feed us better.

Part III:
The Goddess Within

Eve Ensler is an internationally acclaimed playwright whose works for the stage include *Necessary Targets*, *The Good Body*, and *The Vagina Monologues*, which has been translated into over forty-five languages and performed in over 120 countries. She is the founder and artistic director of V-Day, the global movement to end violence against women and girls that was inspired by *The Vagina Monologues*. In ten years, the V-Day movement has raised more than sixty million dollars. www.vday.org

CHAPTER TEN

Peace Is a State of Being

Eve Ensler

I grew up in a middle-class family and neighborhood in the United States. I had plenty of food, clothes. I had my teeth straightened. I took ballet classes. We went on vacations. I had a good education.

This security did not come for free. It was my father's money and he created reality. From early on, my emotional and psychological well-being were sacrificed for this economic security. My father was a raging alcoholic. His anger permeated and infected my world. His fists, his hand, his belts, marked my young body and my being. I was always ready to be hit or yelled at or erased. I was told over and over how lucky I was to have a nice house, to live in a good neighborhood. So early on, I came to equate my economic security with violence.

I never dreamed of growing up and getting married, having children. Never. It simply didn't occur to me. There were many reasons. One, I was born in the early fifties and my consciousness was shaped in the sixties. I was a hippie. I gravitated toward drugs, free love, non-monogamy, communes, and anything that had to do with escaping the nuclear family. That nuclear unit was just that for me: nuclear—an atom bomb that annihilated my self, my worth, my confidence, and my identity. My father's rage, his power, his opinion, his money, his moods, controlled and determined all of us, including my mother. Our house, our family, was his empire. I was his subject. Or his tortured prisoner.

I never dreamed of growing up and getting married and having children because I never dreamed of growing up, living that long. I could never imagine life past thirty, and I came close to making sure I didn't get there. I never dreamed of having children, as I was so scared of repeating what had been done to me. I was so scared that I had my father in me. And in fact, I did. I held his rage, his impatience, and his judgments for many years.

It is not surprising that I have grown up to become nomadic. I was unable to have a dining room table until my early fifties, as it was the set piece of so much humiliation and violence. Until my late thirties I kept my bedroom out in the open in my living room so no one could get me. My dreams were limited, simple. All I wanted was to grow up and not be hit or molested. I lived as a survivor. Happy every day not to be screamed at, ridiculed, beaten, terrorized, or thrown out. I did not care about a career. I did not think what kind of a person might be right for me. It was all about what was *not* happening, all about the pain stopping, all about safety, security. I wanted a man or a woman who would not hit me. This, as you can well imagine, is not the greatest prerequisite for a relationship. Not a very high standard. And it's broad. And, to be honest, until you have gone back and retraced and experienced and purged and transformed that initial violation, it is impossible not to keep being attracted to what you are trying to escape.

I think you have several options when you experience enormous terror and violence as a child. You can shut down completely, you can pretend it didn't happen, you can become violent yourself, or you can create situations that mirror your initial situation in an attempt to understand and master it. I have, at some point, embraced all of these. My life has been a journey to find a way to make sense of violence and terror and make peace with insecurity.

In the last ten years I have traveled to many places—more than forty countries. Looking back, I see that a pattern emerges. I see how I was consistently and compulsively drawn to that which I feared, to those situations that seemed utterly incomprehensible. I see how this search to understand brutality and violence began as a search for logic and security but became the journey that freed me of the false need for these protections, dissolving my moorings, undoing my falsely constructed notions of security.

I have spent time in refugee camps, war-torn countries, battered-women and homeless shelters, prisons, border towns, and postdisaster sites. I have lived through a near plane crash, an almost bombing. I have left a fifteen-year relationship. I have embraced a weeping fifty-year-old man in his burnt-out backyard in Kosova. I have held the hand of a woman whose face was melted off by acid in Islamabad, Pakistan. I have clung to the body of an Afghan woman in the middle of a seizure as she remembered the torture and murder that took place in a stadium in Kabul. I have stood face-to-face with a raging member of the Taliban, his whip in hand as he prepared to flog me. I have watched the World Trade Center towers fall in my beloved city. I have sat with thousands of women from Srebrenica in a stadium as they wailed in grief over their lost men. I have spent days in dusty Ciudad Juárez, Mexico, searching for bodies of dead women, and in the hot sun of Crawford, Texas, as Cindy Sheehan stood up to [George] Bush.

I live alone today after cohabiting with partners for more than thirty years. Many of the vestiges that tied me to the ground, to one person, to one place, are gone. In fact, I have become a traveler, a woman who exists in motion, a nomadic being, a citizen of the world. I have been fortunate that the work I do has literally taken me around the planet. But travel is by no means a prerequisite to getting lost. We are able to cross and dissolve all kinds of borders if we are willing to go to the political, emotional, and spiritual places we most fear and resist.

I write and perform and I love my friends all over the world. I work to stop violence against women. I work to prevent and stop war. I sometimes have anxiety. I have bouts of terrible low self-esteem. I feel lonely on occasion, but mainly I feel alive. I feel myself.

This may or may not appeal to you—this moving, this nomadic existence, and this nonattached life. I am not suggesting we all leave our relationships and homes and children. Not at all. I am proposing that we reconceive the dream. That we consider what would happen if security were not the point of our existence. That we find freedom, aliveness, and power not from what contains, locates, or protects us but from what dissolves, reveals, and expands us.

* * * * *

Freedom can come only from contemplating death, not from pretending it doesn't exist. Not from running from loss but from entering grief, surrendering to sorrow.

Freedom comes not from holding your life more precious or sacred than others'. Not from consuming more than your share.

Freedom is not knowing something when you don't know it.

Freedom means I may not be identified with any one group, but I can visit and find myself in every group. Freedom does not mean I don't have values or beliefs. But it does mean I am not hardened around them. I do not use them as weapons.

Freedom cannot be bought or arranged or made with bombs or guards. It is deeper. It is a process. It is the acute awareness that we are all utterly interdependent. That economic injustice and inequity creates an environment of global despair and rage that, until balanced, will inevitably lead to hatred and violence.

Freedom is not only being able to tolerate mystery, complexity, ambiguity, but hungering for them and only trusting a situation when they are present.

Not owned, not occupied, not bought.

Finding the place in me that connects with every person I meet rather than being different, better, or on top.

Believing there is a power determining everything at the same moment that I know there is absolutely no one in charge.

Wanting to win the award when I know awards mean nothing.

Freedom is not knowing where you are but being deeply there.

Not waiting for someone to save or rescue you or make up for your terrible past. Doing that for yourself.

Not putting your flag in the ground.

Not owning people or ideas. Being willing to get lost in the desert.

Freedom is about becoming vulnerable to one another, rather than becoming secure, in control, and alone.

The increasing insecurity of the world can make us insane or can simply clarify reality, which is that we are going to die and it could happen anytime, anywhere.

The world is indeed a near-death experience, forcing us, if we let it, to let go of certain illusions that separate us from one another. Having this in our consciousness could be the elixir that makes us more feeling, more present, more appreciative, more loving, more generous.

If we are truly interested in security, let's begin with securing all people the basic human right to food, shelter, drinkable water, health care, a place to live, safety, and a livable earth.

Let's make compassion the end goal, human connection the end goal, honoring all people the end goal.

Then, I promise, we may not know security, but we will certainly know peace.

Dana How, EdS, LPC, a licensed professional counselor who maintains a private practice in Virginia Beach, Virginia, has an educational specialist degree in both school psychology and counseling. She has extensive training in alternative therapies, energy studies, and vibrational medicine, including completion of the training program in vibrational healing through the Vibrational Gateways Institute in Kansas City. Dana has spent years combining spirituality, science, psychology, and her intuitive abilities to develop Trans-Consciousness Therapies, which emphasize unique Alchemical Processes. She utilizes these transformational therapies in her private practice, seminars, workshops, and professional training. www.TransConsciousnessTherapies.com or www.DanaHow.com

CHAPTER ELEVEN

Awakening Sacred Self
Dana How

I AM the Sacred Self. I AM connected to the Source of All That Is. I desire to express the Light of this. I seek the experience of fulfillment, joy, passion, love, potency, peace, and bliss. I seek to express my essence, and experience my Divinity in the world of form.

I AM the Feminine, the energy within women and men receiving seed thoughts—sacred, pulsating inspiration, insights, and intuition—from the Sacred Self and delivering these to the masculine radiant forces that live within.

I AM the Masculine, the energy within women and men receiving from the feminine and delivering seed thoughts into action, into form.

The Feminine, witness to the Sacred Self, proclaims to the Masculine, "Know that we are all connected. Hear me and create through your strength, power, and actions, and all the world shall be blessed. Acknowledge, trust, ask, listen, and follow through on what I deliver to you, and feel how your actions will affect the whole. And doing this, your impact will be great, uplifting, and of service to all."

I observe a world that is oriented toward the masculine without the balance of the feminine, a world that is focused on the external. How can I be a good mother, a better partner, or spouse, or be more successful in my career? What is required of me?

How much of our energy goes out to perform these roles, these tasks, these ideas of self? How much conformity—or relinquishment—does it take to gain a sense of acceptance, or power, or to at least avoid rejection or alienation? This is the fear that contracts around the desire to "Be" as we really are, to be our Sacred Self.

The Sacred Self cannot be awakened or imparted into our world without the balance of the feminine, the Goddess Shift. We all must open to this energy, this love, in order to reclaim our nature, balance, unity, and wholeness.

I am often asked, "How do you know there is something within, some Source, something Divine, something Sacred? How do you know there is something delivered through a healed, balanced, unified consciousness? How do you create this balance and begin to live as that Sacred Self?"

I am confident I entered the body with the appropriate grandeur, having reviewed my Soul Blueprint and attributes for this life:

- I AM connected.
- I AM enhancing.
- I AM unique.
- I AM lovable.
- I AM whole.

I merged my awareness with the body that would serve as my temple, the vehicle that would allow me to express and experience Divine Light through my thoughts, emotions, and senses. A Divine Plan. I pushed through the veil...

We establish our belief systems during the first seven-year cycle of life.

I was born into a loving family in a small Virginia town, and the challenges began. I was unable to potty-train effectively due to an undiagnosed blockage between my bladder and kidneys. My mother assumed the accidents were deliberate. She thought I just didn't want to stop playing, and she grew frustrated and angry. In response, I tried to control my body and please my parents. I tried to stop the accidents by holding my urination, but I became constipated and impacted instead. I had more infections, and at four years old, I underwent surgery that left a permanent scar from the navel downward.

I began to express my unique, inner joy by playing with cars, trucks, and dirt piles instead of playing with dolls and playing dress-up. The external world met this with disappointment, rejection, and upset. My brothers were agitated. I would not leave their toys alone, and my mother was disappointed that I did not want to wear the matching dresses she made and that I always came inside covered with dirt.

I also began to express my artistic "enhancing attribute" by painting my toddler table and chairs with my father's paints. I chose my colors by the paints I could reach, and I even mixed my own colors with the wooden stirrers I had seen my father use. I had just created my first masterpiece! My parents, however, admonished me for making a huge mess, ruining the table and chairs, and ruining my father's paints.

The Divine Nature of your Soul Blueprint never alters. Nor does the desire to express and experience Sacred Self. We are designed to cloak the Divine Light and the Sacred seed thoughts that move through us with coherent thoughts and feelings about ourselves and our world. Thus we can express and experience our own Divinity in our own unique ways.

Based on my perceptions of myself in relation to my external experiences, the expression of this Divine Light, this Divine Energy, was beginning to contract and become distorted. I contracted into self-judgment. And the Divine Emotion of (feminine) passion, which was intended to propel me (through masculine action) and deliver me into the world of my choosing and creating, began to distort into anger. My interpretation of myself and my world became "I am less than" and "I am unable to express myself as I choose."

Understand that there is not, nor has there ever existed, the energy of "less than" or of any "limitation on self-expression." These misperceptions are self-constructed, altered perceptions of the truth. Each of us, as a result of our life experiences, creates incoherent thoughts and emotions regarding the truth of who we are.

My desire and the inspiration to paint that table and chairs was an expression of the feminine energy. From my feminine right brain burst forth this amazing idea, this amazing vision. The balance of the masculine energy was required to act, to mix the paint, and to apply the paint. My feminine aspect relished the experience, the beauty, the strong scents, the feelings. I basked in the result and was ready to explore other ways to expand and express through the masculine aspect of Self.

Instead, I was chastised. My feminine aspect was crushed, and I expressed that feeling (through my masculine aspect) by crying and screaming. The messages, thoughts, and intense emotions reinforced the incoherent energy patterns. Through repeated experiences, I interpreted that I had to express myself "appropriately" in order to avoid others' wrath and/or punishment.

Thus, by seven years old, instead of activating my Soul Blueprint as it was designed, I was left with a distorted, incoherent expression of it based on my misperceptions of myself and my world. I believed:

- I am a disappointment to others.
- I am not supported.
- Something is wrong with me.
- I am less than.
- I am different, and that is bad.
- My ways of expressing myself disappoint others.
- I am unlovable.

- *My body betrays me.*
- *I am broken.*

Between the ages of seven and thirteen, our second seven-year cycle, we anchor the beliefs we developed during our first cycle.

Ulcerated colitis began revealing its symptoms when I was seven, but it remained undiagnosed until I was nine, when I lost so much blood that I required multiple transfusions. I had complained about the symptoms, but they were interpreted as excuses not to go to school. I was put on an extremely restrictive diet and a number of medications, including steroids. One of the steroids' side effects was a puffy face, which caused quite a challenge during preadolescence. By thirteen, I had missed a lot of school due to my illness and acquired the nickname "Moon-Face." I closed this cycle by knocking out half of my front tooth in a bicycle accident.

While these external life experiences reinforced my misperceptions and incoherent beliefs about myself and my world, something else was happening in my life as well.

There was an inner voice, Spirit, always in the background. On a good day, I would lie under the dogwood tree in our backyard, look to the sky, and dialogue with my inner voice.

After my mother told me about my diagnosis, the nature of the disease, the medications, and my food restrictions, I lay in bed, alone, and it was the voice of Spirit, delivered through the inner feminine, that rose to support me. In a comforting matter-of-fact way, she imparted, "All is Divine, and this experience shall serve you well in your service to others."

At nine years old, I had no idea what that meant, but I was certain of one thing—everything was going to be okay.

On another good day, I was alone, riding my bicycle on country roads, when the winds suddenly grew strong. I stopped riding and left my bike to smell and taste the honeysuckle nearby. As I approached the honeysuckle, it occurred to me that I was a young girl alone on a country road and no one knew where I was. There was a wave of empowerment—and a subtle thread of fear. As I reached for the honeysuckle, my inner voice whispered, "This energy of the wind is the same energy you experience when your stomach hurts so badly—it is all one energy."

This experience was one of my first realizations that everything is Divine and that there is something in our perception that alters our experience of it. From that time on, I accessed that inner guidance more frequently. In retrospect, I seemed to seek that dialogue most often when I was forced into quietude, when I was ill. Whatever the circumstances, whenever I asked a question, Spirit always responded with a calm, neutral, almost matter-of-fact resonance.

Between the ages of fourteen and twenty-one, our third cycle, we begin to exercise our creative power.

We begin to create our reality, in full force, based on the Divine Light/Energy pouring through the filter of our belief systems, which are based on our perceptions of self and our world—whatever those beliefs are.

When I was fifteen, a girlfriend introduced me to my first love. He lived thirty miles away so knew nothing of my illness! He didn't know I believed I was broken, so I decided not to tell him about my illness or my restrictive diet (including having to abstain from alcohol).

One morning, before we left for a picnic, my mother mentioned my dietary restrictions. This sparked aggression in him, and over the next couple of years, the verbal abuse moved into emotional and physical abuse and betrayal. He had an affair with someone who was not sick and different. He also threw me repeatedly into the car door and pushed me down a set of stairs.

I had never been exposed to abuse before, so it was easy for these experiences to support my beliefs that:

- Something is wrong with me.
- I am less than.
- My ways of expressing myself disappoint others.

- Others will become angry and punish me if I don't behave the way they want me to.

When my parents witnessed the results of the physical abuse, they forbid me to see him again. Being seventeen and in love, I continued the relationship in secret. The secrecy escalated the turmoil. No one knew we were together. So when I became pregnant and could not follow through with the pregnancy due to my medications, it was easy for him to betray me yet again and disappear with another girl.

Though my personal experiences during this third cycle were challenging and supported my incoherent perceptions about myself and the world around me, there was still the matter of Spirit, the inner voice, delivered through the feminine.

When I was sixteen, in the midst of all of this turmoil, my inner voice informed me that I was going to be a psychologist, a counselor. She said I had something to offer others, a way to serve, to enhance. And it was true. By middle school, friends sought my advice for their boyfriend problems or problems at home. And I noticed that while my friends were talking, another part of them gently communicated as well, sharing additional information about the event, what was happening, and what would help resolve the issue.

I grew up assuming everyone communicated on multiple levels within themselves and with others. There was what we said out loud, and there was what we shared at intuitive/energetic levels. The masculine aspect of my friends' communication revealed what had occurred for them and was expressed through their words. And the feminine aspect of their communication revealed the gestalt, the big picture, and offered great insight into resolving their issue using their intuitive knowing.

The inner voice and its message about becoming a psychologist was comforting, uplifting, even hopeful. But the discrepancy between this voice and its message and my external reality was vast.

Neither my family nor I had the financial resources for me to attend college. And my mother felt college was an unrealistic pursuit given my acute episodes with ulcerative colitis and my impending surgeries to remove my large intestines. I had begun a relationship with a man eight years my senior and the practical thing (in many people's minds) would have been to marry him so I could be taken care of.

So, I was nineteen years old, dating an older man, working as a secretary in the same auto parts store where my father worked, and waiting tables. I was having biopsies every six months in anticipation of my illness evolving into cancer, undergoing surgery, and having an ileostomy bag for the rest of my life. Yet my inner voice said I was going to be a psychologist. Again, the discrepancy between my inner voice and its message and my external reality was vast. And it became an abyss into which I plunged.

I refilled a bottle of pain medication and drove several hours to the home of the girlfriend who had introduced me to my (first) abusive boyfriend. I prayed I would find solace in her home. Her father was a minister and a comforting soul.

As I watched her leave each day for college and each evening for work, my abyss grew wider. I reflected on everything I had put my family through with my illness, the associated medical bills, and my abusive relationship. I reflected on the external life in front of me, a life filled with illness, surgery, and uncertainty. I could not catch any glimpse of: I AM enhancing. I AM unique. I AM connected. I AM lovable. I AM whole. I could not see the truth of who I AM. I could not see my Sacred Self. All I could see were the incoherent misperceptions I had been carrying since the first seven years of my life.

One evening, my girlfriend left for work. She was going to pick up her father after work, and then the two of them were going to pick up my girlfriend's mother at the airport. No one would be home until after midnight.

I poured a glass of Kool-Aid, took the bottle of pills, and fell into a deep sleep.

I awoke to the beautiful, questioning eyes of an intern at Duke University Hospital. "What could possibly be so bad that you would do this?" he asked.

"What could be so bad?" I echoed inside. The real question was "Why am I here?"

I learned between bouts of stomach pumping and vomiting that my girlfriend had gotten off work early, listened to her inner voice, and driven back to the house to see whether I wanted to ride with her and her father to the airport.

"Why wasn't I successful?" There must be a reason.

In a fit of desperation, I said to Spirit, "I cannot do this anymore." The discrepancy between my internal and my external worlds was too great. I simply could not reconcile the discrepancy between "I AM a Divine aspect of God" and "I am broken."

As always, Spirit responded, saying, "Then FOLLOW my guidance, heed my directions, follow your path, and know that I will be there to support you every step of the way."

It was as if a veil had lifted. In that moment, I understood that, though Spirit is always there guiding and directing us, we are called to follow that guidance no matter what appears in the external world or how we perceive those experiences or circumstances. In fact, by following that guidance we can change everything in our external world, beginning with how we perceive it.

The Journey Home

So I began the journey home, back to my Soul Blueprint, back to Sacred Self. I realized that it had always been there. I just needed to live from the inside out and allow the external to bear witness to the truth of who I AM.

The years that followed were filled with opportunities, synchronicities, and blessings that affirmed the life I was creating, consciously, according to the Divine Plan of bringing the Sacred Self to the Feminine to the Masculine into action, into form.

I put myself through college. I earned dual graduate degrees in school psychology and counseling, and I was able to support and take care of myself! I underwent a revolutionary surgery, which meant I would not have the ileostomy bag for the rest of my life. At thirty-three, I found Sacred Relationship and was married within seven months. Through an incredible string of synchronistic events, I found and took a Vibrational Healing course that helped me find my voice and figure out how to incorporate Spirit into the world of psychology. I established a thriving, full-time private practice. I gave birth to two amazing boys after years of being told childbearing would be too medically risky. I travel and teach, which I love. And now I am writing this chapter!

As the years flowed, Spirit continued to guide me with information and ideas, teachings, ways to help others connect to their inner voice and change the course of their lives, ways to become more aligned with who they are, to become more aligned with the Sacred Self. A paradigm began forming in my mind, one that combined the information I received intuitively from my inner voice with psychology, science, and spirituality.

Spirit was always there to guide me and clarify for me. For example, I was in the middle of teaching a two-day workshop entitled, "Healing the Mind, Empowering Spirit." I had just taught what I understood about the conscious and subconscious mind and how our beliefs about self and our world block our capacity to express and experience who we really are. I had just taught that those beliefs block our ability to express the Sacred Self, the Divine I AM, the Spiritual aspect that resides within us, the aspect that helps us express and experience ourselves as the Light of Source that we are.

I was getting ready to introduce the Tracking Process and have the attendees "release" those blocking beliefs and create new ones when Spirit interrupted. "Do not have them release anything. This implies that there is something created that is not Divine."

Well, from a professional point of view, Spirit's timing was less than optimal! Twenty people were waiting for me to teach a process that I was apparently not going to teach as it was outlined in the handouts.

With the class waiting, I inquired less than gently, "Spirit, what do I do now?" The inner voice responded, "You are to call this Alchemy. Have them alchemize their beliefs back to the truth of who they are." At that time, I had no idea what alchemy was or meant, but it sounded good to me. As I have done so many times since, I explained to the workshop participants, "I have a non-compete contract with Spirit and, apparently, the process I have created is being modified as we speak." We spent the rest of the afternoon alchemizing consciousness.

In that moment, in that breath, in Spirit's whisper, I understood that we distort the very truths of ourselves and that our incoherent beliefs— once alchemized—are, in fact, messages from the Sacred Self. For example, I understood that my misperception "I am broken" was an incoherent ex- pression of my Soul Blueprint's attribute "I AM whole!"

As synchronicity would have it, I attended the Mary Mag- dalene conclave with Tom Kenyon and Judi Sion a week later in Washington DC. Tom was inspired to activate the Divine Goddess in our nation's capital because our nation's political structure is embedded there and because its masculine use of power needs to be balanced with the feminine energy's reverence for all life.

Tom and Judi spoke about their book *The Magdalene Manuscript*, which describes the alchemy Mary Magdalene and Yeshua prac- ticed. I found this particularly synchronistic, given Spirit's offer- ings the previous week! From the depths of our hearts and souls, we spent three days honoring and inviting the Divine Mother, the Goddess, the Divine Feminine to take her rightful place with the Divine Masculine, to return to our Sacred Balance. It was truly a glorious experience. You could feel the Goddess energy rising, and you could feel the unveiling of something sacred and holy.

During my four-hour drive home, the sound of Tom Kenyon's voice, his chanting, and the other participants invoking the God- dess energies reverberated to my core. I relished the feeling of the Goddess energy rising in *everything,* the emergence of that which had lain dormant. Internally, I relished the feeling of that Goddess energy purifying every personal rejection of the feminine and ev- ery encounter with betrayal I had ever experienced.

Moreover, I deepened my understanding of Alchemy. I got it! It was the masculine energy pushing forward without the balance of the feminine that was the cause of our downfall, our fears, and our pain, that was the cause of discord and disease, that was the cause of all incoherency.

This moment served as a catalyst for an understanding that has grown and expanded in me over the years: the understanding that there is Light that moves into and through each of us, Light that is given as a Sacred Gift that we may use to express and experience this Divinity as we choose, as we will it.

We are born, and our desires are instinctive within our nature—desires of how we can uniquely manifest, create, express self, love another, and fulfill our purposes. As we develop during our first seven years, we deliver our Light outward into the world through the vehicle of our thoughts and feelings, cloaking, if you will, this Divine Energy so it can be propelled into expression and received as experience.

As this energy permeates our consciousness, we have seed thoughts that epitomize the highest way we can utilize this gift of Light/Life. Our feminine energies pass information and insights to the masculine energies, and it is the masculine energies' job to execute them.

The challenges arise during those early years when we are developing our belief systems, and we misperceive and distort these energies in relation to our experience with our world.

The masculine energy and the left brain have come to dominate our Sacred Selves. Our Sacred Selves lie hidden beneath our distortions, unrealized. Rather than living from the inside out, rather than delivering Sacred Self through our feminine to our masculine in order to create and bring Light into the world in the unique, balanced way only our unique Spirit can, we have deified the masculine forces, and we now create without the feminine balance of the Goddess.

We have determined that it is unwise to express ourselves without first considering whether the outside world will affirm our expression. We are designed to consider the impact of our expressions from the feminine aspect: How will it affect the whole in a loving way? Instead, we consider: What does the outside world require of me and how shall I "do" that? What does my career, my spouse, my children, my house, my friends require of me? Where has my passion gone? What emotion energizes these roles? When did overwhelm, frustration, anger, apathy, some distorted, incoherent form of passion replace my Divine birthright, the desire and passion to Be Me?

Awakening within each of us is the Sacred Self, the unlimited, amazing part of us who knows who I AM and who does not hold any misperceptions or incoherent beliefs about who I AM.

Sacred Self is there, lying beneath the dogwood tree, riding her bicycle and stopping to smell and taste the honeysuckle, trusting that illness is a pathway for greater good, knowing that everything is Divine, listening to the voice of Spirit, and, of course, looking for synchronicities.

The Goddess, the Divine Feminine, is the bridge to the Sacred Self. She honors and connects you to your center, to the truth of your Source. She is the Divine Mother. She carries you in the still of her womb. She whispers to you in every moment of who you are. She loves your essence and is joyous, passionate, and blissful. She acts as your guardian while you are carried forward by her partner, the Divine Masculine.

We have lived too long without the Sacred Balance of the masculine and the feminine, without the Alchemy of Spirit. For too long, the masculine energies have dominated without the balance of the feminine. In isolation, they have acted without the balance of love, without the balanced consideration of how every action affects everything and everyone, and without the balanced consideration of how every action affects All That Is.

The Goddess Shift is about balance and wholeness. It is about that which is within and bringing that forward in all its glory. It is about Awakening Sacred Self—expressing and experiencing who we really are, who we are meant to be, our true nature.

I AM the Sacred Self. I AM Spirit. I AM connected to the
Source of All That Is.

Acknowledge me.
Trust me to support you in all things.
Seek my guidance.
Listen to my voice.

I AM the Feminine, the energy within women and men
receiving seed thoughts—sacred, pulsating inspiration, insights,
and intuition—from the Sacred Self and delivering these to the
masculine radiant forces that live within.

Follow through on what I deliver to you!

I AM the Masculine, the energy within women and men
receiving from the feminine and delivering seed thoughts
into action, into form.

I AM the Sacred Self.
I AM the Feminine.
I AM the Masculine.

And in seeking the balanced expression of these,
the Alchemy of Spirit,
we are Awakening Sacred Self.

Julie Gerland, an international lecturer, workshop leader, and professional trainer in the field of healing and conscious evolution for more than thirty years, inspires people to heal and transform their lives from soul to cell. Founder and director of the pioneering Holistic Parenting Program: Preconception to Birth & Beyond, she is an advocate for this primal period and empowers parents for world peace. She is UN representative for a world organization on prenatal education in Special Consultative Status with the Economic and Social Council of the United Nations and author of *Bliss Bonding: Re-Create Your Loving Universe Soul to Cell*. http://julie gerland.com

CHAPTER TWELVE

A Loving Universe

Julie Gerland

Many of us are aware that we are on the threshold of a new era. Some point to the Mayan calendar or to the many other native prophesies that foretell that this "civilization" is drawing to a close. Yes, a new era is dawning in the grand cycle of time. A page is turning on the dark ages in which lies, greed, deceit, and egoism have triumphed under the rule of leaders fed in the womb with fear and violence. Like the ruins of Babylon, this civilization shall lie under the dust of time, an extinct relic of an age when the Goddess was hidden, felled from her grace.

Through the ebb and flow of civilizations such as the ancient Chinese, Hindu, Egyptian, Celtic, Greek, and Roman to name but a few, feminine empowerment, or the Goddess, has been both venerated and feared in her many forms. The Goddess is still worshipped today as the Virgin and also as the Great Mother, for example, and many fear the Temptress and the Crone or the destructive forces of Mother Nature. Carl Jung declared the feminine principle as a universal archetype, a primordial, instinctual pattern of behavior deeply imprinted on the human psyche. He shed further light on the goddess within when he described this devotion to the goddess as "a potent force of the unconscious." He believed that all religions are based on archetypal foundations.

Women have always been endowed with powers thought to be "mysterious," because they differ from those in men. In a struggle to control, men have for a long time now sought to dominate and even stamp out this mysterious power innate in women and in nature, relegating it to a few goddess idols. Woman's mysterious powers of fertility, childbearing, nurturing, and healing have inspired veneration, but they have also brought to her misunderstanding, hate, torture, and often death. When man, separated in consciousness from his own divine origins, treats the "mother of man" in this way, society is surely doomed.

Nature herself shows us, however, that after all death there is resurrection. A resurrection is occurring now in the consciousness of humanity. People are stepping out of their symbolic "stone coffins" that have kept them from connecting with a vast, intelligent, and loving Universe. By living "outside the box," they are beginning to experience freedom in consciousness.

Sacred Archetypes Within

Archetypes are universal blueprints for behavior within our collective superconscious. Many of us have experienced at some time in our lives some form of sixth sense or supernatural power, be it intuition, prophetic dreams, telepathy, or perhaps healing abilities. My life experience has taught me that this need not be left to a random happening; rather, it can become an exciting way of life. It is possible for everyone to connect with these superpowers within and reap the countless benefits. These include such things as feeling safe and unconditionally loved, protected, nurtured, and sustained. Telepathy, healing, clairvoyance, and being able to bilocate are just a few of the capacities that become possible as an integral part of an incredible loving intelligent Universe.

Prayer is perhaps the most common form of communicating with the archetypal Father God, Virgin Mother, or one of the numerous other "deities" to which people pray. My experience has shown me that we no longer need to "pray" to some God out there somewhere, but rather communicate in our own intimate way to infinite loving and wise archetypal parents within our own consciousness.

I was unsuspecting of the possible powerful responses from these deities when at the age of sixteen I had an experience that completely changed my life and my way of perceiving and relating to the world. I was living through the turmoil of adolescence and my parents were going through a particularly difficult period in their own lives. They were out of work and had run out of money. Lying in bed alone one night, feeling lost and not knowing what to do, I chose to turn inward and cried out to a higher power. Then I heard sounds as if someone was entering the room. My body froze, aside from my racing heart. Suddenly, in the middle of the dark room, a point of light shone so brightly that it lit up the whole room. It was different from normal light because, although it shone, I couldn't see anything in the room. Time stood still for me when the light, continuing to spread, engulfed me in its embrace. I felt completely known, unconditionally loved, and "seen." I had never experienced this before. An intense sensation filled my body. I felt protected and no longer alone. My life suddenly seemed to make sense and be meaningful. I fell asleep feeling as though I were cradled in the arms of perfect parents, giving me exactly what I needed and filling me with the knowledge that they would always be there for me. I experienced the bliss of feeling vulnerable yet knowing that I would always have everything I needed. When I awoke the next morning, I experienced a new surge of vitality in my body, and an intense joy filled my heart. I was no longer alone. My archetypal mother and father had just claimed me. I now felt an integral part of an immense, powerful, and loving Universe.

Many people think that I am "special" or "blessed," and indeed I do feel that way. But my experience has shown me that these and other archetypes lie in the transpersonal or superconscious realm of every human being. They are just waiting to be invited to play an active part in our lives. We are all destined to know the blissful blessings of being unconditionally loved, nurtured, provided for, protected, and guided. Isn't this what we are all looking for? In the coming era, every child will know these blessings from the moment of conception as the basis of their life in the new human family. Every woman is currently offered the opportunity to invite the Mother Goddess into her life and let Her lead for a change. She is the power within capable of bringing in the new era, uniting the human family in love, harmony, peace, and abundance.

Womb School

The slumbering Goddess within mothers is one of the most powerful forces in the world. Mothers have the ability to bring into the world a savior or a criminal. Speaking to a group of doctors in 1938, the spiritual teacher Omraam Mikhaël Aïvanhov said that if we were to look after pregnant mothers, in just two generations, or fifty years, we could close our prisons and our hospitals. Discoveries in prenatal psychology over the past thirty years confirm what many ancient civilizations knew: The mother is the child's first universe. Everything that the mother lives during pregnancy, her unborn baby lives with her. During these nine months, the forming prenatal baby is conscious and learning about his or her environment. I recently met a psychiatrist who conducted a study for the British government on reducing violent crimes. He told me that his study revealed that it would be cheaper than the current cost of dealing with rising crime rates, and in the interest of the country, to offer both parents paid leave of absence from their jobs. Each parent would receive parenting education from the beginning of pregnancy and become full-time parents for the first two years of their child's life.

We know that violence in the womb and during the sacred moments of birth, in the many forms this violence takes, brings violence into the world. Ironically, disrespect or respect for the mother herself and our living intelligent Universe, Mother Nature, begins in the womb, too. Mother is the cradle of humanity and every human being is destined by nature to pass through her school. This "prenatal school womb" is the most powerful place in the world. It is here where our deepest subconscious programming takes place and, unless changed, it will last a lifetime. It is the mother who holds the keys to a healthy, peaceful, and abundant civilization in harmony with the Great Mother.

From the moment of conception, a mother has the power of a Goddess over her child. Every mother has been given the divine instinct to love unconditionally, nurture, protect, nourish, and provide for her child. During the period of development in the womb, the baby's subconscious mind, located in the cells, is "downloading" the subconscious program that will greatly determine whether the person will live mostly in fear or love. If the unborn baby is bathed frequently in a poisonous cocktail of the mother's stress hormones or been exposed to a violent environment, he or she will develop in protection, struggle, and violence. This leaves much less energy for the development of the brain. On the contrary, when the mother wants and loves her child and she lives mostly in love, happiness, joy, and security while providing her unborn child with appropriate nourishment and avoiding harmful toxins, her baby will develop optimally in a hormonal love juice. In this way health, intelligence, and creative abilities are all naturally enhanced.

Unfortunately, if the mother herself has never experienced these positive states, it is very difficult, almost impossible, for her to offer them to her child. With no role model to follow, she is most likely to despise and mistrust her own body. Filled with disrespect, she may defile herself, often choosing to fill her cells with highly toxic substances or starve her cells rather than enjoy nourishing, wholesome food. Often she sells herself for a few sensations of care or simply to survive, whether on rice or caviar. It should come as no surprise then that mothers are less present and available to love and nourish their children. In the United States, there is an epidemic of five-year-olds committing suicide. Global juvenile violence and crime is increasing at an alarming rate. Also on the rise are birth defects, miscarriages, and babies being born prematurely.

A great shift must take place! Women can, at any time, turn to the realm of the Gods and Goddesses or the superconscious within for help to make this shift—just as I, and many others, have already done. More than twenty-five years of work and research in the field of early parenting, from the time of preconception to early infancy, has lead to the development of the Holistic Parenting Program. In the program, future parents are given the opportunity to heal their emotional wounds and limitations stemming from their own time in the womb, birth, and early childhood. They learn to connect and bond with the intense sensations of well-being and emotional security that come from having functional inner parents and they make this a new way of life. Both parents learn to build rapport with the intelligence in their bodies and to meet their real needs for a healthy body. Having established their own emotional security, future parents naturally and effortlessly pass this on to their children. Often, almost miraculously, their relationship with their own parents greatly improves, too. Humanity's future is sown in the womb of the Mother Goddess.

Mothers Leading for a Change

Standing on the threshold of extinction or profound change, it is time to realize how far humankind has ventured from the understanding that we are an integral part of an intelligent, loving Universe. Official organizations are recognizing how vital women are to the changes that must occur. The current secretary general of the United Nations, Ban Ki-moon, has spoken up to encourage women to take a more active role in world affairs and particularly peace processes. There is a growing movement of women around the globe, from the grassroots level to the international community of the United Nations, educating on and advocating for recognition of the immense implications of the "primal period" for the world at large.

The period from conception through the first year sets the foundation for health, happiness, the capacity to love and be loved, intelligence, and creativity for every future planetary citizen. The future of our planet depends on how mothers live their pregnancies and how their babies are born and treated. She and her baby must be respected, supported, listened to and, yes, even venerated. This may seem like a daunting task for both men and women. By connecting with the archetypal Mother Goddess, all can access their innate instincts and immense transpersonal qualities to nurture, protect, love, and provide. In connecting with the archetypal parents within, understanding, respect, and support follow.

Governments, those servants of the people, must listen to the "Mother of Man." Mothers must have the right to birth their babies where and how they choose and be supported in those choices. The mother is the keeper of humanity's health. Nature in her infinite intelligence has provided her with all that it takes to nourish and nurture her baby naturally, before and after birth.

We must cease damaging and violating babies by wrenching them out of their mothers' bodies, out of the soft, warm, familiar feel and smell of the loving universe where all their needs are being met. Birth is a natural physiological process where, in the absence of fear, there is no physiological reason for pain. Women are being misled and mistreated, generating the fear-tension-pain syndrome discovered by the British obstetrician Grantly Dick Read nearly a century ago. Nature has perfectly designed women's body for natural calm comfortable birth in the absence of adrenaline caused by fear.

In the absence of "special circumstances," disturbing the skin-to-skin contact of mother and baby after birth, snatching the baby away from the first meeting of their eyes as they bond deeply together, and depriving them of this exceptional peak hormonal experience can be seen as no less than a crime. Babies are aware and intelligent and they record everything. It's time to stop treating women, the Goddess, the Mother, and Mother Nature, who feeds and nourishes us, as if she is flawed or stupid. She is not!

In my work as representative for the World Organization for Prenatal Education Associations, a non-governmental organization with special consultative status with the Economic and Social Council of the United Nations, I have the privilege of bringing this important understanding to the United Nations commissions and the international civil society community. While attending a world family summit in Egypt, I spoke to a minister of family affairs from a European country. When I told him I represented an organization on "prenatal life," his response was to tell me that his wife had wanted him to touch her pregnant belly and speak lovingly to their baby. "Surely, you don't believe all that stuff," he said, shaking his head. I rose to the occasion, telling him that we have had this science now for more than twenty-five years and that I was surprised and shocked that a man in his position was not aware of these vitally important scientific discoveries. Withholding this information from his citizens and thereby robbing parents of the opportunity to make a huge difference in their child's quality of life could be considered a crime against humanity, I continued. In his opening address at the summit, I was delighted and deeply touched that he included this prenatal period in his message on the importance of the foundation of the family for the well-being of society.

It is time to return to the roots of life and empower and support mothers to do what they instinctively know how to do: to give their best to their children; to love, nourish, protect, and empower the life they carry within them. A world movement is needed to believe once again in the Goddess within each woman and her ability to create the happy healthy human family for which many of us pray. Future parents must be informed that they can contribute greatly by beginning the regeneration of humankind, recreating a humanity endowed with the qualities of the "Gods."

What can they do? They can call upon the divine within each other and prepare themselves on all levels of their being—physical, emotional, mental, and spiritual—before consciously conceiving and inviting a soul to join their family. Once the woman is pregnant, both parents become like benevolent deities to their conscious unborn child: communicating with respect their unconditional love, care, protection, understanding, and so much more; and, in so doing, providing a creative, healthy, and loving universe for the next generation. Being present, lucid, and prepared for a sacred birthing experience, parents learn to fill their bodies with their own natural hormones. Sacred birthing experiences will, once again, become the norm as parents welcome their child into the world in a state of bliss. Held, loved, cuddled, talked, and sung to, each baby will develop in the bliss of being alive. Parents will empower their children with positive suggestions and creative images descending from the qualities of the innate Father God and Mother Goddess. Children will grow up free to find their own unique expression in our vast, intelligent, loving Universe. The vocation of bringing into the world another happy, intelligent, healthy, and creative member of this global family must once again be venerated and greatly supported by the whole human family and reflected in the laws and our way of life.

The New Royalty

Not every woman is destined to have children. The Goddess has many powerful roles. As a woman approaches and bonds with the Goddess within, she becomes the conductor of a choice of feminine archetypes. She may develop as a healer, educator, muse, actor, artist, writer, musician, politician, scientist, athlete, or any other creative expression of her divine nature. She can offer the unconditional love, nurturing, wisdom, and feminine strength of the Goddess to any project or calling. I have enjoyed the great fortune of witnessing many people, both men and women, emerge wriggling out of their weary "old genes," where life is experienced as separate and limited, and stepping into their "new selves" to enjoy the abundance and empowerment of their divine inheritance.

New royalty are emerging, the servants of a higher cause, those who have forged a union with their inner divinity. They shall lead the people of the world through these troubled times into the promised land of abundance for all. These "Goddess Queens," or role models of unconditional love and compassion, the nurturers of life-enhancing qualities, will take their place once again in the storybook of human history. Justice, peace, goodness, love, and wisdom shall shine like a sun providing a shield of protection for those who have learnt to live in harmony with the divine intelligence innate in all things. Children will learn from these women leaders and mothers. They will grow up discovering the wonders and infinite possibilities as they take their place as proud citizens of a wise loving Universe, venerating and adoring the Divine Mother.

Joelle (Joey) Berdugo-Adler, president and CEO of Diesel Canada, is a corporate leader, visionary, and philanthropist. In 2003, her husband and business partner, Louis Adler, succumbed to cancer. The following year, Joey began the Lou Adler Foundation to raise funds for cancer-related charities. In 2005, she founded ONEXONE (www.onexone.org) and has since raised millions of dollars for children around the world living in poverty. She also created the Adler/Sheiner Patient Support Program at a Montreal hospital to assist families in coping with serious illness. She is currently collaborating with Mary J. Blige's foundation FFAWN to empower girls and women.

Living with Passion— A Journey to Truth

Joey Adler

Not a single life, anywhere in the world, should be expendable. By combining passion with action, we can inspire others to commit to improving the world for every person, one by one.

Passion is not to be confused with ambition or desire. Passion derives from the decision to open our hearts completely. It prompts us to take risks for something we believe in so strongly that we are willing to expose ourselves to great vulnerability. Passion is about giving 100 percent to someone without expecting anything in return. Only in this way can we reach the highest level of connection in our relationships with spouse, family, and friends and in business. When we bring this philosophy to everything we do, we live life on a completely different level. For me, understanding this perfect truth came after a great loss—a journey I would never have chosen.

The expression "Life turns on a dime" refers to an unimaginable change in direction so quick and sharp that we are unable to stop it. August 30, 2001, brought such a change for me. On that night, my husband, Lou, who had been in the hospital for the past week with an undiagnosed problem, was rushed into surgery for leg circulation completely blocked from clots. He endured two surgeries in less than twenty-four hours to save his foot. His blood was clotting at a rate that no one in the hospital had ever seen. Any first- or second-year resident would have suggested that somewhere in his body was a cancerous mass. The senior doctors in the hospital had ignored the simplest clues. This was the beginning of a seventeen-month journey that would change my life forever.

Lou was eventually diagnosed with lung cancer and Trousseau's syndrome, a condition of recurrent blood clots. Few cases of the syndrome in medical history were as aggressive and as intense as Lou's.

The next four months comprised daily challenges as I fought to save my soul mate. Days into the process, one doctor told me not to waste my time and informed me that the hospital would not spend resources on a patient who would never make it. We were blessed with a few doctors—among them Dr. Nathan Sheiner, our surgeon; Dr. Jack Hirsh, a world-renowned expert on anticoagulation; and Dr. Denny Laporta, head of the ICU—who, along with the nurses, believed in the passion my family and I exhibited. We refused to allow any negativity anywhere close to Lou and we never left him alone.

After the first night and those two surgeries, Lou was put in a medically induced coma and challenges continued to arrive: a lung infection that traveled across the ICU after having killed another patient, gangrene, and middle-of-the-night lifesaving interventions. Every morning I was almost afraid to walk into the ICU for fear of the next nightmare to deal with, but I never gave up hope. I never allowed those whose advice was to let go to dictate my actions.

There was one hematologist whose mistakes, which seemed driven by her ego and an inability to admit she was wrong, caused unnecessary and painful surgeries. I am certain that the surgeries, in combination with the original misdiagnosis, precipitated Lou's death. I don't know, of course, whether Lou would still be alive today, but I do know that had he been taken care of properly two months before this nightmare began, he would have had many more years with a much better quality of life.

The hardships we faced fighting for his life are so painful to remember. Imagine having to fight every day with a few doctors who believe your husband is dying and actually create the circumstances that help generate that scenario while you and a few others fight hard to make sure that doesn't happen. Imagine ten surgeries, of which seven were probably unnecessary. I put every ounce of my energy into bringing Lou out of his coma so I could get him home.

On the morning of Sept 11, 2001, Dr. Sheiner brought the bad news that there was no longer an option: we had to amputate Lou's leg. I was devastated. I knew my husband and I knew the love he had for activities. At 9:00 a.m., I picked up the phone to call my sister at her house. Before I had a chance to tell her my bad news, she began to describe the disaster happening in New York. Sitting on the couch in the waiting room, the one I had been sleeping on for the last twelve days, I put my head in my hands and cried—for me, for my husband, for those people who were in the process of losing their lives. I wasn't sure that tomorrow would matter. It was one of the only times in the seventeen-month journey that I cried.

I left the hospital that night to go home to shower and change. I turned on the television and watched the towers come down. The images were so hard to watch. A few minutes later, during a commercial break, I watched a PSA about a children's organization in Africa. At that moment, I had the epiphany that would one day consume me. I realized that nowhere on Earth was the value of a single human life fully understood. The life of my husband, a beloved community leader, the lives of the thousands of souls in the towers, and the life of that child in Africa had equal value in the world's eyes—no value. I prayed that I would one day have the strength and opportunity to teach and promote the value of a single human life. I vowed to try.

The Talmud says, "If you save one life, you save the universe." We Jews are repeatedly exposed to this expression, but I had never fully understood or appreciated it. Out of that day and night and that profound saying arose the idea for what would become a foundation in honor of my husband.

After Lou had been in the ICU for four months, I was able to check him out of the hospital, minus his leg, which had been amputated in two stages, the second well above his knee. I was committed to getting Lou on his feet, even though doctors told me that would never happen.

I took Lou home from the rehab barely one week after he entered it, and home became our cocoon. I became knowledgeable on every facet of his medical condition and was able to change bandages, perform minor surgery on his limb, take the special blood tests he needed, and clean and fill the two deep holes in his chest. I spent the next ten months living every moment for the man I loved, all the while keeping vigil on the business we had built together.

Maintaining his dignity became a fierce and obsessive mission for me. With the help of my stepsons, Mitchell and Jarrid, and our family, we were able to take care of him at home, which all doctors had told me emphatically we could never do. We were blessed with many resources and that helped tremendously, but the truth is we were passionate about our responsibility. We loved him unconditionally and we gave him every ounce of our being, nurturing, and care.

We spent that summer as a family, having fun and laughing a lot. Mitchell put his dad on his motorcycle even though balancing with one leg was difficult. Lou and I held each other and whispered in the night how much we loved each other. I continued the ritual that I had started in the ICU, whispering, "I love you with all my heart forever and ever." We rehabilitated at home and have pictures of Lou walking on a prosthetic leg, proving wrong those who had said it couldn't be done.

I will never forget those ten months. I learned what love meant. I learned to love unconditionally to a depth I never knew existed.

When I look back at the joyous moments we lived, I get angry at the thought of the influence of naysaying doctors, that other families in similar circumstances might listen to them and give up. Those ten months of joy are a constant reminder that life should never be dismissed and no one has the right or even the ability to tell us when a life is ready to depart.

By late October, the cancer and clotting had returned, and all the unnecessary surgeries had compromised Lou's other leg, which had to be amputated. For the first time, my confidence wavered. I knew Lou would never be able to accept living without both limbs and I was scared. As I write this now, anxiety still consumes me remembering the night he awoke and I had to tell him his other leg was gone. We came home again, and nothing can describe picking up my husband like a child.

The winter brought bleak days of coming to grips with living one minute at a time; planning was no longer part of my life.

On January 20, we went to the hospital for a CAT scan. The doctors couldn't understand how Lou was still living. We started to discuss further options when the head nurse, who had become a close friend, said to me, "Joey, he is living for you and you are living for him. You need to tell him it is okay to let go."

The words were so profound. At that moment, I understood that I had lived the last seventeen months with a heart so open for another that I had given everything to Lou. Passion had consumed me—the passion for a man I loved beyond the love for myself. I went to his room, looked into his eyes, and said, "Honey, if you want to keep fighting, I am right here with you 100 percent, but if you are tired and have had enough, I am okay and I understand."

Lou told me he wanted to die at home and in my arms, so we went home. Three days later, he died as he had wanted. A peace such as I had never experienced came over the house. Although it took me many months to accept it intellectually, I believe that Lou's soul had been freed and he was at peace.

When I returned to work a week later, I felt empowered to make a change. I had a business to run without my partner. Would the banks support me alone, would Diesel SPA support my role as CEO without the front man? More important, how could I personally move forward in a positive way rather than be consumed by anger and bitterness, and how could I put the wheels in motion to honor the vow I had made on September 11, 2001?

My answer was to found a nonprofit organization, ONEXONE (One by One), to share the message that every single life is infinitely precious and that the power of one person to make a profound difference in the lives of others is more powerful than we can ever fathom. Saving and helping the most vulnerable (children), one at a time, became the mantra of ONEXONE. We focus on five factors essential to a child's well-being: water, hunger, healthcare, education, and play. Since the first event in 2005, we have raised millions of dollars for children here at home and around the world. With the help of many, including Matt Damon, Frank McKenna, and Edward and Suzanne Rogers, we have come a long way in a short time. It has been an amazing experience for me to travel and meet people from all walks of life whose sole motivation is to make a change in the lives of others.

Women are at the forefront of bringing passion to all facets of life. I believe that women's ability to open their hearts and give is what will change the world, one person at a time. Passion and compassion are traits that we bring to all areas of life, and our comfort in taking emotional risk is what will bring about change.

My journey has taught me that the phrase "This can't be done" should never be an option. I have learned to trust implicitly and, although I have been hurt a few times (meeting those whose ego is greater than the cause), the joy and love I have experienced far outweigh the few hurts. So much of the past seven years has been a tapestry of people weaving in and out of my life at the most incredibly opportune times, and opening my heart to them has allowed me to achieve what I dreamt about on that fateful night. Every day is a challenge and I must constantly work on myself in order to continue to move forward in the most positive way possible.

I fervently believe that thinking and speaking positively brings positive things, and the opposite is true as well. I remember a young East Indian doctor in the ICU telling me very early in the journey to get pictures of Lou in active life settings (horseback riding, golfing, skiing) and put them around his bed. When I asked why, he explained that those positive images would give the nurses and the other caregivers a positive image of Lou as human and not an inanimate blob.

I had always been a positive person, but after this journey I became more so. I also realized that being positive was not only thinking about positive actions, it was also about not creating negative situations. That is why, after Lou passed away, it became important for me to put back into the hospital. In the same ICU area where I spent four months, I established the Adler/Sheiner Patient Support Program to help families cope with catastrophic illness. An extraordinary woman, Sheila Kussner, created Lou's House, which supports cancer patients in the most unique ways. I was honored to become the main benefactor. Sheila survived cancer at the age of fifteen (more than sixty years ago) and was one of the first people to recognize the importance of emotional support in illness, especially cancer. Giving back to the hospital through creating these programs was cathartic for me, helping me to let go of anger and bitterness about what had happened to Lou.

Along with learning how to think, speak, and act positively, another challenge is learning to love unconditionally. Loving selflessly and unconditionally is the most freeing experience, and being passionate about everything we do is the key to a truly successful and happy life.

My journey continues, as does the pain of the loss of my beloved friend and husband, though it is no longer unrelenting. I will always remember where this journey began, and taking something so negative and turning it into something so positive is a lesson I am proud to share. I am filled with a sense of peace at knowing that Lou's and my experience has been a catalyst for good and that the spotlight that ONEXONE shines on children every day is making a difference in the world.

Azar Nafisi, the bestselling author of *Reading Lolita in Tehran,* is a visiting professor and the executive director of Cultural Conversations at the Foreign Policy Institute of Johns Hopkins University's School of Advanced International Studies in Washington DC, where she teaches courses on the relation between culture and politics. Formerly awarded a teaching fellowship at Oxford University, she also taught at the University of Tehran, the Free Islamic University, and Allameh Tabatabai, earning national respect and international recognition for advocating on behalf of Iran's intellectuals, youth, and especially young women. In 1981, she was expelled from the University of Tehran for refusing to wear the mandatory Islamic veil and did not resume teaching until 1987. www.azarnafisi.com

CHAPTER FOURTEEN

A Home That Cannot Be Taken

Azar Nafisi

I can cite the dates when the war with Iraq started (September 22, 1980) and ended (August 20, 1988), and I can tell you the casualties were high, but I feel helpless when it comes to describing the subtle changes that transformed the fabric of our lives, so that I could walk down the familiar streets of my childhood and feel like an utter stranger. In a diary I started in the fall of 1980, somewhere in between my teaching notes for classes on *Huckleberry Finn, The Great Gatsby,* and Gorky's *Mother,* I wrote, "Home is not Home anymore." Our lives altered, not just by catastrophe and carnage, but also by a different kind of violence, almost imperceptible, that wormed its way into our normal everyday lives.

Like my cousin Majid, who roamed the streets of Tehran in the hope of bringing about a revolution, I had dreamed of change in the political system, but at the core of everything I did was the idea of returning home, to those mountains, to the night sky under which I had slept throughout my childhood, to Naderi Street and the scents of fish, leather, coffee, and chocolate, to the movie houses and restaurants, and cafés with their lively music, to my father who, holding onto my hand as we walked along the wide, tree-lined avenue toward the mountains, would say, "One reason we should believe in God is that poetry like Rumi's or Ferdowsi's exists." Nothing is more deadly than crushed expectations: the revolution was supposed to change the political system, to bring more freedom, to make us more at home in our own home. Now I had returned and nothing was the same. Or, more disturbing yet, everything seemed the same but was in fact different: the streets had new names, Iran had become the Islamic Republic of Iran. Even the language sounded oddly unfamiliar, a language in which citizens were either emissaries of God or Satan, and women like myself were "prostitutes" and "Western agents." The face of religion was changing from the gentle teachings of my father to the ideological rants of a group of people, staunch followers of Ayatollah Khomeini, who called themselves Hezbollah—the Party of God. Their slogan was "Only one party: Hezbollah."

Religion was no longer just a part of Iranian culture, shaping it and being shaped by it; time and again Ayatollah Khomeini reminded us that not Iran but Islam was our real home and that Islam's borders stretched from Iran out into the wide world.

I cannot think of the Iran-Iraq war without remembering that this was a war between two governments who were simultaneously carrying out a brutal campaign against their own people. Ayatollah Khomeini had called the war a blessing; for him it was a great diversion from the mounting domestic problems and opposition. In his mind, now the whole nation would gather against the foreign invader while at the same time the state could suppress any voice of dissent in the name of national security. During the eight years that the war lasted, Tehran was bombed several times, never as heavily as some of the border cities in the province of Khuzistan, but in the intervals between the bombings the fear remained. Every time there was a victory march on the radio announcing the bombing of another Iraqi "nest of spies" in Baghdad, we knew all too well that those spies were ordinary people like ourselves, as we knew that soon Tehran would be targeted and Saddam would announce the destruction of "nests of spies" in Tehran. I felt a great deal of empathy for those ordinary Iraqis, forced to be our foes, but in reality our kin in distress.

About a month after my return to Iran, I started teaching at the University of Tehran and a girl's college whose changing name was symbolic of the constantly changing times: during the Shah's time it was known as Farah Pahlavi, after the Shah's wife; then it became Mottahedin, after a female member of the militant Islamic Mojahedeen Organization who had been killed during the Shah's time. When the divisions between the Mojahedeen and the new regime deepened, the college's name was changed again to Al Zahra, to commemorate the prophet Mohammad's daughter. The first day I entered the cavernous hall of the faculty of Persian and Foreign Languages and Literature at the University of Tehran, I was struck by the buzz of different voices rising and falling. Several tables were laid out with pamphlets, books, and leaflets, each table representing a different political grouping. I soon got used to the noise, the crowds that swelled and receded at the tables, the constant motion.

After a while I myself would become part of the motion: I would rush from meeting to meeting, protesting the expulsion of a professor, attending demonstrations and sit-ins. But my point of focus was always my classes. From the moment I stepped, with fear and anxiety, into the immense room to teach a class irrelevantly called "Research," and wrote on the blackboard the required reading: *Adventures of Huckleberry Finn,* I felt at home. No matter how contentious the atmosphere that reigned over the university, it was somehow calming to know that these books had survived wars, revolutions, famines. They had been there long before we were born and would be there long after we were gone. (What was it that Ferdowsi had said? "I shall not die, these seeds I have sown will save / My name and reputation from the grave.") The novels of George Eliot, Jane Austen, Flaubert, and Tolstoy became a vehicle to express the need to foster a democracy of voices. Tom Jones taught us the value of humor, Tristram Shandy of irony, and each novel we read seemed to offer a lesson in the complexity of moral choices and individual responsibility. All became somehow deeply and urgently relevant to the reality we lived in. Sometimes I mixed in examples from Persian literature, drawing mainly from banned books such as Sadegh Hedayat's *Buf-e Kur,* Forough Farrokhzad's *Another Birth,* or from our classical past, discussing Rumi's exuberant playfulness, or Hafez's mischievous delight in undermining orthodoxy.

On March 21, 1980, on the occasion of the Iranian New Year, Ayatollah Khomeini issued a harsh statement, accusing the universities of being agents of Western imperialism. At Friday Prayer on April 18th, Ali Khamenei (who was to replace Khomeini as the Supreme Leader in 1989) attacked the universities, saying, "We are not afraid of economic sanctions or military intervention. What we are afraid of is Western universities and the training of our youth in the interests of West or East." This was the signal for what came to be known as the Cultural Revolution: the plan to close down the universities in order to Islamize them, create a new curriculum, and purge them of undesirable faculty, students, and staff.

The students and faculty did not give up without a fight. I remember the fiery speeches, the demonstrations and sit-ins, the vigilantes who would suddenly appear with knives and stones to attack the demonstrators. I remember running for cover in dusty alleys. I remember finding a refuge in a nearby bookstore seconds before the owner locked the doors and we all scrambled away from the window to avoid the bullets. Every day we heard news of murdered students, their bodies snatched away by agents of the regime. These scenes appear out of nowhere, still disturbing my sleep.

Soon the tables of pamphlets in the hall would be removed. Many of those who stood behind them, representing different student groups and tendencies, would be expelled, arrested, and in some cases executed. All organizations except the Islamic ones would be closed—though not without bloody protests, sit-ins, more arrests, jailings, and executions. In our faculty, me and two other colleagues would refuse to wear the mandatory veil and soon I would be expelled from teaching along with many other colleagues.

In time, many of the students who pressed for the Islamization of the universities would become disillusioned and start criticizing the regime, staging protests and demonstrations. Could any of us have foreseen how some would become enamored of Jane Austen and F. Scott Fitzgerald, Spinoza, and Hannah Arendt, and begin to question the tenets of the regime they had so ardently supported? Soon they would be asking for secularism and democracy, the ones arrested, jailed, and executed.

I was leaving Al Zahra, the girls' college, for home, admiring as I often did the way the garden with its mown lawn and flower beds, carefully arranged to appear haphazardly strewn together, made one feel secure and serene amid all the turmoil outside the gate, when I heard a loud whisper behind me: "Professor!"

I had not noticed anyone following me and was startled when I turned around to see her standing so very close to me. "May I speak to you?" she asked. "Of course," I said. "That day when you were talking to Miss Bagheri about *Wuthering Heights,*" she said, "I was there." Miss Bagheri, whose sensibilities had been offended by the novel, was an aggressive defendant of morality on campus. She had waylaid me one day after class to protest the book's immorality: she said it set a bad example by condoning adultery. "Novels are about life, they embrace all aspects of existence," I said. I asked her, "When you read Ferdowsi, do you start believing in demons and people living for four hundred years? Do you decide to go whaling when you read Moby-Dick?" "This is different," Miss Bagheri said. "Adultery is a sin." "That is the point of novels," I told her. "The only thing sacred about them is that they are by nature profane. It is a great love story. Can you tell me of one good love story that sticks to the rules?" By the end of the term this same

Miss Bagheri had told me enthusiastically that she was now so in love with Catherine and Heathcliff that the girls in her dorm made fun of her.

"And so," my stealthy stalker said, "I want to know what you meant when you said that the only thing sacred about a novel is that it is profane." She was dressed in a black chador, revealing only the "oval of the face," as the edicts on proper dressing indicated. Her face evaded description. It was rather long, rather pale, almost bloodless, and bony. Serious eyes that, unlike those of so many other students, looked at you directly. I don't remember her name. She was different from Miss Bagheri. There was a tenaciousness, a certain stubbornness in her that I liked—she would not change her mind about *Wuthering Heights* in a matter of months. Her tenacity did not come only from prejudice or her religious beliefs; it seemed to me as if she was trying to solve something as she talked to me. Despite her faith, she appeared to be driven by an inner puzzle, so wrapped did she seem to be in some interior world. The pause between my last sentence and her response was at times so long that I thought she had forgotten we were conversing. Her serious demeanor made me feel frivolous. I wanted to joke and lighten her burden. This was not the kind of discussion I was used to having with my religious students about the morality of a work of literature—I had discovered how boringly similar their arguments were to my own and my comrades' reasoning when I was a radical activist, in the way they reduced all literature into an ideological message.

I said to her, "Perhaps if you and I discussed some of these so-called immoral novels my meaning would become clearer." She asked for a list of books. She said she had read Forough Farrokhzad, and I reminded her that her works were banned. She said, "Everything is permissible, I think, if it is in pursuit of knowledge." Pursuit of knowledge! That was one way of putting it. "Anyway, Forough Farrokhzad was more Western," she said. "She did not follow our traditions." I suggested that she should perhaps take another look at the women in the *Shahnameh* and other classical tales. After all, adultery is not a Western construct, nor is love. In *Vis and Ramin,* the lovers openly commit adultery, because their main moral commitment is to love. But while we are on the topic of adultery and the novel, how about starting with *Madame Bovary* and *Anna Karenina*?

Over the next two months this student and I met at least once a week. We sat on the lawn or walked up and down the leafy street on which the campus was located. Once or twice I brought a cream puff or two and she made sure the next time to bring a big box of pastries. She read *Madame Bovary* and some of *Anna Karenina*. She said these women were repentant in the end. "Not repentant," I said, "desperate. Anna's heart was broken, Emma had reached the end of her rope." "You said it's about love," she said. "That too, but with Emma it's more about illusions, the dreams we impose on a drab and harsh reality. She married because of that dream and she cheated on her husband for the same reason. She had read too many romantic novels and wanted to be a romantic heroine."

"She broke her contract," she said; "she had a contract to honor." "She did," I said slowly, "but Charles Bovary was also partly a victim of his own romantic illusions. He loved the idea of Emma as much as, if not more than, he loved Emma herself. He was blind to who she was and what she wanted from him."

I asked, "Why don't you think women who marry without love are adulterers? It seems to me they are worse." "They are bound by their duty," she said, "they don't lie." "There are so many different kinds of lying," I said. "I know a woman, a very morally correct woman who would never dream of adultery, yet for almost thirty years she has been cheating on her husband, emotionally, with her dead first husband." When I told my student about that woman, she said, "I feel sorry for her and for everyone else too. This woman you talk about, she suffered from the absence of love"—my student said this as if the absence of love were a form of malady. I registered that phrase and returned to it every once in a while when I thought of my mother and grandmother, of Aunt Mina, the poet Alam Taj, and so many other women who felt their lives were wasted not just because of their aborted social ambitions but also because they suffered from an absence of love.

We trailed from there to the meaning of loyalty and self-respect, and, inevitably, time and again to women, women in Europe, in America, in Egypt, in Turkey, who had fought the same fights, tolerated the same humiliations. "But why aren't we told about all that?" she asked. "Why is it never mentioned in school?" We ended up talking about women in our country, who could go to school and read *Wuthering Heights,* but were deprived of the right to make the most basic choices about their lives: whom to marry, how to dress, where to work. Her intelligent eyes took on a new light. "It's funny now that I think of it," she said, "before the revolution I most probably would have given in to an arranged marriage, to spite the government, but now I am not sure anymore. I guess this is what the novel is, it makes us think about these things—or something like that."

Suddenly she stopped coming to classes and the term ended. I left Al Zahra and was immersed in the campus battles that flared up at the University of Tehran. I wanted to ask Miss Bagheri about her, but I did not. Only from time to time I returned to her and wondered what became of her. Did she marry a man of her choice? Was she ever tempted by another man, or the idea of another life?

Often in the morning we would wake up to some new and unexpected event. My mother's sources (she had her "eyes and ears" in every corner of the country, like the emperor Darius) had informed her that soon there would be a reversal of fortunes for the new rulers. Soon, she confided, "the grand Ayatollahs will rebel against Khomeini."

And they did rebel. Many clerics did not believe that the religious establishment should interfere directly with the affairs of state. For centuries the clerics had exerted power by pressuring the state and posing as supporters of the poor and the needy. Although Khomeini seized power in the name of tradition, his ideological interpretation of religion was modern and, according to some, antitraditional, influenced by modern totalitarian ideologies. Around the country traditional religious leaders, further up in the hierarchy than Khomeini, were making their unhappiness known. The most prominent of these, Ayatollah Shariatmadari, began to openly criticize the regime. In Tabriz a million people reportedly participated in demonstrations in support of Ayatollah Shariatmadari, who was calling for the separation of religion and state, which he insisted was one of the cornerstones of Shia Islam.

These rebellions were quashed violently. The venerable Ayatollah Shariatmadari was defrocked and jailed. His supporters were arrested and some murdered, and he died while under house arrest. ("Remember that when Khomeini was in trouble with the Shah this same Shariatmadari sat under a tree weeping in protest," Father would remind us with an ironic smile. "Our new Imam knows how to show his gratitude.") A message was sent by the regime to the faithful: to survive they would have to be loyal to only one interpretation of the faith, and to accept the new political role of the clergy.

Father felt that this spelled the end of Islam in our country, and he did have a point. "No foreign power," he said, "could destroy Islam the way these people have." Later a friend would say, "How can you believe in a religion when, from politics to plumbing, it is held responsible for everything?"

Mother was becoming increasingly interested in my activities at the university. Now, when she called me down to join her and her friends for coffee, she would say, "Tell them, tell them what 'they' are doing at the universities to women." She would count all the injustices committed against women: banning them from serving in the judiciary, from participating in sports, abrogating the family protection law (she conveniently forgot that she had herself voted against it), lowering the age of marriage, and on and on she would go. Then she would turn to me and say, "Tell them." She wanted me to describe the demonstrations and sit-ins staged by women, the battles over the veil. "And then what did your friend Haideh say to the committee on the Cultural Revolution," she would ask, egging me on, and before I could say anything she would turn and say triumphantly, "And this woman, Azar's colleague, gets up and says, 'You have turned the universities, the bastions of knowledge, into torture houses.' Of course, she, Azar, and two of her colleagues went to the meeting without the veil," she would add, with evident pride.

After the Islamic Revolution I came to realize the fragility of our mundane existence, the ease with which all that you call home, all that gives you an identity, a sense of self and belonging, *can* be taken away from you. I learned that what my father had given me through his stories was a way to make a home for myself that was not dependent on geography or nationality or anything that other people can take away from me. These stories could not guard me against the pain I felt at my parents' loss; they did not offer consolation or closure. It was only after their deaths that I came to realize that they each in their own way had given me a portable home that safeguards memory and is a constant resistance against the tyranny of man and of time.

Madonna, singer, dancer, actor, fashion trendsetter, and entrepreneur, has sold more than two hundred million albums worldwide. The Recording Industry Association of America cites her as the best-selling female rock artist of the twentieth century; *Guinness World Records* listed her in 2007 as the world's most successful female recording artist of all time. In the more than two decades that she has enjoyed icon status, she has continually reinvented her music and image. From her controversial songs such as *Like a Virgin* and *Like a Prayer* to her coffee table book *Sex*, Madonna has forged her own way. Raised a Catholic, she now finds spiritual nurturance in Kabbalah, the mystical tradition of Judaism. In 2006, she and Kabbalah scholar Michael Berg founded Raising Malawi (www.raisingmalawi.org), a nonprofit dedicated to aiding orphans and other children in Malawi.

CHAPTER FIFTEEN

I Found an Answer

Madonna

There is an old cliché: When the student is ready, the teacher appears.

I had traveled the world many times over, performed in soccer stadiums, appeared in films, dined with state leaders, collaborated with great artists, and achieved what most people would view as a high level of success, but I still felt something was missing in my life. I was pregnant with my daughter, almost fourteen years ago, and had just finished the film *Evita* when I realized I had spent my whole life worrying about myself and that I would soon be responsible for someone else's life.

I was raised a Catholic and my father was very religious, but none of my questions ever really got answered when it came to trying to understand why people suffered in the world or what the meaning of life was. And suddenly I thought, "What will I teach my child about the important things in life?"

I had been practicing yoga for years and studying Sanskrit. I had read many books by the great yogi masters and Indian avatars. I studied Buddhism and the teachings of the Dalai Lama. I studied Taoism and the Art of War. I read about the Gnostics and the early Christians. I learned a lot and I was very inspired, but I still could not connect the dots and find a way to take this knowledge and apply it to my daily life.

I was looking for an answer.

I went to a dinner party in L.A. A woman sitting next to me was telling me about a class she was taking from a rabbi. She said it was so inspiring and that I should come along. I asked her what it was about.

She said, "Life."

I asked her what it was called.

She said, "Kabbalah."

I told her I wasn't Jewish and she said: "What difference does it make what it's called and what religious upbringing you have had if you are inspired?"

She had a point.

So I went to the class. I sat in the back and I listened to a man named Eitan teach the class. I heard what he had to say and I knew at that moment my life would never be the same.

I began to go to the classes regularly and sit in the class with my notebook. No one bothered me. I took notes.

I met with Eitan privately and asked a lot of questions. The thing that was most encouraged was to inquire further.

All the questions I had about life began to be answered and I realized I had finally found a "belief system" or philosophy that incorporated science and spirituality. I was learning about physics, astronomy, nature, and the laws of cause and effect. All the puzzle pieces started falling into place. Life no longer seemed like a series of random events. I started to see patterns in life. I woke up. I began to be conscious of my words and my actions and to really see the results of them.

I also began to see that being rich and famous wasn't going to bring me lasting fulfillment and that it was not the end of the journey. It was the beginning of the journey.

I have been studying with Eitan consistently since that first class and it was only a matter of time before I met Michael Berg, whose father, Rav Berg, comes from a long line of Kabbalists and was the teacher of Eitan. Michael Berg is a very unique human being. He might be the smartest person I know.

At first he seemed quiet and shy, conservative, and even perhaps a bit naïve. But ask him a question on any subject and you will find yourself swimming in an ocean of information. It's astounding what he knows and what he has accomplished at such a young age. The fact that he translated twenty-two volumes of the Zohar [considered by many the most important Kabbalistic text] from Aramaic into Hebrew and English is remarkable. The funny thing about Michael is that he is as comfortable and knowledgeable in discussing the teachings of the Ari [sixteenth-century Kabbalist Isaac Luria] as he is in discussing his favorite *Seinfeld* episode.

He knows more about pop culture and what's going on in the world than anyone I know. Yet his desire to effect change in the world and the compassion he feels for people who are suffering are unparalleled. When Michael gets up to tell a story in front of a room full of people, there is never a dry eye in the house, including his own.

I am lucky to call him my friend.

He has a child with Down syndrome and it is perhaps because of this that he feels the need to come to the rescue of children who are living in challenging situations or abject poverty. We were both looking for a project to do with children. Lo and behold, a Malawian woman appeared and told us about the plight of over one million children orphaned by AIDS in a small landlocked country in Africa. Before we knew it, we were visiting Malawi, and that was the birth of our foundation: Raising Malawi.

Of course, now that I know what I know, I realize that this did not happen by chance. Once again, the students were ready and the teacher appeared. In this case, the children of Malawi are the teachers. They have taught me so much. And they continue to teach me. As do Michael and Eitan.

Part IV:
Dare to Be

Judy Chicago is an artist, feminist, and writer whose career spans more than three decades. As an artist she has been highly influential, exploring a variety of media and addressing issues of gender, ethnicity, and power. Her best-known work, the massive installation *The Dinner Party*, has been exhibited across the world. In addition to her artistic achievements, she pioneered feminist art education, setting up study programs at Fresno State University, the California Institute of the Arts, and the Los Angeles Women's Building. She has published seven books, including two autobiographical texts, *Through the Flower* and *Beyond the Flower*. www.judychicago.com

CHAPTER SIXTEEN

Women and Art
Judy Chicago

From the time I was five, I began the practice of studying art, visiting the Art Institute of Chicago to take classes, and to wander through the galleries where my ambition was shaped. From very early on, I had set my sights upon becoming the kind of artist who would make a contribution to art history. However, the kind of art on display in the galleries through which I walked was sending a contradictory message.

On the one hand, I felt inspired by the wonderful paintings I saw in the museum and would spend hours studying the millions of colored dots that together form Seurat's *La Grande Jatte* (1884–86), learning a great deal from his use of color opposites. But when I looked at, for example, Degas's sensuous images of women, I could not relate to them or to many other male artists' depictions of the female, primarily because too many of those pictured seemed content to just lie around being gazed at, something I myself had no intention of doing.

One might say that this was when I began to experience "rupture," as it is sometimes described. I set myself against these images because they did not have anything to do with me. Even then,

I knew that I did not wish to become the object of the male gaze. Rather, I wanted to be the one who did both the gazing and the painting. Later, I came to understand that some of the confusion I felt as a female child was the consequence of an art system that privileges male artists, as evidenced by the centuries of discrimination against women artists; the omission of their achievements from the canon of art history; and the fact that even today, only 5 percent of the art found in American museums consists of work by women artists.

Then there were my experiences as a young woman artist struggling to be taken seriously. With considerable effort, I managed to wedge myself into an art system in which few women were visible, primarily by adopting what might best be described as "male drag," i.e., banishing any indication of my gender from my art and assuming an aggressive stance that was false to my nature as a person.

However, I still found myself feeling opposed to and isolated from the type of art-making that has dominated much of what we have considered great art, a good deal of which seems to privilege form over content and technical innovation over human meaning, or at least meaning that affirms rather than denies my experience and feelings as a female person.

My problem was that I did not wish to be marginalized, nor did I want my experiences as a woman to be considered less central to the human dialogue than those of men. And it is crucial to understand that one of the ways in which the importance of male experience is conveyed is through the art objects that are exhibited and preserved in our museums. Whereas men experience presence in our art institutions, women experience primarily absence, except in images that do not necessarily reflect women's own sense of themselves.

Consequently, since the early 1970s, I have been on a path whose goal has been to bring the female experience into the very mainstream of art history rather than its being—as it is too often—an "add-on," at the end of the text as it were. When I began down this path, I was quite alone and, it seemed, without any historical context—at least that's what people said to me.

And here I paraphrase a museum curator who, in an effort to explain some of the intense art-world hostility to which my work and even my very person have been subjected, said that there was no context for my art. As a result, he suggested, people in the art community did not know how to deal with my work, particularly because many of the issues it raised made them uncomfortable, which, according to him, was another reason they reacted negatively to it.

However, I had discovered from the research I had done in the late 1960s and throughout the 1970s in relation to my best-known project, *The Dinner Party* (a monumental, multimedia tribute to women's history), that I did indeed have a context. This context extends back in time hundreds of years and consists not only of countless writings by women but also of a large body of art that, to my mind, evidences a different perspective from the art of men, along with a range of responses to the questions with which I was then concerned, questions concerning the nature of female identity. The trouble seemed to be that this context was not visible to most people.

This was the problem I set out to redress with *The Dinner Party*, one of my goals being to provide a tangible symbol of the many achievements and something of the historical context of women in Western civilization. Like most young women of my generation, I had grown up without any knowledge of this information, and, after I discovered it, I dedicated myself to breaking what seems a terrible historical cycle of erasure, a process which results in successive generations of women remaining ignorant of their marvelous heritage as women.

Not that I believed that this information would be valuable only to women, not at all. In fact, I was and am deeply convinced that men and women alike need exposure to a broader range of human experience than that which is transmitted through our educational institutions, if only so that they might be better equipped to embrace the diversity of the world in which we now live. *The Dinner Party* was, in part, intended to call into question the way history has been written, demonstrating that an equally biased and exclusive historical picture could be assembled from any number of viewpoints—in this case, from the perspective of women. The piece might also be considered a corrective to the notion transmitted to me through my own education that women had made no significant contributions to history and—more pernicious in terms of my fierce ambitions as an artist—the idea that there had never been any really great women artists.

During my years of research for *The Dinner Party*, I stumbled upon dozens of images by women artists that made me feel affirmed in a way that the work of their male counterparts never did. These included, for example, the self-portraits I discovered in basements or dark corners of European museums, which, as a happy result of recent feminist scholarship, have begun to emerge from obscurity to take their place in the art historical canon.

As for the widely accepted argument that many of the famous, even iconical, paintings by men constitute great art, I call into question some of the criteria by which greatness has been measured. After all, how "great" is yet another image of a nude woman displayed upon a couch, not matter how well it might be painted?

One reason I wanted to confront the issue of what constitutes great art is that I am concerned for the ways in which young women develop their sense of self. Still, despite my maturity, when I visit museums filled with work by men, I feel my sense of self challenged to the point that I experience a sense of dissolution—as if I do not exist.

Even when the paintings do not evidence overt hostility toward women or the sense of entitlement with which most male artists approach the female body, I believe that they inevitably produce the same kind of confusion for many young women that I experienced when I was young. And I cannot help but wonder how many of these young women will have the wherewithal to develop and sustain the oppositional gaze (learning to look against the preconceptions of the dominant culture in order to resist its perspective and its expectations).

Almost three decades ago, I was motivated to make visible my own opposition to an art system which, I had come to realize, disempowers women, in large part through the erasure of our aesthetic heritage. Once I began to encounter the rich history of women's art, it changed my life, partly because much of the work I discovered was—to me—important, sometimes even great art. But, more significantly, the knowledge I acquired about the bravery of the women who had made the work gave me strength to continue in the face of innumerable obstacles.

In addition, women's images and the achievements represented by these images helped me to see myself as part of history rather than in opposition to it, even though it was a history which was largely invisible. Thus, one might say that I have lived in opposition to the prevailing system, but in harmony with an alternative system, one which has nurtured my sense of self.

I carried this newfound context within my mind for more than fifteen years, and during that time I was engaged in an image-making whose focus was both an alternative female identity and also the assertion of an oppositional set of values. These values were oppositional in the sense that they challenged many prevailing ideas as to what art was to be about (female rather than male experience); how it was to be made (in an empowering, cooperative method rather than a competitive, individualistic mode); and what materials were to be employed in creating it (any that seemed appropriate, irrespective of what socially constructed gender associations particular media might be perceived to have).

By the mid-1980s, I felt that I had realized many of my aesthetic goals, in particular those which involved the creation of images about my discoveries about women's history and my exploration into what it means to be a woman. My primary intention in terms of this body of art was for it to reach others, especially young women, so that they might be strengthened by it to the point that they might not be persuaded by the plethora of images of women that can so threaten a woman's sense of herself that she ends up retreating from her own perspective.

In the decades since I found my own path as an artist—one whose aim has been to contribute to ending the cycle of erasure of women's achievements, attested to by *The Dinner Party*—women's studies courses have abounded; feminist theory has evolved into a formidable body of intellectual challenges to traditional thought; and women artists all over the world have internalized the freedom that female artists of my generation fought so hard to acquire. As a result, an enormous body of art by women of the past has emerged from the shadows of history through the scholarship of countless feminist art historians. And new and exciting art by women is being created everywhere.

Nevertheless, I receive innumerable letters from female students and, when I lecture at universities in various parts of the world, often hear stories that repeat the same complaint. Too many educational and art institutions continue to present women's work in a token way, and hence, young women are still being deprived of knowledge about what women before them thought, taught, and created. Rather than inheriting a world made different by the infusion of oppositional ideas, new generations of women are experiencing the same identity problems that motivated my own search for a female history and for images which affirmed rather than negated my existence. In terms of young women artists, it is my perception that too many of them continue to feel isolated and contextless with the same sense of belonging nowhere that I had. My goals have always included bringing women's art into the mainstream. As long as women's art is treated as an "exotic other," it will continue to be marginalized.

Another of my goals has always been to demonstrate that women's art could be as interesting to men as men's art has been to women throughout history. In contrast to some feminists, I firmly believe that women's art can and should be understood by men, and that the body of art by women about the female experience can help to expand men's understanding of women and to broaden their views of what constitutes the human experience.

However, too few men have been willing to acknowledge or accept that they have much to learn from women and from women's art. One explanation for this resistance might be that many men find it difficult to be open to a different way of seeing, particularly one which demands the recognition that the universality of perspective too often claimed for male art (especially white male art) is, in reality, a view of the world shaped and limited by men's experience, which has generally been based upon the privilege of being male in a male-dominated world.

My deepest desire is to make a contribution to a more equitable world and to do so through what is dearest to me, which is—and always has been—visual art.

Renée Fleming is an internationally renowned soprano whose artistry has taken her to the world's capitals and great opera houses. The Metropolitan Opera celebrated her in its opening night gala of 2008, an evening starring the singer with the voice of "liquid gold." With many recordings to her name and two Grammy Awards, her latest CD is *Homage—The Age of the Diva,* comprising rarely heard works associated with legendary singers of the past. Among her many awards are the *Chevalier de la Légion d'Honneur* by the French government and an honorary doctorate from the Juilliard School. She has even had an iris named after her, and a master chef created the dessert "La Diva Renée" in her honor. www.reneefleming.com

CHAPTER SEVENTEEN

Generations in Our Voices

Renée Fleming

How does a girl from Churchville, New York, come to be asked to represent her country at a major international musical event, standing on the stage of a theater filled with dignitaries? The answer is unnervingly simple: it all comes down to two little pieces of cartilage in my throat. Those vocal cords—delicate, mysterious, slightly unpredictable—have taken me to unimaginable places. I have slept at the White House after staying up until two in the morning talking music with the Clintons and the Blairs. I have sung for Václav Havel at the end of his presidency and sat beside him at dinner for four hours afterward while he spoke of his life.

Apart from the moments of celebration and commemoration, I have performed at more solemn occasions. I have sung "Amazing Grace" at a ceremony at Ground Zero, only a few months after the attacks of September 11, with nine thousand people crushed into a space that was impossibly small for them, filling up the streets, pressing against one another shoulder-to-shoulder in every direction until they became one single life of sorrow. In the week leading up to that event, I had sung that song again and again, trying to imprint it into the muscle memory of my throat so that when the time came to perform it, I would be able to get through to the end without crying. I remember a young girl who was sitting at the front of the crowd with her family on the day of the ceremony. She was about sixteen years old, and I had no idea whom she had lost, but among the obviously grief-stricken people who carried photographs and signs and wept, her expression seemed utterly empty. Her eyes were dry. It was as if she had lost her own soul when those buildings went down, and when I started to sing I had to look at the sky or I knew I'd never be able to maintain my composure.

Given the fact that most classical musicians are not household names or faces recognizable from television, it's interesting to speculate about why people so often turn to a classically trained musician, and most often a singer, in times of national conflict or grief. Why choose a soprano to represent our collective emotional experience, rather than a familiar singer from the world of popular music who has sold millions of records? Why turn to a far lesser-known voice whose music is appreciated by a smaller audience? I think the answer lies in two places. First, the tradition of music grounds us and connects us to one another through a sort of universal appreciation that transcends taste, particularly in such songs as "Amazing Grace" and "God Bless America." Second, a trained voice has a kind of innate authority that transmits a sense of strength. We can be heard without a microphone. We sing with the entire body. The sounds that we make emanate not just from the head, but from the whole heart and soul and, most important, the gut. The word "classic" has come to be applied to so many things in our culture—cars, rock music, a particular episode of a television show—when in its truest sense it carries the weight of something that has been distilled over time and represents the highest quality in a given field. The music we sing has been loved in many past generations and will continue to flourish and find life and love in the future.

Thanks to the instrument of my voice, I have been fortunate enough to be invited to step onto the stage at great national and international occasions. I have seen the world from the vantage point of the greatest opera houses and recital halls. I have been incredibly fortunate in my career, and people often remark to me, "What a wonderful gift you have—how glorious it must be to open your mouth and have that voice pour out!" While it's a fact that a voice begins with natural talent, any talent must be nurtured, cajoled, wrestled with, pampered, challenged, and, at every turn, examined.

The story of my singing has a plot not unlike those of the horse novels I loved in my youth: A child finds a wild horse whose true potential only she can see. She loves it and cares for it, trains it tirelessly. The girl and the horse have a commitment to each other that no one else can get in the way of. She sticks by the horse through injury and doesn't believe anyone who says the horse is all washed up. When the horse is thriving, she turns down all offers to sell it off. In the end, the horse proves to be a winner, and in return for her work and devotion, it takes her to victories she had never dreamed possible.

*   *   *   *   *

Often in the middle of a performance I find myself completely overcome with a deep feeling of gratitude for the fulfillment inherent in this work. Music enabled me as a fragile young person to give voice to emotions I could barely name, and now it enables me to give my voice the unique and mysterious power to speak to others.

The central challenge I face is making sure I have enough time with my children. I openly discuss everything about my work and my traveling with Amelia and Sage. They know exactly when I'm leaving and when I'm coming home and when they get to go with me. We make calendars; we e-mail and call each other every day.

We never lose our sense of connectedness. I stay completely informed about everything that's going on with them. I work very hard to make it clear to my daughters that they come first with me, and they seem to know that they do. They're also at an age now when they're aware of my Herculean work ethic and the necessity for multitasking to the extreme, but they also know deep down that if push came to shove, there would be no choice: it would always be them. I never close the door on them when I'm rehearsing. They can come and sit in my lap. They can interrupt me if they need to. I've never wanted them to feel they were competing with music for my attention, and so far, so good. They love music. I don't push it, but it's always there, and they're welcome to it. My general philosophy as a parent is to expose them to as much as is humanly possible—as many kinds of interests, as many kinds of people, places, and situations.

Untold amounts of love go into making sure their needs are met on a daily basis, and happily, I'm now finding it possible to better balance my personal life with my professional life overall. I feel grateful that my mother worked and instilled in me an understanding that while she was different from my friends' parents, I could be proud of her. We don't teach our daughters to be dependent anymore, but that wasn't the case in my mother's generation. Recently, Sage performed in the children's chorus of a Russian opera, and when I went backstage to pick her up after the accolades, I said, "Sweetie, you're skipping rope onstage and you're supposed to be having fun. May I please have one of your most stellar smiles next time? And sing out!" I had to laugh when I realized that history was repeating itself. I'm not only caretaker of the girls; I'm also their role model. I tell them that I hope they'll find a life's ambition that makes them as happy as mine has made me: something they feel passionately about.

One beautiful day in Connecticut, I was driving the girls on errands when my older daughter, who was ten at the time, started singing one of the Queen of the Night's virtuosic arias from *Die*

Zauberflöte, complete with high Fs absolutely perfectly in place. I keep a pitch pipe in the car, because I often warm up while driving (make a note to stay clear of sopranos on the road), and with it I verified that she was even singing in the right key. I looked at her and said, "Amelia, that's amazing! Where did you hear that?" I had taken them to see the opera, but that was a year earlier.

She smiled and answered, "Oh, I saw it on television the other night. It was in a movie."

"Oh, so you saw it a few times throughout the week?" I asked, thinking it must have been on the Disney Channel.

She shrugged, seeming totally unimpressed with herself, "No, just once."

Musical memory is such an interesting gift. Of course, for a week after that both girls sang the Queen of the Night's aria every time we got into the car, driving it into higher and higher ranges. It was hilarious to me, but deeply puzzling to any little girlfriends of theirs who were riding with us.

Every time she sang, I told Amelia she was doing a wonderful job, until finally she said to me, "Well, you know, Mom, I *am* considering becoming an opera singer."

Of course, being an opera singer was the furthest thing from her mind three days later, but for a second at least she had seen it, this thing I have known all along: there must be at least one note in my range that belonged to my grandmother, and certainly my mother's soprano and my father's deep love for new music have given much of the color and depth to my sound. Their voices are our inheritance, part of the amalgamation of who we are and what we have learned. We are unique, each human voice, not because we are completely self-generated, but because of how we choose to assemble the countless factors that made us. My voice carries in it the generations before me, generations of my family, of brilliant singers I have admired, of dear friends. Tiny slivers of my voice will be incorporated into a student I teach in a master class or into the young singer who listens carefully, just as little glimmers of

Leontyne Price's shining high C and Dietrich Fischer-Dieskau's expansive breath came into me. If this is the past of my voice, then I must believe it is the future as well. My voice will go forward in the same way, not only through recordings but through my daughters and through their daughters and sons as far as the line will take us. It doesn't mean that everyone will be a singer, but that every one of us will find a passion in life to drive us ahead, and just maybe part of that passion will rest in the voice. People will hear it even in a word that is spoken: the wealth and wonder of all the music that came before.

Shirley MacLaine, actor, dancer, writer, and activist, has appeared in more than fifty films and won countless awards, including the Best Actress Oscar for *Terms of Endearment*. Her acting debut was in 1955 in Alfred Hitchcock's *The Trouble with Harry* and she has worked steadily since. She is the bestselling author of twelve books, both autobiographical and philosophical. With *Out on a Limb* (1983), she began writing about spirituality and sharing details of her spiritual journey, and continued to do so in subsequent books. Her most recent book is *Sage-ing While Age-ing*. www.shirleymaclaine.com

"Women's Pictures"

Shirley MacLaine

I have been blessed with doing some really good "women's pictures." That is to say, films whose subjects and casts appeal to a woman's point of view. I'm not sure what that definition means, though, because the public is not as compartmentalized in its thinking as we often perceive it to be. If pictures with women are termed women's pictures, why are pictures with men just pictures?

The term "women's pictures" never really came up in Hollywood until the middle of the seventies, when women were being redefined in our culture as a result of the success of the women's movement. Until then, pictures about women's lives starring Joan Crawford, Lana Turner, and Bette Davis were pictures for everybody. Those heroines of yesteryear must have made actresses feel they could play anything. There were love stories, family stories, stories of human values, and stories with socially redeeming messages of hope. The stories usually revolved around the female character because they were about feelings. The women were the leavening influence, the inspiration, the anchor. Or, conversely, they were caught in the conflict of ambition, jealousy, love triangles, bad marriages, backstreet affairs, mother-child troubles, or coping with a crumbling world…Feelings…Life.

Nobody is really sure what changed or why. We only know that now the average habitual moviegoer is between eleven and seventeen years old. They prefer action pictures, which are typically inhabited by men. With the advent of high-tech screen techniques, many of these action pictures have developed into showcases for special effects, usually peopled by men who either portray buddies to each other or enact the slave/master role in a story about the triumph of good over evil or vice versa.

When action pictures, science fiction, crime dramas, and stories of sexual perversity prevail, there is not much room for women unless we play dominatrices or outer-planetary dark goddesses. Violent action accelerates and men are required to resolve it.

Why do we need so many pictures like this? Because they reflect what's happening in our society? The violence and deterioration of values? Of course, but there's more. We feel we can't keep up with the changes today—they're all happening too fast. This causes deterioration, until finally we sense, on a visceral level, that we must reach inside ourselves and find some centeredness and peace in order to express what has been suppressed and get on with the badly needed transformation of our consciousness.

In may ways our modern culture has inflicted a kind of velvet control over our inherited, unresolved conflicts. We live with an overlay of civility, but often it's only that—a surface. The violence, sexual perversity, racial hostility, anger at poverty, and revolt to experience human freedom are real. On some level we human beings intuit that we still function as if we lived in a jungle. We need to confront our unconscious jungle brains, and understand how they make us behave, before we can begin to feel the new energy, the jump to a higher spiritual consciousness, and resonate with it.

Movies and television can help us do that, but instead they mainly *reflect* the violence and confusion that is occurring. Our industry is not living up to its responsibility to inspire and nurture the best in ourselves and our audiences. Art has a way of tapping into the subconscious of human life, which lately we've not felt we had the right to look at. Somehow in the last twenty years, looking and feeling deeply has been considered self-indulgent, embarrassing. Films can help relieve this embarrassment. The films of the forties and fifties did just that. They were more conversant with human emotion and, because of that, starred more women—Bette Davis, Joan Crawford, Myrna Loy, Rita Hayworth, Loretta Young, Joan Fontaine, Olivia de Havilland, and so many others. In the sixties came the Vietnam War and with it the violence we witnessed every night on the seven o'clock news.

The more we observed the violence—bodies floating down the Mekong River, children burning with napalm—the more distanced we became from our own feelings. The more distanced we became, the less we found the examination of feeling even palatable. Add to that the technological advancements in communication, and there simply wasn't enough time to keep abreast of it all. We became inundated with events and happenings outside of our own lives, which left precious little time to absorb and process what occurred *inside* our lives. The faster information traveled the less communication there was between human beings.

Slowly but surely, we have abdicated the recognition of our own deep feelings and, more precisely, the spiritual feminine in ourselves. Its presence on the screen, unless it is etched with comic relief or car chases, is usually unacceptable, it makes us squirm and wriggle. We are afraid of oversentimentality, of seeming unintellectual. Yet we *know* that the feminine side of ourselves is nurturing, we *know* our feminine side is intuitive. We know our feminine side is mostly, and at its best, patient and nonjudgmental. *And* our feminine side recognizes that we cannot go on as we are and expect to have a loving and peaceful world. Still, our feminine aspects are not considered commercial. They are not considered politically viable. They are not considered qualities of leadership.

We are afraid that these qualities will not excite audiences, will not elicit cheers and spar competitive rooting. We are afraid and embarrassed because the feminine is more internal, more attuned to a silent knowingness, more connected to the deep core of why we're here and where we're going. We feel, but we are unacquainted with our intuition. We don't acknowledge the quiet recognition of the God spark within us.

All of the above, in my opinion, is why writers, producers, and studio heads are confused and bereft of ideas where the feminine is concerned. They are afraid to empathize with what feminine feels like. Yet pictures like *Terms of Endearment, Driving Miss Daisy, Fried Green Tomatoes, Steel Magnolias, The Piano,* and *Little Women* are successful enough to warrant the production of more like them. So why more movies with women are not produced is a question no one seems able to answer, unless of course it is *because* female profitability is unacceptable. Women in equal economic control would expose everyone's emotional attitudes about women, including those of the female executives who currently make decisions on a playing field controlled by men and according to the cultural dictates of the moment. If more "women's pictures" were made and successful, the field on which Hollywood plays its game would change completely. No longer would women be relegated to decorative cages to be toyed and played with according to the whims of men. And more important than anything, if more women were in economic control, the men would have to face their fear and anxiety at being subservient to the female authority figure again. In other words, it would be a "mama" problem all over again.

The women's movement has tended to amplify this problem, which before was subtly swept under the rug. But the battle between the sexes is exposed full-blown now, and the men and women who commit money to develop projects would rather avoid the "mama" subject than stigmatize themselves by revealing their ignorance of their feelings about their own mothers. In fact, they use politically correct attitudes to obfuscate their deeper conflicts with mama.

Therefore, we have, it seems to me, a crisis of feminine, mother-earth spirituality versus masculine commerciality in *both men and women*. Or more to the point, humanity versus money.

We seem to be shirking the recognition of the missing feminine, mothering parts of ourselves, in favor of focusing on what will keep us afloat in a world of masculine intellectual material-ism. But it doesn't keep us afloat. We are drowning and we know it. Instead of fighting to keep from drowning, we could surrender to the flow of the water and float. But this "law of reversed effort" is suspect. It does not command respect. It is considered weak and untenable, flimsy and emotional. More than anything, it is con-sidered to have no strength, no stamina, no bite, no power. It is a vegetarian concept in a flesh-eating environment.

The notion of "let go and let God" is a spiritual, feminine, mothering fantasy that engenders nervous laughter and rolling eyes. It is too *allowing*.

Yet whenever a man has taken his masculine endeavors to the max, he returns to the serenity and peace of his female counter-part for sustenance, love, hope, and nurturing. He knows in his heart that the world out there is unbalanced and he knows why. The first person he knew and depended upon was his mother. She was allowing. The last person will be the female in his life, because she is allowing. He will want her as he goes to meet his maker. That is one of the few times he really recognizes her and, in so doing, realizes how he has denied the female in himself. Why does it take death to come to terms with such a spiritual truth?

Human beings have always had a general belief in the doctrine of the wholeness of the world, a spiritual belief that we have an ethical purpose for being alive. The purpose supposes a recogni-tion of God within and without us. We live on Mother Earth and reflect Father Sky. The duality makes the power of One. It has al-ways been considered a holy teaching, a philosophical tradition taught to young people as a preparation for their future life—the equal recognition of the masculine and feminine. This has been so in primitive tribes as well as in highly developed civilizations.

In our present civilization, this spiritual background has gone astray. Our Christian doctrine has lost its way. It is religious, but it is no longer spiritual. We have lost our balance because of it. We are drifting without orientation. Our lives are losing meaning because we ignore and negate the spiritual meaning.

In a world that believes we all swim in shark-infested waters, are there no alternatives to masculine solutions?

I believe there are. If we all, including feminists, more fully acknowledged that we have been bereft of the spiritual feminine for far too long, there would be less violence, anger, and hostility in the world.

With that recognition, our culture would be soothed. Our films and television would reflect the resulting serenity and we, I hope, would begin our transformation with a consciousness of stability, balance, harmony, and "allowance." We would return to what we were meant to be—the Power of One.

Whoopi Goldberg, comedian, actor, and singer-songwriter, appeared in one indie film before her starring role in the film version of Alice Walker's *The Color Purple* catapulted her to screen fame. She went on to appear in more than a hundred films, including *Jumpin' Jack Flash, Ghost, Sister Act, Ghosts of Mississippi,* and *Girl, Interrupted.* She has starred on Broadway and on TV, hosted the Academy Awards for four years, and performed in humanitarian aid fundraisers such as *Comic Relief.* She is one of the few people who have won all five awards: Academy, Golden Globe, Tony, Grammy, and Emmy. She continues to break new ground in cohosting, with a panel of women that includes Barbara Walters, ABC's talk show *The View.* A *New York Times* review of the show declared that it "actively defies the bubbleheads-'R'-us approach to women's talk shows."

CHAPTER NINETEEN

Dream

Whoopi Goldberg

I can do anything. I can be anything. No one ever told me I couldn't. No one ever expressed this idea that I was limited to any one thing, and so I think in terms of what's possible, not impossible.

They did sell me on the notion of reality. That I got. I got the laws of physics and nature pretty much down and knew early on there were very specific things I couldn't do. I knew I could never make anyone float, or turn water into wine, or make cats speak French. I knew I couldn't bring people back from the dead. I got that part of it. But I also knew that if I was with someone who had lost somebody I might be able to make them feel better. I couldn't keep someone's house from burning down, but I could help them sort through the rubble and get their shit together and start in on another one. So I realized I wasn't God, which was a slight disappointment, you know. Just a slight disappointment—and a mild surprise.

Movies were my first window to the outside world, and they told me stuff. They told me I could go anywhere, be whatever I wanted, solve any damn puzzle. The right movie was my ticket to any place I wanted to go. But it had to be the right movie, and it had to come from the right place, 'cause I had to bank on it being historically accurate. See, in school, nobody talked about black people unless they had us picking cotton. Who knew there were free blacks? Maybe you heard about Frederick Douglass, but you didn't really know about Frederick Douglass. You couldn't always trust the history books. They told a diluted truth, a truth by committee. It was only later that I learned there was something missing in what went down with the landed Americans and the indigenous people of this country. In movies too. They didn't always get the story right, especially when it came to our nonwhite history. You knew the Indians didn't look like Jeffrey Hunter, but you didn't know what they really looked like either. It was a great mystery. There weren't too many Indians in my Catholic school in New York, so you had to use your imagination a little bit.

In my head, Queen Elizabeth was just like Bette Davis. That's how I saw her. She walked and talked and *poofed*—and made grand statements in staccato sentences. Movies opened doors to a lot of things for me, but for every one they opened another one closed. The casting always messed with the way I saw it. It changed the terms. In this way, books were more liberating, more magical, and so I started to read. To really *read.* Books opened the mind to all kinds of possibilities. There is nothing in Dickens to leave you thinking there were no black people in England, or that Bob Cratchit didn't pass you on the street every single day. But movies made you believe there were no black people, except the ones who were picking cotton, or tap-dancing up a flight of stairs, or birthin' babies. When I was little, this didn't strike me as odd, but as I grew up, all during the 1960s, it bothered the shit out of me. I knew there had to be more to us than that. Now I know there are all-black movies, with gumshoes and heroes, cowboys and harlots, but these were just not shown on the *Million Dollar Movie,* and when I started to figure this out I realized life was what we put in and took out, and we were all in the same soup. Indians, blacks, Asians, women.... Shit, it never even occurred to me that Emma wasn't black. It wasn't a part of the equation. Why shouldn't we have been in a Jane Austen situation? Why wouldn't we have been in a manor house in a Dickens novel? Why couldn't we have been the light in the forest? And don't tell me Robert Louis Stevenson didn't have me in mind when he wrote *Treasure Island* because, you know, even the Muppets understand this notion.

Daydreaming, I used to think I was Sherlock Holmes; it's a part I've always wanted to play. If you're the most brilliant detective, the people will come to you. They won't care if you're black, or a woman. It might even give the story some new dimensions. *The Speckled Band,* starring Whoopi Goldberg. I like it!

This—the possibility—is why I look on acting as such a joyous thing. It's shot through with possibility. Anything can happen. As I write this, I'm appearing eight times a week, on Broadway, in a part originally written for a man, but you'd never know, right? If you come to a thing with no preconceived notions of what that thing is, the whole world can be your canvas. Just dream it, and you can make it so. I believe I belong wherever I want to be, in whatever situation or context I place myself. I believed I could pass as an ancient Roman in *A Funny Thing Happened on the Way to the Forum.* I believed a little girl could rise from a single-parent household in the Manhattan projects, start a single-parent household of her own, struggle through seven years of welfare and odd jobs, and still wind up making movies. You can go from anonymity to Planet Hollywood and never lose sight of where you've been.

So, yeah, I think anything is possible. I know it because I have lived it. I know it because I have seen it. I have witnessed things the ancients would have called miracles, but they are not miracles. They are the products of someone's dream, and they happen as the result of hard work. Or they happen because, you know, shit happens. As human beings, we are capable of creating a paradise, and making each other's lives better by our own hands. Yes, yes, yes... this is possible.

If something hasn't happened, it's not because it can't happen, or won't; it just hasn't happened yet. If I haven't done something, I just haven't gotten around to it. For a long time, I wanted to sit with Stephen Hawking and have him explain all his theories to me so that I could understand them and build on them and find ways to adapt them to my own life. But I never got around to that. I would like to be a diplomat in some foreign country for a couple months. I would like to play for the Knicks, and dance with Alvin Ailey, and ride a camel down Sunset Boulevard. I would like to find a way to stop famine, and to free the children from the orphanages in Bosnia, Rwanda, and Romania, and here at home. I would like to do a lot of things. All I need is time.

Angelina Jolie has starred in more than thirty films, including *Changeling, Lara Croft: Tomb Raider,* and *Girl, Interrupted.* Her acting has earned her an Academy Award, three Golden Globes, and two Screen Actors Guild Awards. One of the highest paid actresses in Hollywood, she is also a humanitarian and serves as Goodwill Ambassador for the UN High Commissioner for Refugees (UNHCR), using her celebrity to bring attention to the plight of refugees in Africa, Asia, and South America.

CHAPTER TWENTY

Notes from My Travels— Visits with Refugees in Africa
Angelina Jolie

Côte d'Ivoire

I am on a plane to Africa. I will have a two-hour layover in the Paris airport, and then on to Abidjan in Côte d'Ivoire (Ivory Coast).

I honestly want to help. I don't believe I am different from other people. I think we all want justice and equality. We all want a chance for a life with meaning. All of us would like to believe that if we were in a bad situation someone would help us.

I don't know what I will accomplish on this trip. All I do know is that while I was learning more and more every day about the world and about other countries as well as my own, I realized how much I didn't know.

I have done a lot of research and talked with many people in Washington, DC, at the United Nations High Commissioner for Refugees (UNHCR). I have read as much as I could. I discovered statistics that shocked me and stories that broke my heart. I also read many things that made me sick. I have had nightmares—not many, but they scared me.

I don't understand why some things are talked about and others are not.

189

I don't know why I think I can make any kind of difference. All I know is that I want to.

I wasn't sure I should go. I'm still not sure, but—and I know this may sound false to some—I thought of the people who have no choice.

It seems crazy to some of my friends that I want to leave the warmth and safety of my home. They asked, "Why can't you just help from here? Why do you have to see it?" I didn't know how to answer them. And I'm not sure if I'm being crazy or stupid.

My dad attempted to cancel my trip. He called USA for UN-HCR, but since I am an adult, he couldn't stop me. I was angry with him, but I told him that I know he loves me and that as my father he was trying to protect me from harm. We embraced and smiled at one another.

My mom looked at me like I was her little girl. She smiled at me through her teary eyes. She is worried. As she hugged me good-bye, she gave me a specific message from my brother, Jamie. "Tell Angie I love her, and to remember that if she is ever scared, sad, or angry—look up at the night sky, find the second star on the right, and follow it straight on till morning." That's from *Peter Pan,* one of our favorite stories.

I am thinking about those people I have been reading so much about and how they are separated from the families they love. They have no home. They are watching the people they love die. They are dying themselves. And they have no choice.

I am sitting in a chair in a UNHCR office in Abidjan. I am having a long morning.

I have come to understand many things, and yet there is so much I don't understand. Most of all I realized how little awareness I had of these people.

I am sitting under a sign—a poster for UNHCR. It reads:

It doesn't take much to become a refugee. Your race or belief can be enough.

I was allowed to sit in on an interview with "asylum seekers."

These "asylum seekers" are here to apply for a chance to live in the borders of a country that is different from their own place of origin.

UNHCR will listen to their stories and sometimes check on the information. They will help them if they can. They have to try to determine if they are eligible to be labeled a refugee, and therefore, seek asylum.

They must prove their need for protection and support; that is, for whatever protection and support is available, and in many countries that is not much at all.

The young couple interviewed today lost contact with their two children. The husband was thirty. The wife was twenty-five. They seemed much older. Their bodies so weary, their eyes so sad, desperate.

Sierra Leone

Jui Transit Centre is situated at the mouth of the capital of Sierra Leone, just some seven miles to the heart of the capital city, Freetown. Established in 2000, Jui Transit Centre was one of the temporary settlements that were primarily put in place by the UNHCR in Freetown in response to the large-scale repatriation of Sierra Leonean refugees in Guinea. Following alleged Sierra Leonean RUF rebel cross-border attack on Guinea, Guineans swooped on Sierra Leonean refugees, who were accused of harboring RUF [Revolutionary United Front] rebels and trying to destabilize Guinea. Many Sierra Leonean refugees were physically manhandled, forcing many to opt for a return to Sierra Leone even though the war in their country of origin was still raging. As a large part of the country then was under rebel occupation, the returnees could not return to their villages. To meet the returnees' need for temporary accommodation, UNHCR established two host communities (Lokomassama and Barri) in the northern and southern provinces. However, as returnees arrived by ship from Guinea, there was need for them to stay overnight not just to recuperate after a long journey but also to make decisions on where they will proceed based on the information they received about other family members. In Jui, like in other transit centres, returnees were provided with such services. In principle, returnees were to stay for no more than five days in the Transit Centre, but in reality, some two thousand returnees were sheltered at the centre.

The Transit Centre is a neighbor to the Jui Village, which is home to an estimated six thousand Sierra Leoneans. There is a primary school and a secondary school as well as a Bible Training Institute. Returnees had to send their children to these schools while they were at the centre. The Transit Centre itself had a health post, a huge water bladder with several water collection points.

Plastic tents, dirt floors. It feels like nowhere. People walk around. Can't help themselves. Can't go home.

A man ran up to UNHCR workers, his hardworking hands begging for them to come quick.

They explained that he wanted them to look at a boy.

I met the boy. He looked about twelve, but he could have been sixteen. It is hard to tell because of the malnourishment. He was very sick.

I didn't want to lean over and look. I kept a distance. I was a woman he didn't know. He was being examined by a doctor.

He was so young and yet seemed so aware of what was happening to him. His legs had become paralyzed. His stomach and his ribs seemed too wide. Later, I was told it looked as if he had been operated on. His spine was severely damaged. Disease was eating away at his body. It is likely this all began with a gunshot wound and a poor operation.

Here he was being released from the hospital. There are no funds and there is no room to care for him past what is considered an emergency (by their standards).

To me, this was an emergency. Now the humanitarian workers will try to look for help—but this boy is one of millions like him.

I will never be able to forget his face. I will never forget the way he moved his legs with his hands.

Nyarugusu Camp (Congo Refugees)

We traveled on an already very bad dirt road that has been made worse by all the rain. So many people were stuck on their way to the Nyarugusu camp.

Fifty-three thousand refugees, all from the Congo, are here for food distribution that is brought in two times a month.

There are 250 births here every month.

All lost tribal members are brought here. Families are reunited.

The numbers are always growing.

Food rations are continually being cut down because of lack of funds. Everyone gets less than usual.

The system is very complex.

My first job was to work chute number 4, helping to pass large bags in bulk to groups. I was focused on families of five. The children ranged in age from one to ten years old.

We were not able to distribute any cooking oil because the truck bringing it to the camp was stuck on a washed-out road.

I had lunch with members of Christian Outreach Relief and Development (CORD). We had cabbage, water, rice, and beans. I was starving.

Local refugees who made instruments wanted to perform for us. While we ate, we could hear the music.

Our next stop was where men were building large structures with mud and bricks. I tried to help for a little while, but I found it to be very hard work. I told one of the workers how I admired him for being able to work there every day, all day long. He said, "Yes, it is hard work, but it is for the children, so it feels good."

I am watching the refugees. I have begun talking and dancing with them. I feel I am making friends.

Someone once said, "You can learn more about someone in an hour of play than in a year of conversation."

I experienced something like that—of the same nature. And that is what I felt.

They asked for my address. We promised to keep in touch.

The sad thing is they know they will not be leaving the camp anytime soon. But the spirit of these people, and their will to survive, continues to amaze me. I wish I could find a better word. I am inspired by them. I am honored to spend time with them.

Mtabila Camp

Ninety-five thousand refugees here (mostly Burundians).

UNHCR brought me to the nutritional and medical center, which is run inside the camp by the Red Cross.

My first job today was measuring the medicine powder at the therapeutic feeding center.

Under the age of five—extra nutrition.

Pregnant—measured.

I wanted to be careful not to measure a spoonful too short.

They have to monitor the children to make sure they are growing and not losing weight. The newborns are measured for height and weight and given vaccines. One little baby was scared and peed on the examining table. The mother used part of her dress to wipe it off. There is no soap available. Keeping safe and clean is very hard for everyone.

The kitchen contains a very small room with three large clay pots on wood-burning stoves.

It was hard to see. All the smoke in the room hurt my eyes.

I helped make milk for the mothers. It comes dehydrated in bulk. With a small plastic pitcher I took two liters of boiling hot water (I measured the best I could) and poured it into an old beaten-up green plastic bucket. It's hard not to let the hot water burn your hands. You leave it in the bucket until it cools down (so it won't destroy the milk proteins), then you mix it.

[In the pediatric ward] there were about fifteen small wooden beds lined up on each side of the room. Nets surrounded each bed—to try to prevent mosquito bites that can lead to malaria. Most of the nets have holes in them. Malaria is very common in this area, almost impossible to avoid. Another big problem is diarrhea. To babies and small children the loss of bodily fluids is deadly.

I have deet spray on at all times, and still I have been bitten by mosquitoes—and not just at night. I am also very lucky to have malaria pills. The pills don't stop you from getting malaria, but they help prevent the severity of it if it comes.

An eight-year-old was sitting with her baby brother on her lap. They were sitting on the last bed. She had him wrapped up. The baby had loss two hundred grams. He has diarrhea and he also might have worms.

This little girl saw her parents and her older brother brutally killed. Somehow she escaped with her baby brother. The baby is so terribly skinny. I don't think he will make it. He is all she cares about. He is her only family.

Everyone who meets these two children is affected. One of the nurses had to quietly walk away. She began to cry, and one of the men walked her outside.

The little girl never looked up into anyone's eyes. She seemed very sweet. She just sat there looking out the window, resting her chin on her little brother's head.

She was too weak to cry.

We got up at 6:20 a.m. There was no electricity. I am packing my final things with a flashlight. I moved so quickly in the dark. I thought, I am leaving today and I will be gone before I know it.

It is very cold this morning, and I think about how cold it must be for the refugees in the small mud homes—the homes they made. They have no electricity. They never know how much food will be available on distribution day. The nights can be so cold. They have to make firewood every day.

All the clothes on the children are rags. Some only wear small sheets of red cloth. When funds were cut for sanitary napkins, the

red cloth was distributed so the women could at least wrap themselves up during their menstrual cycle, but it was explained to
me that the women would go without. How they do it I don't
know. The women would rather the children stay warm, or at
least warmer.

It is cold and foggy. It took the little plane we were about to
board three attempts to land. We waited—our bags on the grass—
looking out at the dirt landing.

I was so hungry. I grabbed the last of the bread as we were running out the door. No coffee this morning—no electricity.

We finally took off and arrived just in time to catch the second plane.

I am so tired and hungry but at least I know when I will eat.
Very soon I'll have a hot shower and food.

I hope I will never forget how much I have learned. I hope I
always appreciate all that I have.

I had no idea what people are going through all over the world.
It is worse than I had imagined, and I know I have only begun to
see things, I have only begun to understand.

I am now on a British Airways flight to London. I realize I am
the dirtiest person on the plane.

Suddenly, the idea of taking off this dirty jacket upsets me.
It has been my blanket. I don't want to clean up or wash off
this place.

These three weeks have been a new world for me—a special
time—I have changed. I like who I became here.

For some reason, taking off my jacket, I feel I am detaching
myself from all the people—the places....

The boy on the dirt floor holding his legs.

The eight-year-old girl with her little baby brother in her arms.

The man in the amputee camp who looked into my eyes and
told me his story.

The images are like a slide show, flashes of their faces, their bare feet.

From this moment on—wherever I am, I will remember where they are.

Helen Mirren, born Helen Mironov of Russian-English parentage, has acted on stage, screen, and television on both sides of the Atlantic in a career that spans more than four decades. Known for tackling challenging roles, her talent in doing so has garnered many awards, among them multiple BAFTAs and Emmys for her starring role in the television series *Prime Suspect* and an Academy Award, a Golden Globe, and a BAFTA for her portrayal of Elizabeth II in *The Queen*. In 2003, she was titled a Dame of the British Empire.

CHAPTER TWENTY-ONE

The Freedom to Work

Helen Mirren

For some reason, even though my parents had a happy and successful marriage, I had no desire or ambition for marriage or children. I love children. I find them funny and inspiring. And I think people like my parents, who sacrifice personal freedom and economic wealth for the well-being and happiness of their children, are the true heroes of our society. But I just do not want that. I loved my life of freedom, and of work.

I also loved the men I had the good fortune to share my life with. They educated me about boxing and rock and roll and fell walking and dry-stone wall building and photography and sailing and gardening, and above all how to love. They made me laugh and I think they loved me and I will forever be grateful for that. However, I did not want to marry them.

I don't mean to be flippant, but I think a part of that was that I did not need to wear the dress. Maybe a lot of women get married because they are longing to wear that big white dress and the beautiful tiara, look lovely, and get their makeup done. They crave to be the centre of attention for a day at least.

I had had the opportunity to experience all that by being an actress. I had beautiful dresses handmade for me, makeup done on me, people looking at me, and so forth as a part of my profession. So that particular reason for getting married was not pertinent. I was also happy not to be particularly responsible to anyone or for anyone except my work and myself.

As soon as I was in my thirties, while giving interviews to promote a piece of work I had done, I found myself being asked about my marital status. It seemed a sexist question to me, as I don't think male actors were asked the same thing. I would always respond that I had nothing against marriage, it just wasn't for me. It was not that I didn't agree with marriage; but that, without being Catholic, I didn't agree with divorce. What I meant was that I simply could not see the point of being married if there was the remotest possibility of being divorced. I mean, what was the point? It was so easy and pleasurable to live together, and obviously such a pain to divorce. Besides, at that time, marriage never seemed such a good deal for the women involved.

In fact, I had a recurring nightmare about getting married. I would be walking down the aisle, big dress, veil, church full of well-dressed people, knowing that in some hotel there was a vast, expensive banquet arranged, knowing it was a horrible mistake but not being brave enough to say so.

All my relationships took second place to my work, the fun of it and the intensity of it and my ambitions within it. I continued merrily along this path, having a series of relationships that had all the requirements of passion and lust and domesticity and tears and laughter and love, until I met Taylor. We met on the film *White Nights*. I was in my late thirties by then and he just a few months older.

I was called in to meet with a director who was preparing a film about Russia. His name was Taylor Hackford. I shrugged my shoulders. "Oh well," I thought, "I guess they think I actually am Russian, from seeing *2010*." The film was about two dancers, and starred Mikhail Baryshnikov and Gregory Hines. I was sent the script. The role was OK: head of the Kirov Ballet, someone who worked within the system. I took exception to certain elements in the script, which I thought reflected too closely American paranoia about Soviet Russia. I felt that not all Russians wanted to leave Russia and that there remained a deep love of country that was independent of the political system, but this was nowhere to be found in the script.

However, I duly went off to meet with this director. I'd had a few meetings like this in LA and had found them always very intimidating and humiliating. There is a completely different attitude to a film audition in Los Angeles. It's a town where every waitress and barman wants to be a film star, so you as the actor are supposed to be incredibly grateful to be auditioning at all. You are one amongst a million. Next, the process has very little to do with acting. It's all to do with whether you are "right" for the part. This is why actors and waiters and every other aspiring star dresses for the role when they go for an audition. If you show yourself to be "right" for the part in your reading and you get cast, that's the end of the story. The performance you are required to give is what you did in the reading. They feel cheated if you then take it off in another direction.

This is the opposite of how I prefer to work. I want to change and experiment and invent. I want the freedom to use my imagination. There are as many ways of playing a line or a part as there are blades of grass. It is only poverty of imagination that stops you. So, actually, although I wanted to stay in America for the sense of personal freedom it gave me, I was not at all suited to the "Hollywood" system.

So off I went to meet with Taylor Hackford, already resentful and cross, and refusing to look anything like the head of the Kirov Ballet. Then he's late and I am waiting in the office, steaming now, glaring at the girl behind the desk. I am insulted. If I can get there on time, then he most certainly can. Fifteen minutes go by. I think,

"OK, I will wait for twenty minutes in total. That is the cut-off point." A further five minutes go by and I stand up to leave, telling the alarmed secretary that I'm off. I walk to the door and, as I reach for the handle, Taylor walks in—and into the next twenty years of my life, and counting.

However, that was not at all clear in this, our first meeting. Well, actually, our second. By now I am very pissed off and I show it. I hardly respond to anything, just wanting to get out of there. Mikhail is there too, and, while I am very impressed to meet the greatest living dancer, I do not want to engage in small talk. "So, do you want me to read?" I ask. I read the scene and when I'm finished, I say, "OK? That's it." And gather my stuff together to get out of there. It's then Taylor says to me, "We've met before, you know."

"I don't think so," I reply snottily.

"Yes," he says, "in San Juan Bautista, while you were working with the Teatro Campesino. I came to watch. I am a friend of Danny Valdez." I was amazed. There and then I knew I was not dealing with the normal kind of Hollywood film director. Most Hollywood film directors would not have sat in a dusty little town far from Beverly Hills watching an experimental theatre workshop. I left the meeting somewhat chastened. My assumptions had been all wrong. A few hours later Taylor called to tell me I had the role. I was not exactly over the moon, as I felt again that the role was flawed in the writing, but it was a job, and in another fully fledged Hollywood movie.

It was certainly not love at first sight. After that meeting in Los Angeles, I would have taken a hefty bet against it if someone had suggested that this was the man I would complete my life with.

Firstly, I had never had a relationship with a director in all my years of work. Somehow that was off limits to me. I could not see how to work properly under those conditions. Also, more importantly, Taylor was married, with two children from two different marriages.

But as soon as the film started, and then as it progressed, our attraction to each other became a clear and unavoidable force. Taylor's strength, which he shares with many film directors, is his positive nature, and his ability to press forward against all odds. One of his faults, albeit usually a charming one, is his precipitous nature. After a separation of six months or so, when I returned to Britain in the hope of putting some distance between the two of us, Taylor turned up in London. With much pain, he had separated from his wife. My fate was sealed.

My first years in Los Angeles as Taylor's partner were very difficult for me. Once he had made that complicated decision to take me on board, I felt for the first time in my life I should put my relationship before my work. It was the least I could do. The geographical distance between our two home and families meant something had to give if this was going to succeed, and I did not want yet another wonderful-but-only-four-years-long relationship.

Taylor had made major changes in his life for me, and I thought I should do the same. So I arrived in LA, was driven to our new, rented home in the Hollywood Hills, in which we were to live with Taylor's older son, Rio, who was fifteen at the time, and then I was introduced to the very equitable Californian concept of joint custody as far as his second son, Alex, was concerned.

It was a whole new world for me, utterly alien and fraught with difficulty. I had no experience with children and I had absolutely no profile in Hollywood as an actress. In spite of my appearance in two Hollywood films, I was not even C list—if anything, I was Y list.

When Taylor took me to my first big "studio head"–type party, the tattoo on my left hand was suddenly a serious embarrassment. I told people I'd got it in prison when I was running with a bad crowd. They were suitably horrified that a risen star of Hollywood filmmaking had hooked up with such a creature. Nowadays, of course, they all have tattoos, but then it was a sign of total depravity.

The people who ultimately got me through the anxiety, the embarrassment, and my feelings of awful displacement were Taylor's sons, Alex and Rio. They were always kind to me, and ultimately loving. They had grown up in a world I knew nothing about. They lived a life so very different from anything I had experienced as a child or even as an adult. My arrival in their world had caused upheaval and pain. Yet they gave me sympathy and courtesy from the beginning, and I loved them.

I also loved Taylor for putting his sons above me. I loved a man whose primary concern in life was his responsibility toward his children.

This does not mean there were not difficult times. Often I wanted to give up and go back to where I was wanted. Work-wise, I could not get started. When I arrived, films were being made almost exclusively for the teenage market, an audience that Hollywood had ignored for a while and recently rediscovered. There are never that many roles for women, and whatever roles I could have played inevitably went to actresses with a bigger Hollywood profile than me. I was at the back of the line, just like that time in primary school, except this time I couldn't even get the "one of the twenty-four blackbirds" role.

At this point, Taylor did a memorable thing. I had gone to meet him for lunch at the Raleigh studios, where he was working. Crying, I started trying to explain all my difficulties. There was a path by the side of the studio that reached far into the distance. He took me to the beginning of this path, took two steps, and said, "Don't worry. Look, we are only this far along in our life together, we have all that way to go. Some will be hard and some will be easy, but we will make it."

I think this was the moment I finally absolutely fell in love with him.

With the help of Alex and Rio, we grew to understand how to live together, and eventually to work parallel to each other, but we still did not get married for many years—fourteen to be exact. Marriage was simply not a necessity for us. I had achieved the aim, impressed upon me by my mother, of being economically independent. I always kept my own home in London, and as the years went on most of my work was in Britain, while Taylor's was in America. Taylor always gave me the same freedom to work as I did him, and that of course is one of the many reasons we are still together.

Barbara Walters, journalist, writer, and media personality, is the first woman ever to cohost a network news program (cohost of NBC's the *Today* show and coanchor of the *ABC Evening News*). She went on to cohost ABC's newsmagazine *20/20* for twenty-five years. In addition to continuing to host the top-rated *Barbara Walters Specials*, she cohosts ABC's *The View*, which she cocreated and co–executive produces as well. In the course of her career, she has interviewed the whole range of the famous and infamous, from pop icons to world leaders.

CHAPTER TWENTY-TWO

Time to Stop Auditioning
Barbara Walters

Becoming Barbara Walters

I was exhausted most of the time I was on the *Today* show. I learned how to go to sleep anywhere, anytime I had a few minutes. That sometimes included three-minute naps on the set during a commercial or while someone else was doing an interview. I was often so tired that if someone touched me, it felt almost like pain. To this day I can nap anytime, almost anyplace, and if for some ungodly reason I receive a phone call at 5:00 a.m., I am instantly wide awake and make perfect sense.

There were some things about waking before dawn that I liked. I really enjoyed drinking my morning coffee at the kitchen table when everything was still and quiet. It was the calmest time of my whole day. I liked the short drive from my apartment to the NBC studio. There was no traffic at 5:00 a.m. The light was just breaking. It was, in its way, so peaceful. Within ten minutes, though, I would be in my dressing room, everyone hovering over me. The peace was over.

Sometimes the whole show traveled.

Al Morgan loved to take *Today* on the road. The most ambitious broadcast, in fact a historical first, took place on May 3, 1965, when *Today* broadcast live from Europe, via Early Bird satellite. This was the inaugural telecast over the satellite, the first time an event taking place in Europe was seen live in the United States. Al ran the show from Brussels, Belgium, and orchestrated the feeds from Hugh Downs in London's Westminster Abbey, Jack Lescoulie in Amsterdam, Aline Saarinen at the Forum in Rome, Frank Blair on the Capitol steps in Washington, and me in Paris, with the singer and actor Yves Montand on his balcony overlooking the city. My job for this broadcast was to add some glamour by reporting on French cuisine, French couture, and French men. Not a bad assignment.

This first satellite broadcast was so significant that it was introduced by Pope Paul VI speaking from the Vatican. (Morgan said later he'd never forget saying, "Cue the pope.") A tough act to follow, but it was almost topped by live shots of adorable little girls in their respective countries saying, "Good morning," "Bonjour," "Buongiorno," and "Goedemorgen—this is *Today!*" The next cut was to London and live coverage of the Changing of the Guard at Buckingham Palace.

The satellite broadcast was widely celebrated as a breakthrough for the future of television. The print media started to take more notice of television—and of me.

There were at that time only two other significant women in television network news. One was Pauline Frederick, NBC's veteran United Nations correspondent, who was a highly distinguished reporter of some twenty years' standing. Pauline truly was a trailblazer, but she was rather stern and unglamorous and got very little media attention. The other was a stylish figure named Nancy Dickerson who had been at CBS before I started appearing regularly on *Today* and was hired away by NBC to be their Washington correspondent. She was a good friend of the Beltway establishment. Lyndon Johnson was particularly fond of her. Nancy sat in for me several summers during my annual vacation and evidently set her sights on my job. She organized a letter-writing campaign suggesting that she would be better at the job than I, which hardly endeared her to me. It also made me quite anxious. I was still very insecure, and Nancy, in truth, was far better known than I. But then she shot herself in the foot.

She was married to a very wealthy man and used to arrive at the NBC studios in a Rolls-Royce, which set some people's teeth on edge. But it was her tendency, when she didn't get the assignments she wanted, to go above the producers' heads and complain directly to David Sarnoff, the chairman of RCA, NBC's parent company. This practice slowly eroded the support she might have had among the people she worked with. Both the producers of the evening news and the *Today* show began using her less and less and finally closed her out altogether. Her career continued for many years, but she never regained the prominence she had had in her early years at NBC.

So that left me, a new face on the air, and the object of curiosity.

To the delight of the NBC publicity department, one article followed another. "That Barbara Walters is a girl no one can deny," began a full-page profile of me in the *New York Herald Tribune* on August 22, 1965. The women's movement had not yet rammed home the substitution of "woman" for "girl," but no matter, I was happy with the media attention, especially the article's title— "They Love Her in the Morning." But not just for my ego. For my status with the brass at NBC.

I'm not sure the top guns at NBC had much confidence in me during my early months on the program until they read the mounting number of articles about me, including one of my favorites, also in 1965, in the *New York Times,* "Nylons in the Newsroom," by the beautiful and, later in her career, extremely influential feminist leader Gloria Steinem. Gloria nailed the television industry's long-entrenched assumption that, as one male executive said, "Women didn't want to watch other women except on girl-type subjects," and used me, as the most visible, nongirly woman on television, to mark a step forward for womankind. I like my quote in Gloria's story, which, more than forty years later, seems so prescient. "If I wear anything below the collarbone, the viewers write shocked letters. I'm a kind of well-informed friend. They don't want me to be a glamour puss and that's fine. It means I won't have to quit or have face lifts after forty. I'm in a different category." (By the way, Gloria and I remain friends to this day. We even performed together at a charity event in Carnegie Hall. Gloria tap-danced and I sang "For Me and My Gal." We received great applause—but no one has asked us to repeat the performance.)

The reaction of NBC's executives to all this media coverage was predictable. Suddenly I was their "baby celebrity," as *TV Guide* put it back then. Before the media onslaught I'd been working in a windowless office. After a feature in *Life* magazine quoted me as saying, "There are days when I don't see daylight"—which was true, given the studio, which was also windowless, and the literal dawn-to-dusk hours I worked—I was given an office with a window. I was also given a secretary, Mary Hornickel, whom I didn't have to share. Wonderful Mary stayed with me for the next twelve years. My picture even went up on the corridor leading to the *Today* office, and NBC executives, including the CEO, actually said hello to me in the elevator.

The network had two radio programs, *Monitor* and *Emphasis*, and I was asked to start contributing to both, which I did, five days a week until I had to cut back my workload to three. Meanwhile the media continued to feed off one another and the brass fed on the media, and there I was, if not the toast of the town, at least a good bite.

In actuality my life didn't change very much. I never asked for and was not offered a raise. I had the same rent-controlled apartment and the same friends. Unlike people in the entertainment division, newspeople did not have a retinue of agents, publicists, personal managers, and hangers-on. I was happy just to have a secretary. I did get invited to premieres and opening nights of plays that I was usually too tired to attend and there was the occasional glamorous party I went to, but basically my life stayed the same. My friends didn't envy me because they know how hard I worked and how tough the hours were. Unlike Hollywood, where an actor can make one smash film and his or her career can take off overnight, working in television news was, and is, a long and, if you're lucky, steady climb. I had begun that climb.

To Be Continued...

Once I announced that I was leaving [20/20], I was deluged with requests for interviews and invitations to be honored by this or that organization. It was like reading my own obituary. I hadn't retired from television, but it looked as if I had. I turned down all the so-called honors and most of the interviews. I thought the "exit" interview I had done for the New York Times said it all. The interviews I did do were with Oprah, one for her magazine O and one for her television program. Oprah is one of the people I could interview again and again. Now the tables were turned and she wanted to interview me.

She and I talked about a variety of things for the magazine, but what affected me most is the last question and answer.

Oprah: What does being "Barbara Walters" mean?

Me: I'm not sure. I realize how blessed I have been but sometimes I still feel inadequate. I don't cook. I can't drive. Most of the time, when I look back on what I've done, I think: *Did I do that? Why didn't I enjoy it more? Was I working too hard to see?*

As I said this, I looked up at Oprah and saw that she had tears in her eyes. I had touched a chord. Without any more words, we both knew what we had achieved and perhaps what we had given up. Most hard-working women would understand what we felt.

I "retired" from 20/20, but I did not, as many thought, retire from television. I am still working every day, what with The View and the Specials. Moreover, I have a new venture: radio. I now do a weekly live program on Sirius satellite radio with Bill Geddie. We take phone calls from listeners, discuss hot topics, argue, agree, and just have a swell time.

So now there is the question of when to truly retire. Let me tell you a final story.

A few New Year's ago, before I went out to celebrate, I watched my very dear friend Beverly Sills host a program on public television called *Great Performances*. Few people have delivered greater performances than Beverly, who was one of the world's most acclaimed operatic sopranos. She was a relatively new friend; I had only known her for about thirty years. After Beverly made the decision to end her operatic career, she went on to become the general director of the New York City Opera, then chair of Lincoln Center, and still later chair of the Metropolitan Opera. When she left the New York City Opera, her husband, Peter, gave her a gold ring with an engraved inscription. When I decided to leave *20/20,* Beverly gave me the ring. She said I should pay attention to what was inscribed. The ring says, "I did that already."

Sadly my darling Beverly died of cancer in July 2007. In September, I spoke at the memorial service the Metropolitan Opera held for her. Thousands of people filled the opera house, up to the highest tier. To me the most important person there was Beverly's daughter, Muffy. Muffy was born totally deaf and has never heard her mother sing. But Muffy is an amazing woman, smart and sensitive, with Beverly's sense of humor. She is truly her mother's daughter. We stay in close touch and share our love of her remarkable mother. I miss Beverly every day.

Memories. Memories. Mine are mostly good. The ghosts have receded, but occasionally they come to the fore. I recently gave a dinner party, and, as is sometimes my custom, at the end of the meal I introduced a question for each guest to answer in turn. The question I posed was, "Looking back at your life, what do you regret the most?" When Sarah Simms Rosenthal, whose husband, Dr. Mitchell Rosenthal, had been so helpful with [my daughter]

Jackie, answered, "I regret not having been with my mother when she died," tears stung my eyes. I, too, still regret not having been with my mother at the end. But no one can undo the past.

This is the most important thing: I am probably happier and more at peace than I have ever been. I know I had a fantastic career. I know I traveled everywhere and met almost every important person there was to meet. I achieved more than I could ever have imagined.

My colleague Don Hewitt repeatedly tells me that he and I lived through the golden age of television news. Perhaps he is right. But I don't want to spend my days looking back. I do know this, however: In this time of instant Internet news, cell phones that take videos, and a profusion of blogs where everyone is a reporter, there will be little chance for any single person to have the kind of career that I've had. If I was, perhaps, atop of the game, I also had the advantage of being ahead of the game. How lucky I was. How lucky!

Perhaps I have made it a little easier for some of the women who followed in my footsteps—maybe even for some in other careers. Television is no longer a man's world. Perhaps, too, I helped to change that. If so, I am very grateful. I am blessed seven times over. And there are even some days when I think I deserve it. But I also think it may possibly be time for me to finally say, "I did that already."

It is time to stop auditioning.

Part V:
Speaking Truth to Power

Michelle Obama, First Lady of the United States, is an attorney, mother of two daughters, and former executive director of Chicago's Public Allies, a nonprofit organization that encourages youth's work on social issues. Though some media persist in focusing on the First Lady's fashion sense, likening her to Jackie Kennedy (she has been dubbed Michelle O), Michelle has already shown that she will give them much more to report on than what she is wearing. She visits homeless shelters and schools, advocates for military families, and has had an organic garden and bee hives installed on the South Lawn of the White House. With a law degree from Harvard, she is the third First Lady to hold a postgraduate degree. Integrally involved in her husband's presidential campaign, she continues her support of his policies from the White House by publicly endorsing legislation that furthers them, stepping out of the traditional First Lady role.

Dream Big
Michelle Obama

Every woman that I know—regardless of race, education, income, background, political affiliation—is struggling to keep her head above water. We try to convince ourselves that somehow doing it all is a badge of honor, but for many of us it is a necessity and we have to be very careful not to lose ourselves in the process.

More often than not, we as women are the primary caretakers in our households—scheduling babysitters, planning play dates, keeping up with regular doctor's appointments. Usually, we are the ones in charge of keeping the household together.

And for those of us who work outside of the home as well, we have the additional challenge of coordinating these things with our job responsibilities. How many of us have had to be the ones, when a child gets sick, who is the one to stay home?

To top it off, we have the added social pressure of looking good, staying slim. Don't add pounds. Got to look good with wardrobe pulled together. And we have to be in good spirits, right? Ready to be there for our significant others. I'm tired just thinking about it.

These are not challenges that are unique to me. I say this all the time and people think I'm being modest. But the truth is that my experiences tell me that we as women are facing what I call the next level of challenges. Balancing work, family, and ourselves differently than ever before. My mother says this all the time. She's like, "I don't know how you do it," and she means it.

We have made great strides with regards to equality at all levels of society. And because of the struggles so many have fought, I know that my daughters can dream big. They really can. There is no ceiling. They can envision themselves any way that they want: surgeons, Supreme Court justices, basketball stars. They have images that I never had growing up.

I wonder what the unspoken cost that having it all takes on us. If we're scurrying to and from appointments and errands, we don't have a lot of time to take care of our own mental and physical health. For many women, juggling this adds another layer of stress. We see it in our health: women with increased heart attacks, diabetes, asthma. We're up in the numbers and this is no coincidence.

We have to really think through what the next level of challenges is for us. There just aren't enough hours in the day, so we do what we can. What is happening is that we do what we can in spite of the fact that we're not getting the needed support from the government and society as a whole.

The reality is that women and families are not getting the support that they need to thrive. We've spent the last decade talking a good game about family values, but I haven't seen much in my life that really shows that we're a society that actually values families.

We have essentially ignored the plight of women and families. We've told them, "You go figure it out." Figure out how you're going to support a family on minimum wage and no benefits. You go figure out who is going to watch your children while you are at work without access to adequate, affordable childcare. You figure out how to keep your family healthy without access to quality health care. Figure out how you're going to ensure that your children get the best education possible. You figure out how you're going to live without access to affordable housing.

Essentially, we've told women, "Dream big, but after that, you are on your own."

My husband is a man who understands my unique struggle and the challenges facing women and families. It is not just because he lives with me—someone who is very opinionated and makes my point. I am not a martyr, so he hears it.

It is because he actually listens to me and has the utmost respect for my perspective and my life experience.

It is also because he was raised in a household of strong women who he saw struggle and sacrifice for him so he could achieve his dreams.

He saw his grandmother, the primary breadwinner in their household, work her entire life to support their whole family. He saw his mother, a very young, single parent, trying to finish her education and raise two children across two continents. He sees his sister, a single parent, trying to eke out a life for herself and her daughter on a salary that is much too small.

He sees it in the eyes of women he meets throughout the country. Women who have lost children and husbands in the war. Women who don't have access to adequate health care, to affordable daycare, or to jobs that pay a living wage. Their stories keep him up at night. Their stories, our stories, are the foundation of what guides Barack throughout his life. Barack is someone who recognizes that society, our community, is only as strong as our women and our families.

We have the opportunity now. We can be part of changing the way women are viewed in this country. We can build a government that doesn't just encourage women to dream big but one that provides women and young girls with the support and resources to pursue those dreams.

I want that for my daughters; I want that for your daughters; I want that for this country.

Congresswoman Barbara Lee (D–CA) began her political career as an intern in the office of her predecessor, Ron Dellums. Upon his retirement, she won the seat in a special election in 1998. Her willingness to stand on principle earned her international acclaim when she was the only member of Congress to vote against giving then-President Bush a blank check to wage war after the 9/11 attacks. She continues to be one of Congress's most vocal opponents to the war in Iraq. Chair of the Congressional Black Caucus (CBC), she also serves on the powerful House Appropriations Committee, among others. In 2006, Mills College (her alma mater) established the Barbara Lee Distinguished Chair in Women's Leadership in recognition of her courageous leadership in politics, policymaking, and human rights.

❦ CHAPTER TWENTY-FOUR ❦

Peace and Justice

Barbara Lee

*Never think you are alone when you stand for right because
GOD is with you. We are very proud of you. It makes us feel good
that you are a Congressional Member.*

Rosa Parks wrote these kind words to me in a letter some
years ago, and when I read these two sentences I was so moved
that a woman of her stature—and a hero in her own right—felt
that I was carrying the torch for peace and the nonviolent struggle
for human rights. By sharing my life story with others, I want to
help people realize that bad choices, adversity, and all of the other
obstacles life places before us can be overcome. There is always
hope! Rosa Parks was the mother of the civil rights movement,
and her willingness to put her life on the line in the face of threats
and violence confirmed for me that each time I stood up for what
was right, I was never truly alone. No, standing behind me was
God and the teachings of Christ. Moreover, I was standing on the
shoulders of giants—all the people who came before me who
risked it all and whose bravery and sheer force of will changed the
face of history. These freedom fighters' quests to end war, fight
poverty, eradicate injustice, and eliminate discrimination continue

to be shining beacons for us all, and their causes have not dimmed with the passage of time. I have drawn strength from their courage and indomitable spirits. Rosa Parks' single act of defiance created a storm of bigoted fury and retaliation, yet she always remained a pillar of calm and determination. Her peaceful resistance inspired her contemporaries and led to a true civil rights movement that continues to galvanize new generations—and she has been a reminder to me that one person truly can make a difference.

I never set out to be a champion for peace or human rights or to chart new territory by going against the tide. But like Esther of the Old Testament, I was taught that if I witnessed an injustice, then I had no choice but to stand and be counted. I had to do something. To do nothing has never been an option for me, and if it fell to me to lead, then that was the path destined for me. I have been fortunate to have met, worked with, or read about incredible people who have shown me that having faith and doing what is right is its own reward. I certainly never consciously decided to become a lightning rod of political controversy. Each time I have been thrust into the center of conflict, it has been the hands of fate at work and my sincere wish to follow my conscience and to right a wrong. I often wonder what my life would have been like if I hadn't met or worked with some of my most important influences and mentors, like the Catholic Sisters of Loretto, Reps. Shirley Chisholm (D-NY) and Ron Dellums (D-CA)—now mayor of Oakland, California, Gloria Steinem, Bobby Seale, and Dolores Huerta. No one accomplishes anything completely alone in life, and I have been blessed by a wonderful loving family and friends who have supported me. My faith also has helped me face each new challenge. I have been fortunate to receive recognition for my work throughout my life, and these confirmations of personal and professional accomplishments have sustained me as well. It started in high school when I won a Bank of America Achievement Award and a Rotary Club Music scholarship. Later, going to Mills College became a positive and enriching, life-altering experience that instilled me with the confidence I needed to achieve my goals.

When I worked on Rep. Chisholm's (D-NY) campaign for President, I saw firsthand that there were important women of color who could give young black women an idea of just how far they could go in life if they worked hard and never lost faith in themselves. Had I not so admired "Mrs. C," as she was affectionately known, I might not have worked on her campaign and not have had the chance to meet my future mentor and boss, Rep. Dellums (D-CA). His faith in my abilities gave me the work experience of a lifetime and enabled me to become one of the first African American women as a top key staffer. During my eleven years in his office, I watched him take unpopular stances on peace, the war in Vietnam, and the issues of race, poverty, and human rights. I saw how he struggled with his conscience and how he often stood alone for or against an important issue. When he resigned from the House of Representatives in 1998, I was able to run for his seat and carry the baton, which he passed to me, for the work he had begun. Winning his seat has been a professional and personal milestone in many ways. I became the first woman to be elected to represent the Ninth District of California, which includes Albany, Ashland, Berkeley, Castro Valley, Cherryland, Emeryville, Fairview, Oakland, and Piedmont.

As a member of the House of representatives I have worked hard to represent my district and the American people. Like Ron, I have been forced to make difficult votes that have earned me the admiration of many and the hatred of some. In some cases my votes famously foisted me on to the front pages and into the history books, but I try to vote for what is right. Being in the limelight can be a blessing if you are trying to bring attention to an issue, but it can also be dangerous and frightening. My vote against giving the Bush administration a "blank check" to use force after 9/11 didn't feel momentous—just morally, ethically, and constitutionally correct. It never occurred to me that I would be the only person voting against it. I had made other controversial votes like that when the Clinton administration wanted to use force in Kosovo. Again I was the sole "no" vote, and I am sure that in the future I will vote for or against a bill that will earn me the enmity of other members of Congress and the public. But each time I contemplate taking on a difficult cause that is sure to be met with resistance and strife, I know that I can persevere if I remember who else faced dogged opposition, whether it was my mother who fought her own battles to do the right thing or Rosa Parks.

Mahatma Gandhi was a man whose method of nonviolent resistance and civil disobedience introduced the Western World to a new way of bringing about change and created in India a free and democratic nation of three hundred million people, where once there had been colonial oppression and subjugation. I was very moved when I visited his burial site and house in Mumbai, India, several years ago.

Martin Luther King Jr. saw the dignity and power of Gandhi and Rosa Parks' actions and began a groundswell of political action that would change American history.

Gloria Steinem changed the dialogue about women and the future of the women's movement by challenging what it meant to be a woman and a feminist. She showed us that as women, it's up to us to define ourselves, not men, or society, government, advertisers, or the media.

Dolores Huerta, the mother of the United Farm Workers Union, has for forty years used nonviolent resistance to fight for the rights of farm workers, women, legal immigrants, and Latinos, and she did it in a time when Latinos were still considered indentured servants by many Americans. She has been arrested more than twenty times and has been brutally beaten by police only to return and resume her struggles with grace and dignity. I have worked with her, marched with her, and greatly admire her struggles and accomplishments.

Bono, the lead singer for the rock band U2, could have sat back and enjoyed the money, fame, and opportunity that his success afforded him. Instead, he has decided to work with politicians like myself, former Sen. Jesse Helms (R-NC), Speaker of the House Nancy Pelosi (D-CA), and [former] President George W. Bush to try to end the senseless and unnecessary spread of the HIV/AIDS pandemic and to help treat and cure the millions of people dying in Africa. Every time I talk with him, I feel his heart and his soul.

Each of these people, in his or her own way, has left a mark on the world. I hope that by telling my story, other people are encouraged to follow in our footsteps and help make the world a more compassionate, safer, cleaner, and healthier place to live. Throughout my political career, I have brought my training as a social worker to my work confronting the challenges that face people of my district, across the nation, and throughout the world. I have tried to build bipartisan coalitions to protect the fundamental human rights of all people: health care, housing, education, jobs, and the quest to create livable communities in a peaceful world. I am merely carrying on the work begun by others, and I hope to pass the baton to the next generation who can continue my work to represent the voice of reason in the campaign to reshape our national budget and our vision for what America will look like in the future. If we choose, Americans can reclaim our lost esteem and prove to the world that we are a nation of people who value freedom and condemn any attempt to shackle or stifle expression. I try to live by a code that respects life and recognizes that our diversity is a strength that should be celebrated, not a weakness that should divide us. When we are divided by fear, hatred, ignorance, and lack of understanding, we cannot live in harmony with other nations. My philosophy on life, politics, government, and the fight for peace and justice has been guided by tenets wonderfully expressed by one of the great leaders of our century, the Dalai Lama, who once said:

Peace, in the sense of the absence of war, is of little value to someone who is dying of hunger or cold. It will not remove the pain of torture inflicted on a prisoner of conscience. It does not comfort those who have lost their loved ones in floods caused by senseless deforestation in a neighbouring country. Peace can only last where human rights are respected, where the people are fed, and where individuals and nations are free. *

---

* Dalai Lama, "Nobel Lecture," December 11, 1989, www.nobelprize.org.

Sonia Gandhi, the widow of former prime minister of India Rajiv Gandhi, is president of the Indian National Congress and chair of the Coordinating Committee of the ruling coalition, the United Progressive Alliance. She rose to her influential position in Indian politics despite the fact that she is Italian by birth. In 2004, *Forbes* magazine cited her as the third most powerful woman in the world. In both 2007 and 2008, *Time* magazine listed her as one of the hundred most influential people in the world. The author of two books on her husband, *Rajiv* and *Rajiv's World,* she also edited two collections of the correspondence between father and daughter prime ministers Jawaharlal Nehru and Indira Gandhi, entitled *Freedom's Daughter* and *Two Alone, Two Together.* www.soniagandhi.org

CHAPTER TWENTY-FIVE

The Art of the Impossible
Sonia Gandhi

I was born in Europe, but was soon claimed by another world more diverse and more ancient. Mine was a middle-class family from a provincial town in the north of Italy. It was a close-knit family typical of its time, conservative and in essence not very different from a traditional Indian family: strong in adherence to values such as loyalty and obedience, to modesty and truthfulness, to generosity and respect for elders. Yet my father, for all his forbidding ways, was progressive enough to encourage me to learn languages and travel abroad. At school, I learnt of the Risorgimento, of Mazzini and Garibaldi, and the unification of Italy. But of India, its great history and its emergence as a modern nation-state, I was taught nothing. My discovery of India happened differently, through the encounter with a remarkable human being. This discovery would take up the rest of my life!

I first met Rajiv Gandhi when I was enrolled in a language school in Cambridge. It was very soon evident to both of us that we would spend our lives together. Two years later, I came to India to marry him. That was almost forty years ago. Not in my wildest dreams could I have imagined then the course my destiny would take. My husband was not in politics when we began our married life. He was a pilot, absorbed and fascinated by the world of aviation; a devoted husband and loving father to our two children; a man of wide interests who pursued his passion for nature, wildlife, and photography in the company of his family and a few close friends.

Though his mother, Indira Gandhi, headed the government, and we lived in the prime minister's house, the life that we made together was essentially private. This was the life we had chosen, a life that brought us joy and deep fulfillment. Yet it was a life permeated by the turbulence of politics. Looking back, I can say that it was through the private world of family that the public world of politics came alive for me: living in intimate proximity with people for whom larger questions of ideology and belief as well as issues relating to politics and governance were vivid daily realities. There were other aspects of living in a political family that had an impact on me as a young bride. I had to accustom myself to the public gaze, which I found intrusive and hard to endure. I had to learn to curb my spontaneity and instinctive bluntness of speech. Most of all, I had to school myself not to react in the face of falsehood and slander. I had to learn to endure them as the rest of the family did.

My mother-in-law was regarded as a strong, rather formidable personality. Indeed, she had the calm authority of a natural leader. She had come a long way from the shy and agonized young woman she had been. But I knew her also as a sensitive, intuitive person with a love for the arts and for the conservation of nature, a sense of humor and the ability to laugh at herself. In the midst of preoccupation with affairs of state, she never failed to make time for personal concerns—a grandchild's birthday, the illness of a friend or a relative, the problems of a staff member. Her breadth of spirit was evident: although rooted in a traditional society, she had accepted her son's decision to marry a girl from a distant land. She opened her heart, her family, and her culture to me, treating me like the daughter she never had. Along with my husband, she guided me patiently through the confusions and hesitations of my early adjustments to India. In time I came to relish the flavors of India's many cuisines, to feel comfortable in Indian clothes, to speak Hindi, and acquaint myself with the cultural heritage of my new homeland. The glorious and multi-hued palette of India came to be as dear and precious to me as it was to them.

Over the years we drew closer together. She shared her experiences about her personal life, her loneliness as a child with her mother ailing and her father imprisoned, of her involvement from her childhood in the freedom movement, of the values that took shape in those formative years. I watched her deal with crises and triumphs. I saw her interact with the common man and with heads of state, with allies and with opponents. She faced adulation and acclaim as well as criticism, slander, rejection, and imprisonment.

At the time I entered my new family, India was not quite twenty-one years independent from British colonial rule. The Congress Party, now led by my mother-in-law, was still preeminent, but was beginning to face a resurgent political opposition. Her father, Jawaharlal Nehru, had passed from the stage less than four years earlier, and his successor, Lal Bahadur Shastri, was prime minister for less than two years.

Indira Gandhi, who succeeded him, was as yet untested in statecraft. She had come to power in the wake of two wars and two famines. Her first challenge was a trial by fire, as she strove to establish her authority over her party and government. In that struggle, her shield was her ability to connect directly with the people; her sword was her empathy with the poor, and the policies she initiated on their behalf.

My first political classroom thus echoed to momentous unfolding events. Two stand out in my memory. The first was the 1971 crisis that transformed Mrs. Gandhi into a statesman. Following a crackdown by the Pakistan military in what was then East Pakistan, more than ten million refugees flooded into India from across the border—that is, about two-thirds of today's population of the

Netherlands. Obviously, India could not shoulder such a burden. My mother-in-law traveled to all the major world capitals, striving to convince the international community to intervene in what was a humanitarian catastrophe. She was met largely with indifference, and in some cases, opposition. When India was attacked, her response was swift and sure. She withdrew Indian forces immediately after a representative government took charge in the newborn country of Bangladesh. Evident here was the importance in politics of patience and tenacity, of daring and courage, and, above all, of action at the opportune and decisive moment.

Another memory I have of her as a political leader is of her steely determination to raise India out of the cycle of famine and dependency on imports of food grains. She took tough decisions that laid the foundations of the Green Revolution that transformed our economy. Her actions saw India move from being seen as indigent and helpless to becoming self-sufficient in food grains production. This reflected the driving force of her passion to uphold the dignity and independence of her country. That was the mainspring of her political creed.

With all the political twists and reversals that formed the background of our first thirteen years of marriage, our domestic life had remained relatively tranquil. Then suddenly our world was devastated by a succession of tragedies. In June 1980, my husband's only brother died in an air crash. My mother-in-law was shattered. Her younger son had been active in public life. She now turned to my husband for support. He was tormented by the choice he had to make, between protecting the life he had chosen and stepping forward to his mother's side when she needed him most. Months elapsed before I could bring myself to accept that if he felt such a strong sense of duty to his mother, I would stand by his decision. In 1981, he was elected to Parliament.

Though I often traveled with him to his constituency and became involved in welfare work there, my main concern remained to ensure a warm and serene environment at home. Politics had now entered our lives more directly, but I resisted its further ingress.

Four years later came the event that shook our nation and forever altered the destiny of our family. My mother-in-law, the pivot of our lives, was assassinated by her own bodyguards in our home. Within hours of her death, the Congress Party asked my husband to take over the leadership of the party and government. Even as I pleaded with him not to accept, I realized that he had no option. I feared for his life. But his sense of responsibility to the country, and to the legacy of his mother and grandfather, was too deeply ingrained in him. The life we had chosen was now irrevocably over. One month later, he led the Congress Party to a landslide victory in the general elections. He was forty years old when he became prime minister.

I now had official duties as the prime minister's wife. But I also had to balance this with our family life, bringing up our children and ensuring they had as normal an existence as possible, given the extensive security restrictions around us all.

Our world had been overturned with the death of my mother-in-law. As often happens when one loses a loved one, I sought to reach out to her through her writings. I immersed myself in editing two volumes of letters between her and her father. Through most of her youth, while her father was in British jails, their loving and close relationship found expression in a flourishing correspondence, recording a rich and vivid interplay between two lively minds. These exchanges brought alive to me the freedom struggle as it was felt and acted by two people who went on to play important roles in shaping modern India. Along with the books of Jawaharlal Nehru, which I had read earlier, they provided a philosophical and historical underpinning to my direct experience of observing my husband as he carried forward their vision for India.

I accompanied him on his travels to the remotest and poorest parts of the country. We were welcomed into people's huts and homes. They opened their hearts to him, speaking of their

sufferings, as well as their hopes and aspirations. I came to understand and share his feelings for them, to see what it was that drove
him to work as he did with so much energy, enthusiasm, and attention to detail. His commitment to making a real difference in their
lives brought a fresh and vigorous approach to the imperatives of
combining growth with social justice. He mobilized Indian scientists and technologists to tackle basic areas like telecommunica-
tions, drinking water, mass immunization, and literacy. It is a matter of satisfaction to me to see so many of the seeds he sowed now
yielding flourishing harvests. To name a few: India's recognition as
an IT power in the world owes much to him; space satellites and
telephone networks are improving the living standards of large
segments of our population, especially the rural and urban poor;
India's entrepreneurial talents, which began to be unshackled in
the early 1980s, are now spearheading our country's impressive
rate of economic growth; the revival of local self-government
institutions is strengthening the foundations of our democracy.
These were all cherished endeavors of his. But the time given to
him by Fate was all too short.

My husband remained prime minister for five years. Soon after came the moment I had been dreading since the trauma of my
mother-in-law's death. On May 21, 1991, while campaigning in
the national elections, he was assassinated by terrorists. The Congress Party asked me to become its leader in his place; I declined,
instinctively recoiling from a political milieu that had so devastated my life and that of my children.

For the next several years I withdrew into myself. I drew comfort and strength from the thousands of people who shared our
grief, cherished my husband's memory, and offered my children
and me their love and their support. We set up a foundation to take
forward some of the initiatives closest to his heart.

The years that followed saw change and turbulence in India.
Economic growth was accelerating. New groups and communities,
long deprived, were seeking their legitimate share. Democracy

was making India much more egalitarian, but it was also giving new power to some old forces—forces that sought to polarize and mobilize communities along religious lines. They threatened the very essence of India, the diversity of faiths and cultures, languages and ways of life that have sprung from its soil and taken root in it.

The Congress Party was being buffeted by these currents. This was the party that had fought for India's independence and nurtured its infant democracy till it became a robust institution. It now found itself in the midst of uncertainty and turmoil. In 1996, it lost the national elections. Pressure began to build up from a large number of Congress workers across the country urging me to emerge from my seclusion and enter public life.

Could I stand aside and watch as the forces of bigotry continued in their campaigns to spread division and discord? Could I ignore my own commitment to the values and principles of the family I had married into, values and principles for which they lived and died? Could I betray that legacy and turn away from it? I knew my own limitations, but I could no longer stand aside. Such were the circumstances under which the life of politics chose me.

I was elected president of the Congress Party in 1998 when it was in opposition. This gave me an opportunity to travel to all corners of the country. I found the people at large responded to me spontaneously. Intuitively, they seemed to understand that, like them, I too valued their traditions, their philosophy, and their way of life. This seemed to build a bond between us, especially with the poor who welcomed me and opened their hearts without hesitation. Again and again, I have been moved and humbled by the gaze of trust and hope in people's eyes.

This link between successive generations of Indians and my family is no abstract one. I had witnessed it in the case of both my mother-in-law and my husband: the almost electric charge that sparked between them and the people: a meeting of eyes, sometimes hands, a communication that surged across all barriers. The attachment accorded so generously to this family is to some extent in recognition of their sacrifices, achievements, and selfless devotion to the country. But perhaps their appeal also lay in their transcending the four basic markers of the Indian identity: religion, caste, language, and region. They came to embody the all-inclusive ethos of our country, its essential oneness.

At times people refer to the Nehru-Gandhi "dynasty." What this word fails to signify is two crucial elements: one is the sovereignty of the people. Through the democratic process, they have repeatedly vested their expectations in one or another member, and equally on other occasions, they have chosen to withdraw their support. The other essential factor, one that lies at the heart of this relationship, is not the exercise of power but the affirmation of a sacred trust. It is this love and faith that imposes its own responsibility and obligations, that has inspired even a reluctant politician such as myself to enter the public domain.

Success in the 2004 national elections came after six years of political work. I was unanimously elected as my party's leader in Parliament. The next step was to form the government. But I always knew in my heart that if I ever found myself in that position, I would decline the post of Prime Minister of India. I have often been asked why I turned it down. In trying to explain that choice to my colleagues in the party, I described it as dictated by my "inner voice." Indeed, that voice has been my wisest guide in political life. The plain fact is that power for itself has never held any attraction for me. My aim in politics has always been to do whatever I can in my own way to defend the secular, democratic foundations of our country, and to address the concerns and aspirations of the many whose voice often remains unheard.

Too often, we think of politics as a public arena, quite apart from our private world—let alone the inner life. But experience has taught me that such separations are illusory: to pretend a distinction between the values we bring to our personal lives and to our public dealings inevitably deprive both of meaning. Practical considerations aside, I have tried to see that, as far as possible, the significant political decisions of my life flow out of the inner experience of emotion and belief, and of the need to be true to myself.

Politics may be the art of the possible, but it must be anchored in truth. In India, we are fortunate to have the example of Mahatma Gandhi so clearly before us: a visionary who shunned expedient strategies, who frequently chose the most difficult way because it was the right way. For him, the means had to be worthy of the ends. His transparent commitment to truth was such that it inspired millions of Indians from all walks of life to participate in the freedom struggle and to face untold hardships, including long years of imprisonment. This created a new model for mass movements in the world: one based on an unflinching moral core, on personal sacrifice, and a dedication to absolute nonviolence.

Mindful of this history, I believe that politics must have at its heart one guiding principle: to achieve its goals through just and ethical means. It is my conviction that coercion, expediency, and the cynical manipulation of popular sentiment and public opinion to attain one's ends, no matter how worthy they are, can never be justified. But I do recognize that this is easier said than done. Very often, practice and precept diverge, sometimes consciously and sometimes unconsciously. When we compromise, we must have the courage and candor to admit to it and not abandon our commitment to basic principles.

Politics is not just the art of the possible; it can also be the art of the impossible. To have won freedom and forged nationhood through a unique nonviolent movement and to have launched universal adult suffrage more than half a century ago, in a society that was then 85 percent illiterate and desperately poor, was a daring act of faith. To have helped democracy take root, and to have nurtured it through sixty years amidst continuous challenges, has been a stupendous achievement. Politics everywhere is an exacting mistress, nowhere more so than in India, with its multiplicity of political parties and ideologies pulling in different directions.

Its sheer size, diversity, and variety; the huge development tasks it is undertaking in a framework of open democracy; the growing aspirations of over a billion people all make it a formidable mission. The exuberance and vitality of our people, especially our youth, gives me the confidence that India will continue to push the boundaries of the possible, for its own well-being and for that of the world.

My journey from the placid backwaters of a contented domestic life to the maelstrom of public life has not been an easy one. Yet, despite its sorrows and difficulties, I have found in my new existence both fulfillment and a larger sense of purpose. The family to which I first pledged my fidelity was in the confines of a home. Today my loyalty embraces a wider family—India, my country, whose people have so generously welcomed me to become one of them.

Sue Monk Kidd is author of the spiritual memoirs *When the Heart Waits* and *God's Joyful Surprise* and the bestselling novels *The Secret Life of Bees* and *The Mermaid Chair*. *The Secret Life of Bees* has sold more than six million copies, was made into a feature film starring Queen Latifah and Alicia Keys, and has become part of high school and college curricula. She is writer in residence at the Sophia Institute in Charleston, South Carolina, where she lives with her husband on a salt marsh. www.suemonkkidd. com

CHAPTER TWENTY-SIX

The Dance of Dissidence
Sue Monk Kidd

The female soul is no small thing. Neither is a woman's right to define the sacred from a woman's perspective.

It was autumn, and everything was turning loose. I was running errands that afternoon. Rain had fallen earlier, but now the sun was out, shining on the tiny beads of water that clung to trees and sidewalks. The whole world seemed red and yellow and rinsed with light. I parked in front of the drugstore where my daughter, Ann, fourteen, had an after-school job. Leaping a puddle, I went inside.

I spotted her right away kneeling on the floor in the toothpaste section, stocking a bottom shelf. I was about to walk over and say hello when I noticed two middle-aged men walking along the aisle toward her. They looked like everybody's father. They had moussed hair, and they wore knit sportshirts the color of Easter eggs, the kind of shirts with tiny alligators sewn at the chest. It was a detail I would remember later as having ironic symbolism.

My daughter did not see them coming. Kneeling on the floor, she was intent on getting the boxes of Crest lined up evenly. The men stopped, peering down at her. One nudged the other. He said, "Now that's how I like to see a woman—on her knees."

The other man laughed.

Standing in the next aisle, I froze. I watched the expression that crept into my daughter's eyes as she looked up. I watched her chin drop and her hair fall across her face.

Seeing her kneel at these men's feet while they laughed at her subordinate posture pierced me through.

For the previous couple of years I had been in the midst of a tumultuous awakening. I had been struggling to come to terms with my life as a woman—in my culture, my marriage, my faith, my church, and deep inside myself. It was a process not unlike the experience of conception and labor. There had been a moment, many moments really, when truth seized me and I "conceived" of myself as woman. Or maybe I reconceived myself. At any rate, it had been extraordinary and surprising to find myself—a conventionally religious woman in my late thirties—suddenly struck pregnant with a new consciousness, with an unfolding new awareness of what it means to be a woman and what it means to be spiritual *as a woman*.

Hard labor had followed. For months I'd inched along, but lately I'd been stuck. I'd awakened enough to know that I couldn't go back to my old way of being a woman, but the fear of going forward was paralyzing. So I'd plodded along, trying to make room for the new consciousness that was unfolding in my life but without really risking change.

I have a friend, a nurse on the obstetrical floor at a hospital, who says that sometimes a woman's labor simply stalls. The contractions grow weak, and the new life, now quite distressed, hangs precariously. The day I walked into the drugstore, I was experiencing something like that. A stalled awakening.

Who knows, I may have stalled interminably if I had not seen my daughter on her knees before those laughing men. I cannot to this day explain why the sight of it hit me so forcibly. But to borrow Kafka's image, it came like an ice ax upon a frozen sea, and suddenly all my hesitancy was shattered. Just like that.

The men's laughter seemed to go on and on. I felt like a small animal in the road, blinded by the light of a truck, knowing some terrible collision is coming but unable to move. I stared at my daughter on her knees before these men and could not look away. Somehow she seemed more than my daughter; she was my mother, my grandmother, and myself. She was every woman ever born, bent and contained in a small, ageless cameo that bore the truth about "a woman's place."

In the profile of my daughter I saw the suffering of women, the confining of the feminine to places of inferiority, and I experienced a collision of love and pain so great I had to reach for the counter to brace myself.

This posture will not perpetuate itself in her life, I thought.

Still I didn't know what to do. When I was growing up, if my mother had told me once, she'd told me a thousand times, "If you can't say something nice, don't say anything at all." I'd heard this from nearly everybody. It was the kind of thing that got cross-stitched and hung in kitchens all over my native South.

I'd grown up to be a soft-voiced, sweet-mouthed woman who, no matter how assailing the behavior before me or how much I disagreed with it, responded nicely or else zip-locked my mouth shut. I had swallowed enough defiant, disputatious words in my life to fill a shelf of books.

But it occurred to me that if I abandoned my daughter at that moment, if I simply walked away and was silent, the feminine spirit unfolding inside her might also become crouched and silent. Perhaps she would learn the *internal* posture of being on her knees.

The men with their blithe joke had no idea they had tapped a reservoir of pain and defiance in me. It was rising now, unstoppable by any earthly force.

I walked toward them. "I have something to say to you, and I want you to hear it," I said.

They stopped laughing. Ann looked up.

"This is my daughter," I said, pointing to her, my finger shaking with anger. "You may like to see her and other women on their knees, but we don't belong there. *We don't belong there!*"

Ann rose to her feet. She glanced sideways at me, sheer amazement spread over her face, then turned and faced the men. I could hear her breath rise and fall with her chest as we stood there shoulder to shoulder, staring at their faces.

"Women," one of them said. They walked away, leaving Ann and me staring at each other among the toothpaste and dental floss.

I smiled at her. She smiled back. And though we didn't say a word, more was spoken between us in that moment than perhaps in our whole lives.

I left the drugstore that day so internally jolted by the experience that everything in me began to shift. I sat in the car feeling like a newborn, dangled upside down and slapped.

Throughout my awakening, I'd grown increasingly aware of certain attitudes that existed in our culture, a culture long dominated by men. The men in the drugstore had mirrored one attitude in particular, that of seeking power over another, of staying up by keeping others down.

Sitting in my car replaying my statement back to those men—that women did not belong on their knees—I knew I had uttered my declaration of intent.

Nearing forty, I needed to rethink my life as a "man-made woman." To take back my soul. Gradually I began to see what I hadn't seen before, to feel things that until then had never dared to enter my heart. I became aware that as a woman I'd been on my knees my whole life and not really known it. Most of all, I ached for the woman in me who had not yet been born, though I couldn't have told you then the reason for the ache.

When this disenchantment, this ripeness, begins, a woman's task is to conceive herself. If she does, the spark of her awakening is struck. And if she can give that awakening a tiny space in her life, it will develop into a full-blown experience that one day she will want to mark and celebrate.

Conception, labor, and birthing—metaphors thick with the image and experiences of women—offer a body parable of the process of awakening. The parable tells us things we need to know about the way awakening works—the slow, unfolding, sometimes hidden, always expanding nature of it, the inevitable queasiness, the need to nurture and attend to what inhabits us, the uncertainty about the outcomes, the fearful knowing that once we bring the new consciousness forth, our lives will never be the same. It tells us that and more.

I've given birth to two children, but bringing them into the world was a breeze compared to birthing myself as woman. Bringing forth a true, instinctual, powerful woman who is rooted in her own feminine center, who honors the sacredness of the feminine, and who speaks the feminine language of her own soul is never easy. Neither is it always welcomed. I discovered that few people will rush over to tie a big pink bow on your mailbox.

Yet there is no place so awake and alive as the edge of becoming. But more than that, birthing the kind of woman who can authentically say, "My soul is my own," and then embody it in her life, her spirituality, and her community is worth the risk and hardship.

Today, eight years after my waking began, I realize that the women who are bringing about this kind of new female life are brand new beings among us. I keep meeting them; I keep hearing their stories. They confirm my own experience, that somewhere along the course of a woman's life, usually when she has lived just long enough to see through some of the cherished notions of femininity that culture holds out to her, when she finally lets herself *feel* the limits and injustices of the female life and admits how her own faith tradition has contributed to that, when she at last stumbles in the dark hole made by the absence of a Divine Feminine presence, then the extraordinary thing I've been telling you about will happen. This women will become pregnant with herself, with the symbolic female-child who will, if given the chance, grow up to reinvent the woman's life.

This female-child is the new potential we all have to become women grounded in our own souls, women who discover the Sacred Feminine way, women who let loose their strength. In the end we will reinvent not only ourselves, but also religion and spirituality as they have been handed down to us.

Nothing happens neatly on journeys such as this. There is no one-two-three program. There are no guarantees, and no two journeys unfold the same way. Every woman's story of finding the Sacred Feminine brims with its own unique events, risks, complexities, pains, and rewards. And every story is a luminous thread that becomes part of a larger fabric, a fabric we are weaving together for the whole world, and this fabric is a thing of immense importance and beauty.

I look back now and I am grateful. I recall that whenever I struggled, doubted, wondered if I could pull my thread into this fabric, someone or something would always appear—a friend, a stranger, a figure in a dream, a book, an experience, some shining part of nature—and remind me that this thing I was undertaking was holy to the core. I would learn again that it is all right for women to follow the wisdom in their souls, to name their truth, to embrace the Sacred Feminine, that there is undreamed voice, strength, and power in us.

And that is what I have come to tell you. I have come over the wise distances to tell you: She is in us.

Aung San Suu Kyi, long-time activist for democracy in her homeland of Burma (Myanmar), is the daughter of assassinated Burmese revolutionary and nationalist Aung San. Suu Kyi is general secretary of the National League for Democracy (NLD) and was elected prime minister in 1990. The military junta refused to step aside, however, and placed her under house arrest, thus preventing her from taking office. She has been under house arrest for nearly fourteen of the past nineteen years. During that time, she received the Nobel Peace Prize and the Sakharov Prize for Freedom of Thought. The military government keeps her under house arrest on the grounds that she is "likely to undermine the community peace and stability" of Burma. Her detention sparked and continues to spark international outcry. www.dassk.org

CHAPTER TWENTY-SEVEN

Freedom from Fear
Aung San Suu Kyi

On August 26, 1988, after the military junta had violently suppressed mass demonstrations for democracy throughout Burma, leading to the deaths of many, Aung San Suu Kyi addressed the public for the first time. Her speech, "Freedom from Fear," reprinted here, was heard by several hundred thousand people. It was first released for publication in commemoration of the European Parliament's award to Aung San Suu Kyi of the 1990 Sakharov Prize for Freedom of Thought. The award ceremony took place on July 10, 1991, in Strasbourg, France. She was unable to attend due to being under house arrest.

It is not power that corrupts but fear. Fear of losing power corrupts those who wield it and fear of the scourge of power corrupts those who are subject to it. Most Burmese are familiar with the four *a-gati,* the four kinds of corruption.

Chanda-gati, corruption induced by desire, is deviation from the right path in pursuit of bribes or for the sake of those one loves. *Dosa-gati* is taking the wrong path to spite those against whom one bears ill will, and *moga-gati* is aberration due to ignorance. But perhaps the worst of the four is *bhaya-gati,* for not only does *bhaya,* fear, stifle and slowly destroy all sense of right and wrong, it so often lies at the root of the other three kinds of corruption. Just as *chanda-gati,* when not the result of sheer avarice, can be caused by fear of want or fear of losing the goodwill of those one loves, so fear of being surpassed, humiliated, or injured in some way can provide the impetus for ill will. And it would be difficult to dispel ignorance unless there is freedom to pursue the truth unfettered by fear. With so close a relationship between fear and corruption, it is little wonder that, in any society where fear is rife, corruption in all forms becomes deeply entrenched.

Public dissatisfaction with economic hardships has been seen as the chief cause of the movement for democracy in Burma, sparked off by the student demonstrations 1988. It is true that years of incoherent policies, inept official measures, burgeoning inflation, and falling real income had turned the country into an economic shambles. But it was more than the difficulties of eking out a barely acceptable standard of living that had eroded the patience of a traditionally good-natured, quiescent people—it was also the humiliation of a way of life disfigured by corruption and fear.

The students were protesting not just against the death of their comrades but against the denial of their right to life by a totalitarian regime that deprived the present of meaningfulness and held out no hope for the future. And because the students' protests articulated the frustrations of the people at large, the demonstrations quickly grew into a nationwide movement. Some of its keenest supporters were businessmen who had developed the skills and the contacts necessary not only to survive but to prosper within the system. But their affluence offered them no genuine sense of security or fulfillment, and they could not but see that if they and their fellow citizens, regardless of economic status, were to achieve a worthwhile existence, an accountable administration was at least a necessary if not a sufficient condition. The people of Burma had wearied of a precarious state of passive apprehension where they were "as water in the cupped hands" of the powers that be.

Emerald cool we may be
As water in cupped hands
But oh that we might be
As splinters of glass
In cupped hands.

Glass splinters, the smallest with its sharp, glinting power to defend itself against hands that try to crush, could be seen as a vivid symbol of the spark of courage that is an essential attribute of those who would free themselves from the grip of oppression. Bogyoke [General] Aung San [my father] regarded himself as a revolutionary and searched tirelessly for answers to the problems that beset Burma during her times of trial. He exhorted the people to develop courage: "Don't just depend on the courage and intrepidity of others. Each and every one of you must make sacrifices to become a hero possessed of courage and intrepidity. Then only shall we all be able to enjoy true freedom."

The effort necessary to remain uncorrupted in an environment where fear is an integral part of everyday existence is not immediately apparent to those fortunate enough to live in states governed by the rule of law. Just laws do not merely prevent corruption by meting out impartial punishment to offenders. They also help to create a society in which people can fulfill the basic requirements necessary for the preservation of human dignity without recourse to corrupt practices. Where there are no such laws, the burden of upholding the principles of justice and common decency falls on the ordinary people. It is the cumulative effect on their sustained effort and steady endurance which will change a nation where reason and conscience are warped by fear into one where legal rules exist to promote man's desire for harmony and justice while restraining the less desirable destructive traits in his nature.

In an age when immense technological advances have created lethal weapons which could be, and are, used by the powerful and the unprincipled to dominate the weak and the helpless, there is a compelling need for a closer relationship between politics and ethics at both the national and international levels. The Universal Declaration of Human Rights of the United Nations proclaims that "every individual and every organ of society" should strive to promote the basic rights and freedoms to which all human beings regardless of race, nationality, or religion are entitled. But as long as there are governments whose authority is founded on coercion rather than on the mandate of the people, and interest groups that place short-term profits above long-term peace and prosperity, concerted international action to protect and promote human rights will remain at best a partially realized struggle. There will continue to be arenas of struggle where victims of oppression have to draw on their own inner resources to defend their inalienable rights as members of the human family.

The quintessential revolution is that of the spirit, born of an intellectual conviction of the need for change in those mental attitudes and values that shape the course of a nation's development. A revolution that aims merely at changing official policies and institutions with a view to an improvement in material conditions has little chance of genuine success. Without a revolution of the spirit, the forces that produced the iniquities of the old order would continue to be operative, posing a constant threat to the process of reform and regeneration. It is not enough merely to call for freedom, democracy, and human rights. There has to be a united determination to persevere in the struggle, to make sacrifices in the name of enduring truths, to resist the corrupting influences of desire, ill will, ignorance, and fear.

Saints, it has been said, are the sinners who go on trying. So free [people] are the oppressed who go on trying and who in the process make themselves fit to bear the responsibilities and to uphold the disciplines which will maintain a free society. Among the basic freedoms to which [humans] aspire that their lives might be full and uncramped, freedom from fear stands out as both a means and an end. A people who would build a nation in which strong, democratic institutions are firmly established as a guarantee against state-induced power must first learn to liberate their own minds from apathy and fear.

Always one to practice what he preached, Aung San himself constantly demonstrated courage—not just the physical sort but the kind that enabled him to speak the truth, to stand by his word, to accept criticism, to admit his faults, to correct his mistakes, to respect the opposition, to parley with the enemy, and to let people be the judge of his worthiness as a leader. It is for such moral courage that he will always be loved and respected in Burma—not merely as a warrior hero but as the inspiration and conscience of the nation. The words used by Jawaharlal Nehru to describe Mahatma Gandhi could well be applied to Aung San:

> *The essence of his teaching was fearlessness and truth, and action allied to these, always keeping the welfare of the masses in view.*

Gandhi, that great apostle of nonviolence, and Aung San, the founder of a national army, were very different personalities, but as there is an inevitable sameness about the challenges of authoritarian rule anywhere at any time, so there is a similarity in the intrinsic qualities of those who rise up to meet the challenge. Nehru, who considered the instillation of courage in the people of India one of Gandhi's greatest achievements, was a political modernist, but as he assessed the needs for a twentieth-century movement for independence, he found himself looking back to the philosophy of ancient India: "The greatest gift for an individual or a nation...was *abhaya,* fearlessness, not merely bodily courage but absence of fear from the mind."

Fearlessness may be a gift but perhaps more precious is the courage acquired through endeavor, courage that comes from cultivating the habit of refusing to let fear dictate one's actions, courage that could be described as "grace under pressure"—grace which is renewed repeatedly in the face of harsh, unremitting pressure.

Within a system that denies the existence of basic human rights, fear tends to be the order of the day. Fear of imprisonment, fear of torture, fear of death, fear of losing friends, family, property, or means of livelihood, fear of poverty, fear of isolation, fear of failure. A most insidious form of fear is that which masquerades as common sense or even wisdom, condemning as foolish, reckless, insignificant, or futile the small, daily acts of courage that help to preserve self-respect and inherent human dignity. It is not easy for a people conditioned by fear under the iron rule of the principle that might is right to free themselves from the enervating miasma of fear. Yet even under the most crushing state machinery courage rises up again and again, for fear is not the natural state of civilized [humans].

The wellspring of courage and endurance in the face of unbridled power is generally a firm belief in the sanctity of ethical principles combined with a historical sense that despite all setbacks the condition of [humans] is set on an ultimate course for both spiritual and material advancement. It is the capacity for self-improvement and self-redemption that most distinguishes man from the mere brute. At the root of human responsibility is the concept of perfection, the urge to achieve it, the intelligence to find a path towards it, and the will to follow that path if not to the end at least the distance needed to rise above individual limitations and environmental impediments. It is [the] vision of a world fit for rational, civilized humanity that leads [us] to dare and to suffer to build societies free from want and fear. Concepts such as truth, justice, and compassion cannot be dismissed as trite when these are often the only bulwarks that stand against ruthless power.

Part VI:
The New Marketplace

Suze Orman, financial expert and internationally acclaimed public speaker, is the author of numerous books, among them five consecutive *New York Times* bestsellers, including *The 9 Steps to Financial Freedom, The Courage to Be Rich,* and *The Laws of Money, The Lessons of Life.* She is the host of her own award-winning CNBC-TV show and a contributing editor to *O, The Oprah Magazine.* She has written, coproduced, and hosted five PBS specials based on her bestselling books, making her the single most successful fundraiser in the history of public television. Her hosting role earned her two Emmy Awards. www.suzeorman.com

Imagine What's Possible

Suze Orman

Women today make up nearly half of the total workforce in this country. Over the past thirty years, women's income has soared a dramatic 63 percent. Forty-nine percent of all professional- and managerial-level workers are women. Women bring in half or more of the income in the majority of U.S. households—a growing trend that made the cover of *Newsweek* and was front-page news in many of the nation's newspapers. Women-owned businesses comprise 40 percent of all companies in the United States. There are more women than ever before who can count themselves among the country's millionaires, more women in upper management, and more women in positions of power in the government.

We have a right to be proud of our progress. I am so honored to witness this revolution in my lifetime. I only wish it told the whole truth.

Now, would you like to hear the other side of the story? Ninety percent of women who participated in a 2006 survey commissioned by Allianz Insurance rated themselves as feeling insecure when it came to their finances. Ninety percent! In the same survey, *nearly half* the respondents said that the prospect of ending up a bag lady has crossed their minds. A 2005 Prudential financial poll found that only 1 percent of the women surveyed gave themselves an A in rating their knowledge of financial products and services. Two-thirds of women have not talked with their husbands about such things as life insurance and preparing a will. Nearly 80 percent of women said they would depend on Social Security in their golden years. Did you know that women are nearly twice as likely as men to retire in poverty?

For years now, I have been in the privileged position of talking to thousands and thousands of women a year—from the callers to my TV show, to those who come to hear me speak, to those who write me e-mails on my website, to my very own friends and family. So I hear, see, and feel your fears, insecurities, and troubles, very often firsthand, and I have come face-to-face with this painful truth: For all the advancements women have made in the last thirty, forty years—and without a doubt they are remarkable accomplishments—I am stunned by how little has really changed in the way women deal with money. There are huge disconnects in play here—between what we know and how we act; between what we think and what we say; between our ability as achievers and our financial underachieving; between how we present ourselves to the world and how we really feel about ourselves inside; between what we deserve in our lives and what we resign ourselves to; between the power we have within reach and the powerlessness that rules our actions.

In 1980, when I was hired as a financial advisor for Merrill Lynch, I was one of the few women in the Oakland, California, office. In the eyes of my (male) boss, that made me the perfect candidate to work with all the women who walked through the door. Back then, women who came to a brokerage firm looking for financial advice had, for the most part, either inherited money, received it in a divorce, been widowed, or were suddenly thrust into a position of helping their parents handle their money. In only a few instances had women come in with money they'd made on their own. No matter the circumstances that brought them to the brokerage firm, they all had the same reason for being there: They did not want the responsibility of managing their money. I always felt they hired me simply to baby-sit their money for them.

More than twenty-five years later, the story is much the same. Regardless of the gains in our financial status, I know and you know that women still don't want to take responsibility when it comes to their money. Yes, women are making more money than ever before, but they are not making more of what they make. What do I mean by that? Your retirement money sits in cash because you haven't figured out how to invest it properly, so you do nothing. You've convinced yourself that you'll be working forever, so the value of each paycheck becomes meaningless—after all, there will always be another one. Your closet houses the wardrobe of a powerful and stylish woman, but the dirty secret is that your credit cards are maxed out and you don't know how you're going to pay them off. But it's not just about saving and investing. It's about not asking for a raise at work when you know you are being undervalued. It's about the fear and loathing you feel when it's time to pay the bills every month because you don't know exactly what you have, where it's going, and why there isn't more left when it's all said and done. It's about how you berate yourself all the time for not knowing more and doing more...yet stay resigned to this feeling of helplessness and despair as time ticks away.

Ask yourself this:

Why is it that women, who are so competent in all other areas of their lives, cannot find the same competence when it comes to matters of money?

I have asked this question—of myself and others—over and over. Of course, there is no one answer. After much contemplation, here is what I have come up with.

The matter of women and money is clearly a complicated issue that has much to do with our history and traditions, both societal and familial. These deep-seated issues are major hurdles to overcome, major tides to turn—and that doesn't happen over-night. It can take generations to effect change of this magnitude in our daily behavior. These issues are absolutely a root cause of this problem. But we have to look at this on a behavioral level, too, since traits that are fundamental to our nature clearly affect how we approach money as well.

Consider this: It's a generally accepted belief that nurturing comes as a basic instinct to women. We give of ourselves; we take care of our family, our friends, our colleagues. It's in our nature to nurture. So why don't we take care of our money? Why don't we want to take care of our money as well as we take care of the spouses, partners, children, pets, plants, and whatever else is in our lives that we love and cherish?

I want you to think about that question. The answer is critical to uncovering what is at work here and what is holding you back. So I'll ask it again:

Why don't we show our money the same care and attention that we shower on every other important relationship in our lives?

Because we don't have a relationship with our money.

Correction: We do have a relationship with our money. It's just a totally dysfunctional one.

Let me tell you why I say this. Across the board, I see women refusing to engage with their money until they are forced to—because of the birth of children, or divorce, or death, for example. In other words, we do not relate to it until we are in extreme, life-changing situations in which we have no choice but to confront money matters. Until then, we don't apply that same primal, nurturing impulse when it comes to taking care of our money—and by extension, *ourselves*. We can't even accept this as a fact—that **our money is indeed an extension of ourselves.** Instead, we persist in a dysfunctional relationship—we ignore our money, deny its needs, we are afraid of it, afraid of failing, afraid it will expose our shortcomings, which leads to shame. What do we do with all these uncomfortable feelings? We suppress them, we put them away, we don't deal with them. It becomes far easier to ignore the money issue altogether. And the longer we ignore it, the worse the situation becomes; we grow even more fearful as time passes that it's too late for us to learn, too late to even try. So we give up. Who likes a failed relationship? Nobody. Better to have no relationship at all than a failed one…

But money is not a person you can write out of your life. You need money to live.

So then let's turn this relationship theory around and ask ourselves the following question: In order to become competent and successful in handling our money, in order to become the fully responsible women we know we should be, what does that require of us?

We have to develop a healthy, honest relationship with our money. And we have to see this relationship as a reflection of our relationship with ourselves.

I can't put it any more simply or emphatically: How we behave toward our money, how we treat our money, speaks volumes about how we perceive and value ourselves. If we aren't powerful with money, we aren't powerful period. What is at stake here is not just money—it's far bigger. This is about your sense of who you are and what you deserve. Lasting net worth comes only when you have a healthy and strong sense of self-worth. And right now, the money disconnect, this dysfunctional relationship, is a barrier to both.

Once you fully appreciate this and hold it as an absolute truth, you will also understand that your destiny depends on the health of this relationship. Are you honestly prepared to roll the dice on this one, or would you rather feel that you have the ability, the determination, the power to make this relationship work—as surely as you know how to nurture and give care to all the people you love in your life?

How do you repair this relationship?

The same way you would repair any relationship that is damaged: by acknowledging your mistakes, taking responsibility, and resolving to act in a way that will bring about change for the better. In the case of you and your money, that means making strong money moves, moves with the goal of making you feel more powerful and secure. If you show money the respect it deserves today and carry it through in all your actions, then one day, when you can no longer take care of it, your money will take care of you. Respecting your relationship with money, you see, is the key not only to your security and independence, but to your happiness, as well.

Now let's talk about happiness for a moment.

The simple fact is that **nothing more directly affects your happiness than money.**

Oh, I know, some of you are just horrified by this notion, maybe even offended. Suze, *how could you?!* Happiness is about all the things money can't buy—health, love, respect—right? Absolutely true—all of these are essential to a happy life. All are determined by who you are and not what you have. But the kind of happiness I am talking about is your quality of life—the ability to enjoy life, to live life to its fullest potential. And I challenge anyone to tell me that such things aren't factors in your overall happiness.

Let's just walk through this together for a moment. Yes, I know that your health and the health of your loved ones is paramount, but explain to me what would happen if, God forbid, any one of you fell ill. Wouldn't you want the best care that money can buy? Wouldn't you be grateful that you were in a good health plan? And isn't it money that puts the roof over your head, and money that allows you to move to a neighborhood with a great public school system? And money that allows you to retire early, or quit your job while you go back to school to pursue a new career?

So why is it, then, that we are so reluctant to embrace this concept fully—that money is a factor in determining our happiness?

Why is it that in a recent survey called "Authentic Happiness" there was not a single question or answer that contained the word *money*? What bothers me about this is that I think it's a lie not to acknowledge the power money has to make our lives better and happier. It's not a subject for polite company? Is that what you've been raised to believe? Well, I'm here to tell you that this isn't just a problem of semantics. I believe that this "conspiracy of silence" is another reason why so many women are in the dark about financial matters. I have often said that we must be careful of our words, for words become actions. Well, the opposite of that is true, too: Silence leads to inaction. We don't talk about money with our friends, our parents, our children—and that's where we get in trouble. How are we supposed to teach our children, how are we supposed to educate ourselves, if there isn't a free and frank flow of information about money? Why do we behave so carelessly with money? Would we do that if we believed our very happiness depended on it? Let me put it this way: If we persist in denying money its place in our lives, if we don't give it the respect it most certainly deserves, then it will surely lead to unhappiness.

What you really have to understand and believe is that every one of you already has more than what it takes to own the power to control your financial destiny. I am asking you now to harness the incredible intelligence and competence that serve you so well in so many other aspects of your life and apply it to your money. Anyone who has it in them to run a household, run a company, run a department of a company, run a car pool, or run a marathon is fully equipped to take control here. Anyone who is a supportive and caring wife, partner, mother, sister, daughter, best friend, caretaker, aunt, grandmother, or colleague has all the skills necessary to forge a solid relationship with her money and to make the kind of smart money choices that support you rather than sabotage you. **That's what controlling your financial destiny comes down to: knowing what to do and what not to do—and having the conviction and confidence to go out and do**

it. Not just think about it. Or intend to do it next week or next month. To actually do it. Right now.

Make that commitment to yourself first. And together, let's imagine what's possible when you do:

Imagine: Opening the credit card bill each month and knowing you will be able to pay it off.

Imagine: Knowing you have done everything to take care of your family if something happens to you.

Imagine: Staying in a relationship purely for love, not because you have no idea how you would make it financially on your own.

Imagine: Loving yourself enough to choose a partner you don't have to rescue.

Imagine: Owning your home outright. No more mortgage payments. No one can ever take it away from you.

Imagine: Knowing you will be able to retire comfortably one day.

Imagine: Raising children who've learned from you the wisdom of living within your means, rather than living out of control.

Imagine: Knowing you have helped your parents live full lives, without fear or uncertainty, right to the end.

The payoff for your commitment extends beyond your finances. Having a healthy relationship with money puts you in a position to have better relationships with everyone in your life. It all flows together. A woman who is more financially confident and secure is a happier woman. And a happier woman is going to be better able to nurture, share, and give support to all those in her life.

All of it is possible.

Linda Denny is president and CEO of the nonprofit Women's Business Enterprise National Council (WBENC), the leading advocate for and authority on women's business enterprises as suppliers to corporations. WBENC, which provides a national and international "gold standard" third-party certification that a woman's business is at least 51 percent woman owned, operated, and controlled, helps hundreds of major corporations, states, cities, and other entities use their supplier diversity programs to cultivate business with WBENC's ten thousand certified women's business enterprises. Ms. Denny draws on a wealth of experience in corporate, financial service, and entrepreneurial arenas to lead this multifaceted organization. www.wbenc.org

CHAPTER TWENTY-NINE

Women Entrepreneurs— The Voice of New Leadership

Linda Denny

Women entrepreneurs are great leaders.

I can make this statement without hesitation because as the president and CEO of the nonprofit Women's Business Enterprise National Council (WBENC), I work with thousands of women entrepreneurs, whose businesses range in annual revenues from a few hundred thousand to several billion dollars. My constant interaction with them has shown me their exceptional qualities as leaders in their families, businesses, industries, and communities.

To include their insights in this chapter, we conducted a survey of our membership on the topic of entrepreneurial women's leadership. More than five hundred generously responded, and I share their views with you here. First, let's consider a few facts on women entrepreneurs, an often neglected topic in the world of business.

Entrepreneurial women are key drivers of America's small business economy, owning over 40 percent of all businesses and providing 23 million jobs, and with an economic impact of $3 trillion, their companies pump life into the nation's economy. If U.S.-based women-owned businesses were their own country, they would produce the fifth largest gross domestic product

(GDP) in the world, trailing closely behind Germany, and ahead of France, the United Kingdom, and Italy, among other countries. They would have a greater GDP than Canada, India, and Vietnam combined.*

What the Women Say

What are the characteristics and personalities of the women leaders behind these remarkable statistics? While the universe of ten thousand WBENC-certified women's business enterprises is diverse in size and industry, it is also surprisingly consistent in two ways: Women entrepreneurs share an ability to build a dream into a profitable company, and they uniformly seek to channel that success into positive change for their clients, their employees, their industries, their families, and their communities.

When we asked our women *"What are the top two characteristics of a successful woman business leader?"* we received hundreds of responses represented by the following:

- Integrity and values
- Visionary and risk taker
- Confidence and perseverance
- Flexibility and problem-solving skill
- Commitment and tenacity
- Emotional intelligence and courage

In other words, women business leaders are fierce yet grounded in principles. These characteristics create a foundation from which women entrepreneurs build their businesses toward ambitious, often lofty, goals. And although women express these goals in multiple ways, the first among many is "to make a difference."

To understand how women meet this common goal of making a difference, we asked our women entrepreneurs *"What motivates you as a woman entrepreneur?"*

---

* Center for Women's Business Research, October 2009.

What we found was striking: Although money and financial security play an important role, they are far from the top of the list of motivations. Rather, most women's interest in money was tied to what the business owner could do with money to help others: secure their family, participate in philanthropy, invest in employee benefits and training, or plow money back into business to allow innovation or expansion.

When taken from a personal standpoint, our women's motivation was clear: freedom. The women business owner places very high value on flexibility, being her own boss, and defining success in her own terms.

Survey question:

As a woman entrepreneur, what motivates you most as a leader?

What WBENC women said:

- Making a difference in other people's lives—the way they think, the way they lead others, the way they influence their teams, families, and communities.
- Being my own boss. Controlling my own future.
- Keeping the family legacy alive—eighty-four years and counting!
- Providing the best products and services to my customers, which creates financial security for my family, employees, and vendors.
- Encouraging other women and young girls to pursue their dreams and goals, no matter what obstacles get in the way.

Given these motives, how do our women business leaders define and measure success? Although our women are innovative, growth-oriented, and profitable, they are not geared purely to acquiring "money and power," which has tended to be the case in the traditional male-run corporation. Rather they are focused toward "means and autonomy." Money is a means to an end that will benefit the entire community that the woman entrepreneur touches: her employees, her family, her city, and her country. And a woman's autonomy achieved by business success enables her to create a workplace culture and hierarchy that works for her. This culture is often collaborative. The hierarchy tends to be flatter, more flexible, and empowering to managers and employees alike. And, of course, autonomy means that the woman business owner has choice over how she spends her time at work and beyond.

"Means and Autonomy" Leadership

This modern woman's brand of leadership has its roots in earlier times and other countries and cultures. An iconic role model for the woman entrepreneur is Queen Elizabeth I. She saved the "family business," the monarchy of England, by transforming it from a weak and turbulent island nation entangled in religious and secular wars into the greatest power on Earth by the time of her death in 1603 after a reign of forty-five years.

Even as she maneuvered to retain and deepen her authority, Elizabeth created an unusually open environment for ideas at that time. She surrounded herself with the best and brightest, highly valued diversity of thought, encouraged free and frank expression, communicated her views for all to know, built consensus, bucked convention by refusing to marry or produce an heir, and compensated her advisors well. Though great power and wealth were hers and she was a role model of commitment and tenacity, her authority and the motivation for Good Queen Bess was her love for her people. She changed the country, inspired an English Renaissance, and made a real difference in their lives.

Today we see hundreds of women who seize the opportunity to lead their family business and have taken that business to new levels of expansion and success.

Take Julie Copeland, president and CEO of Arbill, a family business that has provided workplace safety products and services since 1945. Since taking over, she has reengineered Arbill into an award-winning company positioned for long-term growth. She shifted Arbill's customer base from regional to national to global, expanded the company's scope beyond strictly manufacturing and distribution of industrial safety products, and diversified Arbill's global operations. Today Arbill is known as the leading architect of workplace safety, enabling its corporate clients to build a culture of safety across their organizations to reduce costs and protect their number one asset, their people. Julie instituted multiple channels of open communications among employees, managers, and departments, including quarterly Town Hall meetings that engage all employees in the future of the company.

Making a Difference

Most entrepreneurs perceive a need in the marketplace, identify the product or service to fill that gap, and apply their particular creativity and skills with persistence over time. Success is seldom overnight, always involves taking a risk, and tends to be a roller coaster of highs and lows. Yet throughout the turbulence, most entrepreneurs hew back to the principles that guided them from the start—often "making a difference."

Michelle Tunno Buelow, founder of Bella Tunno, a babyware company whose products are used by celebrity moms, started her business in the wake of a tragic event. She left the corporate world to deal with the grief of losing her beloved brother, a brilliant student about to finish his doctorate, to alcohol and other substance abuse. She dreamed of doing something to honor his memory and to help others facing the curse of this disease. A new mother, she began to create accessories for her daughter to wear and use. Friends and strangers loved what she created and asked to buy them. Over time, she realized her beautiful and unique babywares could produce the money she needed to deliver on her dream. Today her products are available throughout the country and a portion from every sale goes toward the Matt Tunno "Make a Difference" Memorial Fund, supporting drug and alcohol abuse education, prevention, and rehabilitation. She is doing well while doing good, and exemplifies that distinctive drive of women business owners to make a difference.

A profound illustration of the power of women's businesses to nurture the long-term health of a community can be found in the women receiving micro-loans in extremely impoverished conditions and countries. Not only do the women repay micro-loans at a rate close to 100 percent (in sharp contrast to men), but they also plow their profits toward their children's education and the community. They create products or services that fund family, home, and community improvements and health care. The microenterprises they create often bring entire communities together, providing jobs and improving life for all while growing into thriving small businesses. In a recent interview, one of these "micropreneurs" said her purpose was "to make a difference." Many women entrepreneurs from around the world now participate in programs allowing them to provide funds for micro-loan programs for other women.

Redefining the Company Culture

Women are also making a difference by empowering their own employees. We are all familiar with the pyramid-style or hierarchical organization in which the power and authority is concentrated at the top with communication flowing down to the ranks of workers below. The military and most large corporations exemplify this, with the generals and CEOs at the top. The leaders of these organizations expect their directions to be followed and authority respected as those in the increasingly lower ranks carry out the directions given. Many men, but certainly not all, are more comfortable with this organizational model and structure their businesses accordingly. Many women, however, use a more egalitarian leadership style and do not view their authority as a matter of power or see themselves as a person in a superior position. This may be an underlying reason why many women jump off the corporate ladder and become entrepreneurs—it fits their style of leadership better.

Women leaders are more likely to dismantle the pyramid of hierarchy and use a new kind of organizational chart. Rather than a pyramid, it can be described as more like a spider web, with everyone on the same level with the leader in the middle. In the web model, communication and contact with the leader comes from and goes in many different directions. This style of leadership values and enables a flow of diverse thought by being inclusive and consultative as decisions are made. This allows the leader to be in an inspirational role rather than working as a director. Although the vision for the business starts with the founder, this egalitarian approach allows the business owner and her employees to participate together in refining the vision, creating buy-in, and identifying mutual goals, which they share going forward. Employees are more dedicated to delivering on goals they helped create.

The entrepreneurial women building their businesses with this inclusive, participatory style of leadership view their employees as colleagues rather than subordinates, so the resulting "followers" are also different. From the many conversations I've had with employees of female entrepreneurs, it is clear they share a sense of empowerment; they are challenged to lead in their own right, in the projects and jobs for which they are responsible.

LetterLogic is a perfect example. Sherry Stewart Deutschmann, a single mother, founded the company just seven years ago using a small savings account. LetterLogic prints and mails invoices, statements, and letters for businesses, with a money-back guarantee if not delivered. A very customer-centric company with $18 million in annual revenues, Sherry strongly believes if she takes care of her thirty-two employees, they will take care of her customers, creating satisfaction and growth. She pays them for suggestions, with 75 percent being implemented within thirty days. She provides them with fully paid health, dental, life, and disability insurance. She also provides 10 percent of profits in equal shares (no job is more important than another) to employees each month, allows them to bring a child or pet to work if necessary, pays them to bike or walk to work (some make an extra $120 a week), pays 100 percent of public transportation or car pool expenses, helps them buy a home (85 percent are now owners), provides seed money to start new businesses, and more. She empowers employees to make decisions and involves them in setting goals. With no debt, the goal they have set together is to grow the business to $100 million by 2018.

Overcoming Obstacles

The average WBENC-certified business is fifteen years old, has forty-five employees, and has an annual revenue of nearly $10 million. These statistics prove these owners know something about running a sustainable, successful business. The obstacles and challenges they face every day vary based on their industry, market, and resources. Some challenges are beyond control, such as weather, economic downturns, and attitudes, but others can be anticipated and managed.

When I asked our business owners *"What is your greatest obstacle as a leader?"* they had a lot to say. The overall response was that obstacles can be handled, that they are simply problems to be solved. For example:

- I choose to see any obstacle as an opportunity.
- My greatest challenge is that it is hard to decide on which opportunity to focus my time, effort, and development money. If I spend time on the right ones, that means growth and success for my company, security for my employees, and money for everyone—employees, suppliers, and myself. If I spend my time focused on the wrong ones, the actual cost is significant, not to mention the lost opportunity cost.
- What obstacle? Unless they are physical, a business obstacle is an illusion. Get over it, create another solution and move on!

The Gender Issue

Despite the optimism reflected in their response to dealing with obstacles, women business owners report still having to deal with an uneven playing field due to gender. Even highly successful, well-established women entrepreneurs too often face not being accepted for the value they bring as leaders and not being regarded as true equals on a level playing field in business. Women still face not being included or being patronized in business settings. Female business owners frequently express frustration or anger about having sales professionals, customers, or prospects address their comments to male employees, even when they clearly know she is the owner and decision maker. As one woman commented, "Old habits die hard."

A surprising number of our survey respondents wrote about difficulty in dealing with "the good ol' boys network" (which is apparently still alive and well) and "not being taken seriously," which can lock them out of opportunity. Women business owners in the United States and around the world face these challenges to their business and industry leadership every day. Their reactions range from mild annoyance, with a decision to just ignore the "unenlightened" and keep on going, to carefully measured responses to situations with far more serious consequences.

One woman who owns a manufacturing plant in Saudi Arabia, the largest of its type in the Middle East, addressed the issues faced by businesswomen there. Dressed in the required traditional *abaya* and dependent on others to drive her, she shared the following:

> I was born a leader but had to create the style of followers I needed because I couldn't move forward without them. I want my followers to be leaders in their own right, in their place, time, and with their responsibilities. I believe everyone should do something to move forward. Too many Saudi women bow to religious tradition and don't believe it can be challenged, which is what keeps them in "their place." I have learned not to believe those things, not

to bow to the challenges of tradition but to love them, to view them as roadblocks that I can successfully confront or sometimes just quietly go around. I have to be persistent and have real strength of character. I have learned to take what I do seriously, but not to take myself very seriously. The "vice police" (Saudi authorities that monitor the activities of women) don't like me, but because I'm not afraid of them, they don't challenge me. I live my life and run my business *my way!*

So what is the result of "my way"? This brave, entrepreneurial woman has added strict safety standards for her large complex of plants that cover *all* workers, not just Saudi workers, a first in her industry, which has many hazardous jobs filled by foreign nationals allowed into the country to work in these jobs. She is also the first in the industry to set and enforce strict environmental standards for her company, which produces much waste. She has received international recognition for her efforts and leadership.

The Imbalance of Work and Life

We cannot have a discussion of women's leadership without touching on the Holy Grail of work-life balance. Every business owner has to make choices about what is most important to her. Does she take a trip to see an important client or go see her child's school play? Does she buy another company that will require her to work away from home for several months or not? Women entrepreneurs often have a strong survive-and-thrive mentality, but many struggle with how to prioritize the demands.

Survey respondents stated they gave themselves permission not to do everything at 100 percent, not to be perfect, and to expect other people to help. Help comes in many different forms: husbands, mothers, friends, great babysitters, housecleaners, dog walkers, cooks, and executive assistants. Running their businesses well is important to them, but their families are their strength and top priority. Where did they learn how to handle this balancing act? From each other. The support of other women entrepreneurs lets them feel that everything is possible.

Survey question:

As an entrepreneur, what type of support, if any, does a woman need to achieve work-life balance?

Here's what WBENC women said:

- You must have managers that help make decisions and work toward the same goals. Pay them well and they will run things as if they are owners.
- An intelligent family, who can see the long-term benefits, can put aside their needs for the short term to encourage and assist in reaching the business goals.
- My husband and I are "independently together"—we equally share the household work, child rearing, etc.
- Understand that you can have it all but probably not at the same time.
- Having "gal pals" that are entrepreneurs is a great joy! We support, share, and relate to each other in ways that are impossible for me with others, even my husband.
- Organizations such as WBENC are so important for the people they bring together. I connect with other women for inspiration, commiseration, and celebration. They are mentors and role models, and charge my "battery" to keep me going!

The Marks of a Leader

At the end of the day, women business owners are willing to look at themselves in the mirror and remind themselves why they lead, how they lead, and what it will take to lead tomorrow. When we asked, *"What enables you to step into the leader's role?"* our WBENC women said:

- Vision, confidence, courage, and a willingness to take risks.
- Strength to live with my failures and wisdom to learn the valuable lessons that come from those experiences.
- Ability to be both strategic and tactical: seeing the forest for the trees and the trees in the forest.
- Creativity to start from scratch with nothing at all and grow it into a successful business.
- Great time management and organizational skills.

Women entrepreneurs must be significant leaders or they couldn't be doing what they are doing: setting the vision, serving clients, creating new cultures, engaging employees, building strong personal relationships, supporting their communities, and impacting the nation. Just as Elizabeth I revolutionized the monarchy in the sixteenth century, the brave women entrepreneurs of today are advancing—and succeeding—with a new style of leadership that will change how society views women as leaders in the twenty-first century.

Jean Thompson is the owner and CEO of Seattle Chocolate Company (www.seattlechocolates.com), makers of premium, all-natural truffles, dessert shells, truffle bars, and chocolates, including the chocolate brands Frango, Choxie, and Chick Chocolates. In addition to running Seattle Chocolate Company, Jean serves on the Board of Trustees for the National Confectioner's Association, one of the oldest trade associations in the United States. She is also an active member of Entrepreneur's Organization Seattle and the Women Business Owners, a leading nonprofit organization for women entrepreneurs in the Seattle and Puget Sound area.

CHAPTER THIRTY

For the Love of Chocolate
Jean Thompson

If someone had told me ten years ago that I would be running a chocolate company, I would have wondered who could ever be so lucky and how does one go about pursuing that career? Today I stand at the helm of a small, eighteen-year-old chocolate confectionery manufacturing company, still amazed at my good fortune.

I've always loved chocolate. Even as a young girl, I would sneak into the pantry and take a handful of semi-sweet morsels that my mother stored for baking cookies to get my daily fix. I remember going back-to-school shopping with my mother every fall and my favorite memory of these trips was stopping at the candy shop in the G. Fox department store for some chocolate that we would share on the car ride home. My favorite souvenir from trips overseas was always a giant Toblerone bar, which you couldn't buy in the United States at that time. Others bought more lasting treasures for show-and-tell, but I was forging a love for chocolate that would alter my life course.

My childhood love for chocolate was awakened when my husband and I invested in the Seattle Chocolate Company back in the late 1990s. He was impressed with the two highly automated candy-making lines and I was enthused because I knew I would have my own private supply of fabulous chocolate. Within a few years, we became the primary investors and soon after, the sole owners of the company. Meanwhile, I developed a bit of an addiction to the creamy mint truffle. But it wasn't until 2002 when the CEO came to us for another infusion of cash that I decided to pitch in and help the floundering company with their sales and marketing.

Six weeks into this new "part-time" job, the CEO quit and I was left holding the reins. I surprised myself by knowing instantly that this was a challenge I needed and wanted, and that selling the company or hiring a CEO was simply not an option. At this point, I had never read a profit and loss statement or a balance sheet. I had never run a business. I had never stepped foot in a warehouse or manufacturing plant until six weeks prior when I walked into Seattle Chocolates for the first time. I look back now and wonder how I had the courage to take this on with no MBA, no direct experience, and no operator's manual.

Ask Any Woman

Within weeks of joining Seattle Chocolates, I noticed that many in the chocolate industry didn't seem to understand that women are passionate about chocolate. We need it. We want it. We absolutely have to have it. It seemed pretty obvious to me that the target audience for chocolate sales and marketing is women. Yet I saw ads by the big companies depicting sexy women draped across settees dipping into a box of chocolates gifted to her by someone else, no doubt a man. I thought of my friends and me, buying our own chocolate and eating it every day; while driving, working, relaxing, and socializing; as a pick-me-up, to salve an emotional wound, or in celebration. I knew there was a need for a chocolate company that understood how important chocolate is to women. I found my mission.

In the early 2000s, research was starting to surface about the health benefits of chocolate. As women, we always knew it was good for us, and at last, there were scientific facts to support our instincts. There were antioxidants in chocolate that would actually improve our health. Not to mention mood elevators that simulate the feelings of being in love. The fat in chocolate was proving to be one of the few, rare healthy saturated fats that don't impact your cholesterol in a negative way. One of the natural components found in cocoa beans, a polyphenol, occurs naturally in a woman's brain and produces a calming effect. Is it any surprise that women seek out chocolate every day? Men may eat chocolate for the flavor or energy boost, but women eat it for the ahhhh. As women, we have always known chocolate was fattening, but we ate it anyway. Now it was becoming socially acceptable to eat it, even in public, even if you were a little overweight.

The timing seemed right to take Seattle Chocolates to new places. Thank God that I had no idea how hard it would be or I might not have had the courage to try. I didn't understand the obstacles that small companies face in the world of manufacturing or consumer packaged goods. It was time for me to get my business degree, the hard way.

The first thing I had to do was gain the respect and confidence of the Seattle Chocolates staff. This turned out to be harder than I thought because I hadn't yet earned it. I brought new ideas to the table almost immediately and they were met with skepticism and doubt. So to prove to them and me that I could lead this company, I became a student of our products, our manufacturing plant, and our administrative departments, and I studied the market and researched the chocolate category. I spent many hours on the phone with customers learning about what they needed from us. I met with each employee to get their input on and opinion of our company. I fired some employees and tried to develop deeper relationships with the ones who knew the most. I hired a right-hand man to run operations for me and he turned out to be a chronic liar. I developed an ulcer and ended up in the ER thinking I was having a heart attack. I never felt so alone in my life. After confirming with the doctor that chocolate was not the cause of my ulcer, I returned to work the next day with a fire in my belly.

Six months into the job, I had my first breakthrough. Seattle Chocolates won a big and important private label account in the northwest. It is a household name in Seattle, an eighty-five-year-old brand of chocolate sold by one department store. We had to reproduce the original formula and prove that we could make it exactly as it had always been done. After a lot of research and trial, the final test came when they brought in a panel of chocolate tasters who were none other than the women who ran the original chocolate kitchen for this brand for forty years. If it passed their discriminating palates, then it would be approved. The sage taste testers gave us their seal of approval and the company subsequently awarded Seattle Chocolates the business. I called my first company meeting to make the announcement and the employees assumed that I was shutting the company down. Instead, I announced to them that we had won the account, which increased our sales by 50 percent in the first year. I developed instant credibility and the confidence of my staff. There is a chocolate god.

The second breakthrough came when one of the engineers that worked for my husband at Microsoft decided to join me in my chocolate adventure. He understood manufacturing, warehousing, shipping, and transportation. He could fix things and think outside the box, and brought skills to the table that fully complemented my own. More important, he was committed and firmly on my team and I would no longer be alone on this journey.

"Like you, fabulous!"

In the first weeks on the job, my best friend and I were on a walk discussing my early observations of the chocolate business. We agreed that it was all about women and yet the current marketing was not singularly focused on that. We brainstormed a new product line made by women for women. She said, "It's chocolate for chicks," and we came up with our first new line of chocolate:

Chick Chocolates. We gave them personalities that reminded us of certain friends: Extreme Chick, who has to have more cacao than anyone else; Strong Chick, who wants a little more calcium in her chocolate; and Nutty Chick, who eats chocolate strictly because it tastes good. We put the chocolates in lipstick-shaped boxes and gave women permission to eat these three pieces with no guilt. Our motto was that if you feel like chocolate, eat it, and if you're going to eat chocolate, eat the good stuff. Our tagline is, "Like you, fabulous!" Our Chick booth garnered huge attention at the industry trade show and earned us a spot on the Food Network. The Chicks continue to be sold in every state.

Because I believed that women eat chocolate every day, I decided that we needed to be in grocery stores because that's where busy women shop. Who has time to visit a chocolate boutique to get a daily fix? How often does chocolate make it on to the shopping list? Our machinery had the capacity to do this and on a national scale. So that's what we did. We hired a network of brokers and distributors and negotiated our way onto the shelves in eight thousand retail outlets. We ranked number eleven in top-selling premium chocolate bars after two years of working this new market. We had succeeded! At least we thought we did—until we learned that we weren't making any money doing this. These stores operate on miniscule margins and have made an art form out of getting extra margin from their manufacturers. They're big, we're small—who do you think wins in these battles? It was maddening and seemed so unfair, but there wasn't a thing we could do—until we realized that being there was our choice. We decided to pull back and regroup on our marketing and sales strategies. It was better to be small and profitable, than big and broke.

One of my former colleagues from Microsoft, a marketing powerhouse, decided to join me at Seattle Chocolates. She got to work immediately trying to understand who we were in the market and what our brand meant to consumers. What we learned in our research was that we are a contemporary American chocolate that consistently delivers an all-natural taste. We updated our branding to reflect this and our early understanding that chocolate is a delicious treat to enjoy every day. And our new tagline was born: "Seattle Chocolates. What happiness tastes like." We updated our packaging to reflect our philosophy about chocolate. We used bright, vibrant colors and lots of them. We used contemporary patterns that pop off the shelves. We did this with the finest materials to match the quality of the chocolate inside. Retailers and consumers alike loved our new direction. As new trends arise in the industry, such as percent cacao and country of origin, we consider them using our benchmark of "Does this taste great?" And if it doesn't, we won't engage in the trend. The mission of bringing great-tasting chocolate to women remains our paramount objective.

We continue to try new things: new product lines, new markets and channels, new strategies, and most recently a new brand, called JTruffles, to compete at the highest end of the chocolate market on a national basis. It represents everything we've learned collectively about chocolate, the industry, and the market.

Sometimes I promise myself that I'm going to write a book to help the next generation of chocolatiers. I have encountered so many challenges that one cannot ever plan for or predict, and at times it seems a perfect storm of obstacles. Seattle Chocolates has survived an earthquake that condemned our building; broken air conditioners that turned our cool warehouse into an oven, destroying $500,000 worth of chocolate; broken pipes that flooded our warehouse; customers that declared Chapter 11 after we shipped them truckloads of product; skyrocketing commodity and fuel prices; a nut recall; a recession; and, perhaps most difficult of all, my learning curve.

What are characterized as problems have become my opportunities for growth and change. As bad as they were, I ask myself, "Would I have preferred a smooth path with an intact stomach lining?" I don't know that this mission would still hold my interest if it had been easy. Not to mention the satisfaction I have in overcoming these obstacles. My dearest friend once encouraged me by saying, "May your day have just enough clouds to make a beautiful sunset."

A Woman's Touch

Historically, women in business have been measured against their male counterparts. They have had to prove their stoicism and their ability to strategize and analyze with the best in order to be considered worthwhile. There was a time that men and women alike felt that women could not lead because they are too emotional. So women dressed like men and hid their feminine side as much as possible in order to be professional and be considered capable. I see daily evidence of this changing.

Although it is true that spreadsheets tell no lies, the business-people who will stand out are the ones that feel their business. Time and time again, it has been my instincts that tell me what to do before there is any data to fill a spreadsheet. There isn't a spreadsheet in the world that will tell you where your competition or opposition will strike next. But your instincts will. A spread-sheet won't tell you when a design is passé until it is too late to do anything about it. Trusting instincts has faithfully carried me through the storms. I have not had to be or act like a man, for this business and industry required a woman's touch. I would argue that this world needs more balanced brains, not left brains and not right brains, but the balance and use of the left and the right in concert. We need inventiveness, empathy, joyfulness, color, variety, happiness; we need love. None of these should be masked by nonemotional numerical madness that we may deem as progress. Women follow their intuition and their hearts as much as their heads, and are therefore very well suited to excel in today's competitive and changing world.

Women are compassionate. We feel for our employees, vendors, and customers. We can negotiate with unreasonable toddlers; Lord knows opposing viewpoints between employees is a breeze relative to that! Women are peacemakers—only don't push us too far. We pick our battles, we let others win, we are free with a compliment, and we are quick to reward an accomplishment. We understand the importance of an employee's child's second-grade recital even if it's in the middle of the workday and we have to postpone a meeting to accommodate it. I have many mothers and fathers on my staff and they know they can always take the time to be with their kids. They are amazingly productive workers; they get more done in their day than any employee forced to sit at a desk and miss welcoming their child home on his first day of school. I have never felt such loyalty and devotion in my life, and couldn't do what I do today without them.

Women are adaptable. We are not afraid to ask for directions or admit we don't know something. Women are resilient. I have learned how often you need to course-correct in the journey of running a company. Women rule with our hearts, follow our guts, and take each challenge and each day as it comes. If we occasionally stomp our feet out of frustration with a roadblock or burst into tears because of an injustice, it's because we take our jobs and our businesses very personally and we know that our companies matter to a lot of people, most especially us.

Looking back at my past seven years as the captain of this chocolate ship, I still marvel at my good fortune. I still relish the journey and have much to learn. As I earn success and learn more lessons and achieve by all business standards, will that complete my mission? The love of chocolate goes way beyond the profit and loss business challenge set before me many years ago. I see my horizons expanding and the world getting smaller as time marches forward. I know my opportunities will become more global as my personal capacity increases. Chocolate is grown and consumed by people all over the world. I know I was put on this chocolate path to make a difference. They say that where much is given, much is expected. I have been given much and every day I start with the fervent desire to give more.

Frances Green, an attorney at the national law firm Epstein Becker & Green, P.C., is a trial lawyer, counselor, motivational trainer, and international lecturer. She coheads the firm's Women's Initiative, dedicated to enhancing the careers of women at EBG and in the legal profession as a whole. With nearly half of its attorneys being women, EBG is one of only four law firms to make the top 20 lists for the number of women attorneys in the *American Lawyer*'s 2009 "Women in Law Firms" study and the number of minority attorneys in the *Minority Law Journal*'s 2009 Diversity Scorecard. www.ebglaw.com

CHAPTER THIRTY-ONE

One Thousand Small Steps, a Few Giant Leaps

Frances Green

Driving forces have shaped my life. Perhaps the most significant is, indeed, the most universal: the search for fulfillment—that endless journey of the soul that led me to places I never wanted to go and, once I arrived, never wanted to leave. Then there's the drive for attention—that is, for me, being the center of attention and *paying attention* to who I am. This is not a selfish preoccupation, but a worldview of being ready, willing, and steadfast. I believe one of the greatest gifts we can give to ourselves and to each other throughout our lives is full attention to who we are, what we are doing, and who we are becoming.

This kind of focus has contributed to the success of Epstein Becker & Green's Women's Initiative, which I cofounded eight years ago. The mission of the Women's Initiative—to enhance the careers of professional women by providing opportunities both inside and outside the office to network, share information, acquire skills, and develop rewarding professional relationships—essentially mirrors my life. Our Women's Initiative presents lectures by accomplished women leaders and events that educate, entertain, and facilitate networking with other women professionals. We have set the scene for great women to accomplish great things.

The Women's Initiative has provided me with some of the most gratifying experiences of my legal career—which, itself, is the culmination of rather unconventional personal and professional journeys. These journeys are so intertwined that, looking back, it is hard to see where one begins and the other ends.

Family Influences

In both the figurative sense (with respect to my father) and the literal sense (with respect to my mother), my parents loomed large in setting my professional journey in motion.

My father, a naturalized U.S. citizen, born in Ireland, was a U.S. Army paratrooper during World War II, who sustained debilitating injuries in North Africa and Anzio, Italy. A recipient of numerous medals and citations for bravery and valor, my father joined the Veterans Administration of the American Red Cross after the war and advocated for veterans' rights. Although not an attorney, he was well educated, due to his postgraduate Jesuit Seminary studies in the United States and abroad, and, given his Irish roots, was quite the raconteur. Most of all, he was a highly effective and tireless advocate. His experiences helped define my life.

As the second of four children, I yearned, like some others in this unfortunate birth order, for my parents' attention. And I devised creative ways to get it. I would slip on my mother's outfits and then parade around the neighborhood in them. Memories linger of my being plucked off the sidewalk by a neighbor who reported my antics to my mom.

When costuming grew old, I retreated to the companionship of an imaginary friend, Mrs. BB. She was forty-something years of age, a great listener, and one of the best mentors I ever had. Even back then, older women lighted my way. I spent a lot of time confiding my aspirations to Mrs. BB, and she was unceasingly encouraging. With nary a criticism nor a frown, Mrs. BB was my bulwark against any adversity I conjured in my little world.

My fuller world was shattered at the age of nine when my father died of a heart attack—right in front of me. My mother was left to raise four children on her own. She struggled to keep our young family afloat. Our faith in each other and her faith—a brand of heavy-handed Catholicism—helped pull us through the roughest patches. A remarkable woman at any time, but particularly when "single moms" were virtually unheard of and certainly not touted as an alternative lifestyle, she tended to her disparate brood, ranging in ages from eleven months to eleven years.

While I loved my mother, I had always admired my father. After his death, admiration was transformed into hero worship, abetted by my mother's colorful tales of my dad's adventures. I reveled in the thought that one day, I, too, could be that adventurous. Diane von Furstenberg once remarked, "I had always had this fantasy of having a man's life in a women's body." For me, it was the same. Indeed, my mother, distraught over the seemingly endless parade of young men I dated, once told me, "You don't want to marry someone like your father; you want to *be* your father."

However, my quest to "be [like my] father" followed a somewhat unorthodox route. Frantic that I might somehow become a ward of the State if I could not earn a living, my mother decided that secretarial training would assure me not only a living, but also possibly a husband. So off I went to a finishing school run by the Sisters of Charity in New York. Ironically, or presciently, a nun who was my instructor there approached me one day and, apropos of nothing in particular, remarked, "*You* would make a great nun." Although this comment was both amusing and offensive at the time, it was also prophetic.

Corporate Career

My criterion for accepting a job offer after graduation from finishing school was simple. The corporation, where I ultimately began my professional odyssey, had a cafeteria. Bored as a secretary, but enabled by wonderful male mentors (unfortunately, there were virtually no women in the management ranks), I moved up—and out—to become one of the first women to hold a position in senior management.

My sense of accomplishment was tempered, however, by the realization that I was a woman without a college degree, advising PhD graduates on issues related to the management of personnel in a corporate world of more than 120,000 employees. So I enrolled in night school to pursue my baccalaureate degree.

Although my corporate career and college studies were progressing nicely, the itch for adventure was unabated. During a business trip to Texas in the 1970s, while rummaging through a pile of mail that my secretary had labeled "junk," I happened upon a "women in business" type of magazine. (Because of the liberating decade of the sixties, which spawned a new concept of feminism, as well as affirmative action programs by the federal government, a new genre of women's publications, which included the magazine in my junk mail, began sprouting up like clover. Religious orders, too, got on the bandwagon.) As I turned the magazine's pages, an advertisement by the Maryknoll Sisters—Catholic nuns who devote their lives to service to the poor and disenfranchised throughout the world—caught my eye. The ad asked, in essence, "Are you the kind of person who wants to stand with the poor and disenfranchised and live a vowed life in community with other women?" I was ready for a radical commitment, not to mention an adventure. When I arrived in Texas, I attached my business card to the ad and mailed them to the Maryknoll Sisters.

A couple of weeks later, I received a letter addressed to "Mr." as the sisters perhaps couldn't conceive of a woman having her own business card. Once my gender was sorted out, the sisters gratefully accepted my application, and I made the decision to join this religious order. My choice to walk away from a promising corporate future was greeted by collective shock and disbelief. Simply put, my colleagues thought that I was in the throes of a breakdown. Joining a convent at a time of a newly dawning age for women's rights, and forsaking a place at the corporate table, was considered tantamount to insanity.

Faith and Focus

Becoming a nun made perfect sense to me. At twenty-nine years of age, I was burning the candle at both ends. I was the party girl who dated constantly and had already broken off two engagements. With a milestone age just around the corner, I sought major changes in my life—a focus on faith, a sense of stability and order, and a new career path. Needless to say, my mother was horrified.

Admittedly, adapting to life in a "community" made up entirely of women was extremely challenging. I embarked on a vigorous program of running (the allegory should not be missed here) six to eight miles each day. Although I considered myself a "new woman" with radical viewpoints, I discovered that I was surrounded by like-minded women, not "new" (some really, really old, in fact), but equally radical, who shared the same sense of adventure and challenge as I did. It was transformative. Again, my world was rocked.

My epiphany was complete in a most unexpected moment. A Maryknoll sister, who had spent most of her vowed years in Japan living in a Buddhist monastery, had returned home to the Maryknoll community for a short visit. After we dined together, I was washing dishes—a chore that I wanted to complete as quickly as possible so that I could take a nice, calming six-miler before darkness fell. This sister graciously offered to help me with the dishes. She drove me crazy! She gently caressed each dish she handled, wiping the water away with a slow, calculated circular motion. Sensing my obvious frustration, she remarked, "When you dry a dish, you dry a dish." I did not intend to discuss the metaphor. Although she was fully present in the moment, in my mind I was three miles down the road in my Nikes.

We finished the dishes, finally. I went out for the run, but I was changed, and I knew it. Meeting her was a milestone in my life, a point of enlightenment. As a result of our encounter, I was determined to become more attentive and present. And I wanted to learn about Japan and Buddhism.

Advocacy and Law

By the early 1980s, I took my vows as a nun and, to my delight, was sent by the community to live and work in Japan. While studying Japanese each day, I was fortunate to work with another sister in inner-city Tokyo, ministering to men suffering with alcoholism and AIDS—problems as serious in Japan as elsewhere at that time. I learned to speak Japanese, fell in love with Japan and its people, and relished the opportunity to help in the rehabilitation of some and to comfort others with no hope of recovery. I learned that my shoulder-length, curly blonde hair transcended the language barrier. Most Japanese were not used to seeing blondes and were utterly fascinated. I have come to believe that, both in work and in play, you bring all your assets to the party. Even as a nun, I knew this to be true.

My time in Japan was all too short. I learned that my mother's cancer had returned after a ten-year period of remission. Soon after receiving this news, I was back in New York.

Coming home had its challenges. The order okayed my living at a convent near my mom and approved my request to restart my college studies—at thirty-three years of age. Juggling my studies, a dying mother, and a sisterhood community at the same time was no mean feat. Whether due to those circumstances, or the inchoate knowledge that much more was awaiting me, I made another leap of faith, and probably the hardest decision of my life—to leave the Maryknoll Sisters. Perhaps I was lost. But I was also blessed.

In a surprising turn of events, the next phase of my professional journey was about to commence. I was introduced to the director of admissions of a local, but solid law school. She encouraged me to take the law school admission test. Here was yet another women showing me a new way of living my life. Starting on the path to a legal career seemed to make perfect sense. I was drawn to law because of my interest in biblical law and the realization discovered in Japan that most of us, at one time or another, need an advocate—someone to speak for us, petition on our behalf, give us a voice, and make us heard.

So at the age of thirty-five, I went off to law school. I was broke. In my desperation to get money to pay bills, I took a job hoisting cargo at John F. Kennedy International Airport. I thoroughly enjoyed law school and eventually became a Moot Court Scholar (emphasis on "scholar" because with that came scholarship money to pay my tuition).

I had a bit of a scare during the bar admission process, though. The character and fitness portion of my bar exam required me to disclose that I had been arrested as a nun for acts of so-called civil disobedience before I went to Japan, while demonstrating with a well-known Jesuit priest, Daniel Berrigan. My greatest fear was that the character and fitness committee would be horrified by my arrests, and my legal career would be over before it had begun. My fear, fortunately, wasn't realized, and I was admitted to the bar.

While at my first legal job for a brief nine months, I received a telephone call that dramatically changed my life. A partner at a leading law firm, who had been one of my former colleagues, told me that his firm was considering opening an office in Japan. He was aware of my strong Japanese background and invited me to join the firm—the same firm where I am today, Epstein Becker & Green. It is an exceptional firm. In fact, about half of the firm's current professionals are women. The firm was founded nearly forty years ago by men who were smart enough to hire bright and talented women who were turned away from other firms, in large measure, because of their gender.

Accepting that invitation was another transformative step in my journey. I was offered an opportunity to serve as an advocate for Japanese and non-Japanese clients, travel internationally, and develop rewarding professional relationships. And because the firm had hired so many capable women attorneys, I was able to become a better attorney by interacting with, and learning from, these women. I also met the man who is now my husband.

In 2002, a couple of my female colleagues and I decided that the firm would benefit from a women's initiative designed to coalesce the diverse energies of our women attorneys and create more women leaders in the firm. Throughout my professional journey, I was fortunate to have received attention, guidance, and support from women. Indeed, without the women in my life I would not be where I am today. Through the firm's Women's Initiative, I have been able to offer women guidance, encouragement, and opportunities to build their networks.

My career is still going strong after two decades. Even though I am beyond the midpoint of my life, I know that there is more to come, more steps to be taken, and more leaps to be made. I feel content and fulfilled by both my work as an attorney and my involvement with the Women's Initiative.

Leaps of Faith

Looking over my professional journey, I am thankful that I took the giant leaps of faith that were necessary to attain fulfillment—from relinquishing a bright future at a major corporation for a life at a convent and work in Japan, to departing the convent for a legal career, and then leaving my first law firm job for a position at Epstein Becker & Green. I never let naysayers stand in my way.

Everything that I have done during my journey has been part of a winnowing process that has helped me become more attentive, centered, and focused. I do not regret any of my choices.

I have learned to be fully present in my journey, both professionally and personally. I have finally found peace.

Rayona Sharpnack is founder and CEO of the Institute for Women's Leadership, an organization renowned for transformative work around the world. Drawing from her successful careers in education, professional sports, and business, Rayona is an inspirational teacher, coach, and mentor for executives in Fortune 500 companies, government agencies, emerging businesses, and global nonprofit organizations. She is also the author of *Trade Up: 5 Steps for Redesigning Your Leadership and Life from the Inside Out* and one of the featured authors in *Enlightened Power: How Women Are Transforming the Practice of Leadership*.
www.womensleadership.com, www.tradeup.bz

CHAPTER THIRTY-TWO

Redesigning Leadership from the Inside Out

Rayona Sharpnack

The scale of global challenges that we face requires us to forfeit our comfort in being lone rangers.

After twenty-five years in the women's leadership business, I know that the most important work we have to do first is "an inside job." That is to say that, we can only go out into the world and lead change if we know what we are asking of others and if we are willing to lead those changes inside ourselves first.

Fundamentally, leaders are in the context-shifting business. Context is the preestablished belief system you use to interpret and move through every situation you encounter. It ignites the automatic reaction you have when you don't have the option of making your response a conscious one. Why should you care about what context or set of conclusions makes up your reality? We care because context is what determines our actions and behaviors.

There are ten thousand books on Amazon.com that tell you what you need to experience, know, and do in order to lead more effectively. But it takes more than skill development to influence others and make change happen. In my book *Trade Up: 5 Steps for Redesigning Your Leadership and Life from the Inside Out,* I assert that it is more important to work on revealing who you are being—because who you are being is a force that influences and affects everything around you. Once you discover who you are being at the deepest levels, in other words, what contexts you are operating from, you will be prepared to "trade up" to become a more authentic leader and have greater impact in the world. Therefore, demonstrate your ability to lead change *inside* yourself first, which allows you to move *out* to relationships, organizations, communities, and the world.

For example, "I'll never get anywhere in life if I don't keep my nose to the grindstone" was a deeply embedded conclusion I inherited from my parents. In my world, that meant if you didn't work hard on everything, you didn't get anywhere. It wasn't until I was able to surface that context that I could see that not everyone shared my view of reality. My desire to shift out of that context arose because I was unhappy with the impact of my unintended behaviors on my life and on the lives of people around me. I was creating unnecessary stress for my employees, I was micromanaging my perfectly competent daughter in doing her homework, and I was unable to find and nourish a romantic relationship.

Now, let's look at how a trade-up in context affected my behavior and the subsequent impact I could have. When I traded up to the context "It all turns out with grace and ease," I recognized an environment that my body and spirit could settle into. That doesn't mean it was easy to develop my new behaviors. To do so, I needed to rely on the discipline of practice, the support of others, and an openness to feedback. But having established the right environment or context for my new behaviors, I was able to help them grow and ultimately flourish. This inside work allowed for a breakthrough in what I could accomplish with my staff, my clients, and my overall effectiveness with others. In other words, I needed to redesign myself *inside* before I took on transforming people and circumstances *out* in the world around me.

There are five steps you can take to "redesign" yourself for more effective leadership. This process requires that you complete the steps sequentially and thoroughly. If each preceding step isn't done thoroughly, then the succeeding step cannot get the traction required for transformational change.

Before you begin the Trade Up process, you will want to identify one of two things as a prerequisite. You must be experiencing some "pain" in the form of some recurring upset, annoyance, frustration, or area where you are suffering as a leader. Alternatively, you may be standing before some ambitious possibility that requires you to upgrade your leadership capabilities. Without compelling pain or possibility, the seduction to remain in our familiar patterns of behavior is overpowering.

Step 1: Reveal Your Prevailing Context

Leaders create fields of influence. As a leader, your job is to illuminate all the conscious or unconscious beliefs, myths, assumptions, and preconceptions that underlie your own conclusions and the conclusions of the people around you. From there, your job is to jettison conclusions that are limiting, and ensure that new contexts take root that will allow you and your group, organization, or community to improve. Your ability to see and invent conclusions that empower you, your team, or your organization determines what kind of future becomes available. If that ability is limited, it will limit the scope of what can be achieved, putting a lid on the creativity, energy, and enthusiasm of others. When that ability has been honed and exercised, it can be inspiring in ways that you can't anticipate.

One easy place to begin this inquiry is to look at places in your life where you are dissatisfied. What conclusions do you have about yourself, others, or the circumstances in which you find yourself? If you get stuck, ask a close friend to help you sort this out. Revealing all this answers the question: What is shaping or limiting who you are, what you do, and how you learn? That examination can take place at the individual level or in an organization of many thousands of people. What emerges from such an investigation is the choice to achieve new purpose, a new self-awareness about how you operate and why.

If it were possible to fundamentally shift your context, what opportunities would become available? Why do those opportunities matter to you? What different results could you, your team, or your organization produce? Our automatic responses to life are based on the system in which we are firmly embedded. We can choose a different reaction once the patterns of that system are revealed.

Here is an example of the Reveal Step. Alice found herself continuously overlooked for promotions even though she was one of the top performers in her business unit. Having been raised female in a traditional Asian family, her underlying context (conclusion) was: "If I do an excellent job, people will notice and reward me with career advancement." It did not occur to her to make her accomplishments public because that would be boastful and therefore unacceptable. If Alice hadn't taken the time to reveal her prevailing context, she would have continued to be a victim of her organization and never discovered that, in fact, she was the arsonist in her own fire.

To reveal your context, it is important to state it in a short, pithy, sound-bite form that clearly reveals a conclusion operating as "reality."

Step 2: Own Your Context

Once your context has been revealed in Step 1, the most important thing is to "own" it before moving on. Owning your context means taking responsibility for it and being accountable for changing it. Unfortunately, the idea of owning the context you currently operate within is also a bit of a paradox. How can you own something you inherited, that might even feel like it was forced on you? Your context is a mishmash of overwhelming influences. You've got your parents, and their parents, some of your relatives and teachers, the other kids you grew up around, the culture that surrounded you, including whatever church, community, school, or political system in which you found yourself immersed, not to mention the tenor of the times. Conduct an upside-downside analysis of your context. How has it served you? How has it helped you produce amazing results in your lifetime? How has it hindered you as a leader? What unintended consequences or collateral damage has it caused?

Sarah, a highly successful entrepreneur, provides an example of the Own Step. She had completed the first step of Trade Up in discovering that she had always believed: "No one is going to take care of me so I have to take care of myself." This context had served her well in earning positions of leadership in 4H, in the high school drama performances, and on her college basketball team. In fact, starting her own business at twenty-three and growing it profitably for four successive years was proof that she could take care of herself.

Unfortunately, the downside of her tireless autonomy was a number of casualties, including failed relationships with guys who wanted to demonstrate their love for her by taking care of her but were met with a reluctant girlfriend who could take care of herself. In addition, she had hit the wall of how far and fast her company could grow because she was working sixteen hours a day instead of empowering her staff to do things for her.

Essential to completing the Own Step of Trade Up is seeing that the downside or impediments of your context outweigh the upside or virtues of it.

Step 3: Design a New Context

When you come to the realization that the context from which you've long operated is a conclusion about life, and you didn't choose it, a natural question arises: If I were in charge of my own life, what context would I invent to create the future I want? We call this choice point the "trade up."

The third step of Trading Up , known as "design," is both free-ing and paralyzing. Often I ask people, "If you were really the author of your own life story, what story would you write?" Of course, the question is a trick. You *are* the author of your life story, the page is before you, the screen is blank: it's time to start writ-ing. Intimidated? You bet. Very few of us ever have to confront the power of authorship. But the reality is that it is up to you to author your life for the next ten, twenty, or fifty years. Such an act is not for the faint of heart. Create a context that will open up new hori-zons for your leadership. Trade up to the life you want.

An example of the Design Step is found in the experience of Christina, a director of sales for a large apparel company. She grew up in a migrant farm family in central California and had accom-plished more than she had ever thought possible. Her prevailing context, "I must prove to my family that life can be better," was the driving force behind late-night study in high school that enabled her to graduate at the top of her class and receive several college scholarships.

Christina had assessed the virtues and impediments of this context and decided that it was time to Trade Up if she was ever going to get promoted to vice president. After long discussions with her best friends and many hours of entry in her journal, she designed a new context for herself: "Using my gifts in the service of family and community is a life worth living." This new context resulted not only in a huge release from always feeling that she had to prove something, but also provided an internal compass that directed her toward the kind of career opportunities that fit both her skill set and her life passion.

Step 4: Sustain Your New Context

Designing a new context is an exciting and exhilarating expe-rience, but if you don't operationalize it, the changes won't stick. Absent any practices for sustaining your new context, it's folly to expect it to stick. By practices, I mean securing reliable feedback on how you are impacting others, creating a visual display that tracks and rewards new behaviors, communicating your new context so that other people will hold you accountable, and any number of things that will create sustainability. What do you need to stop or decrease? What do you need to start doing or decrease?

What motivates us to want to trade up? The only thing that really inspires change is pain—the desire to stop doing something that is causing suffering through unintended consequences, or the frustration of not accomplishing something we desperately want. No matter where your pain point comes from, you can work backward from it to understand how to shift your context, and then forward again to learn how to adopt supportive new practices.

For an example of the Sustain Step, I turn to my own experience of moving from "nose to the grindstone" to "grace and ease" as a context for the rest of my life. Sustainable practices are the only way to get a new context to stick. The easiest way to approach this is to ask yourself, "What do I need to stop or do less of, and what do I need to start or do more of?"

In my case, I needed to stop saying yes to every opportunity that came my way. In a "nose to the grindstone" world, you do not see the collateral damage of over committing because you know that with a little more hard work and effort you can get it done! I also needed to start recognizing the things that were already happening with "grace and ease." Several times a day, something great would happen, but if it didn't take effort or struggle, it didn't show up on my "scoreboard" of accomplishments. I began a practice of ending each day with a list of what happened that day that was easy or came from an unexpected source. Needless to say, the list grew longer the more I paid attention.

Step 5: Engage—Identify and Enlist Others

All your work of revealing, owning, designing, and sustaining a new context will go by the wayside unless you engage others in the journey. The next step, then, is to enlist your own support team.

This can be done through creating a groundbreaking project that can only be accomplished by living from your new context and engaging a community of support. For instance, a dear friend of mine has taken on transforming the practice of medicine as a project that will require her to stop operating from her default context: "I'm the leprechaun who leads from the back of the room."

Determine whose support you will need to sustain your new context. When I ask people to do this, the answers are usually self-evident. Frequently, a spouse or partner comes to mind immediately. Next, there is often a close friend, or a group of close friends, who can be trusted. More creatively, there are usually a number of key figures in a person's life whose support is necessary in a variety of ways. Many of the top executives I've worked with have enlisted their secretary or administrative assistant. Often, such a person is able to provide a watchful eye and a helping hand in innumerable ways, from assisting in shaping a schedule that permits the openness and space needed for context shifting to letting the leader know how the impact of his work is registering—positively or negatively.

A final group, however, comprises those people you may not find it easy to approach or to enlist in your cause, but whose support would raise the quality of your environment and generate a greater sense of possibility and creativity. This list includes those people you spend a lot of time around, such as your manager, peers, or subordinates at work.

An example of the Engage Step is found in Gretchen who led the Visa team accountable for creating a new global billing system. She knew that to sustain her team's new context of "We are one team in the service of our customers" she needed to create a feedback-rich environment. She encouraged people to give regular feedback to her and each other. The feedback to her was in three areas: 1) What should she keep doing because it was working? 2) What should she do more of to sustain the team's new context? 3) What should she do less of to sustain the team's new context?

In addition to the feedback sessions, she needed to engage her partner, her family, her friends, and her colleagues at work to speak up if she was doing anything inconsistent with what she said she was committed to as a leader. She also participated in our alumnae network of women leaders who are equally committed to redesigning themselves as leaders. She realized that she, like all of us, was never meant to go on the leadership journey alone, but if we don't put in the proper support structure, we default to being the lone ranger.

Trade Up is not just a five-step model for leadership; it is a way of life. If you practice and master the five skills of Trade Up, you will likely find yourself with the biggest challenge of all, which is confronting how good are you really willing to be as a leader and just how good are you willing to have your own life be?

Part VII:
Visionary Medicine

Susan Kolb, MD, FACS, is a medical doctor with a specialty in plastic and reconstructive surgery. A founding diplomate of the American Board of Holistic Medicine and a member of the American Holistic Medical Association, she is the director and founder of Millennium Healthcare, a holistic integrative medical center; Avatar Cancer Center, an alternative cancer treatment institute; and Plastikos, a holistic plastic surgery center. Her practice is an international healing center for women with breast implant disease and other immune disorders. One of the pioneering authorities on the health hazards of breast implants, she is the author of *The Naked Truth about Breast Implants: From Harm to Healing.* www.templeofhealth.ws.

The Spiritual Healer and Synthesis Medicine

Susan Kolb

My journey as a medical doctor and a spiritual healer reflects the archetype of the "wounded healer." In alchemical lore, a physician initiated into the healing arts must first undergo a "sacred ordeal." She may contract an illness for which there is no known cure, suffer a life-threatening injury or endure a severe emotional wound. This wounding forces the initiate to journey deep within her psyche to find the means to cure herself. The initiate emerges from the ordeal, not only healed, but also transformed, returning from her journey with the knowledge that her wound is not only deeply personal, but also reflective of the larger society in which she lives. She returns from her "dark night of the soul" with an exceptional knowledge of healing, not only for herself, but for others as well. A new path of service unfolds divinely before her, because once the healer finds the remedy for her own ills, she can use her medicine to bring healing to others.

I experienced the initiation of the wounded healer. In retrospect, it makes sense that I would have to experience what my patients were going through in order to understand their illnesses. I would have to confront an illness so unconventional that many doctors would not even believe it existed. I would also have to face the toxic forces of society that created the disease in the first place. Most important, I would have to find a treatment by trusting my own internal guidance.

Transcending Victim Consciousness to Reach Transcendent Feminine Consciousness

In 1978, in my third year of medical school, I had been assigned to a vascular surgeon who felt women shouldn't be doctors (and in fact had not been assigned any female medical students for some time due to this belief). He had a strong Southern belief system that women needed to be mothers and in the home. He asked me lots of questions and I got the answers right. At the end of the assignment, he actually gave me a high pass, which is between a pass and honors. I spent six weeks with him and what he said in his evaluation is "She knew the answers to all my questions." That's all he said for an evaluation of six weeks' of work. Normally, the professor would write a lot more. I think I changed his mind about what being a female doctor was about. He thought of me less as a female and more as a doctor. In other words, I challenged his belief system, but the evaluation he gave me was as far as he could go. If I had been a man, I would probably have gotten honors and a glowing recommendation, but he didn't say anything bad and that was probably the best recommendation he ever gave a woman.

I joined the United Stated Air Force in order to pay for medical school. I did my plastic surgery residency in the military in 1982 and, at that point, I was the first female plastic surgeon to go through the military. Much of plastic surgery was actually developed in the armed forces because of war injuries. On my first day there, the head of plastic surgery looked across the operating table at me and said, "I don't think women should be doctors." I made the conscious choice not to be a victim of his belief system. I refused to internalize his (or anyone else's) negative beliefs about me or any other woman and what we might be capable of accomplishing. At that time, the military protected women (and other minorities) from discrimination through a program called "Social Actions." I chose, however, not to report my supervisor and opted instead to perform at a very high level. I took great satisfaction in showing him that I was indeed qualified to be a plastic surgeon. This act of resisting victim consciousness and instead internalizing a sense of personal power is typical of successful women everywhere. Even if the rewards of hard work and devotion are not apparent in the external world, the internal rewards are great. Engaging in a challenge and overcoming adversity is an opportunity. It builds character.

Surgeon, Heal Thyself

When I was in the military, I read books on spiritual practices and spiritual medicine because I had the time. I also began a meditation practice and further developed my internal guidance. My internal guidance had led me into plastic surgery in the first place. I was originally interested in OB/GYN, but I received a clear directive through meditation that I was meant to go into plastic surgery. Though I was born with what we call the gifts of the spirit—the gift of healing, the gift of prophesy, the gift of spiritual hearing, and the gift of spiritual seeing—I would still need to suffer the wounds of the patients I would ultimately treat.

When I was a preteen, I was hospitalized for *Mycoplasma* pneumonia and my chest was x-rayed every day for two to three weeks. I believe the radiation exposure halted the growth of my breast buds and, as a result, I had very little breast development. Throughout my youth, my underdeveloped breasts didn't concern me much since I had other ways of defining myself. In 1985, however, at the age of thirty, while I was a busy plastic surgeon in the Air Force, I felt strongly guided to get implants. I followed my guidance and thus stepped into my initiation as a wounded healer.

When I received this guidance, the problems with breast implants had yet to emerge. My sense is that it was necessary for me to experience breast implant disease so I could help the many others who would soon suffer from problems with their implants and be guided to our clinic in Atlanta. I believe these diseases (and other illnesses that are baffling to conventional medicine) are sent to more spiritually evolved people (like Dr. Garth Nicolson who became ill with Gulf War syndrome). Through treating their own illnesses, these healers learn to help other people who also have these complex disorders. Such is the path of the wounded healer.

For almost ten years, I had no symptoms and actually enjoyed having breast implants. But in 1995, I became very ill. My choice was either to go on disability and quit medicine or figure out how to heal myself. Conventional medicine had no answers for me and, in fact, denied the connection between my illness and the implants. I chose to figure out how to heal myself.

Breast Implant Disease

By that time, I was seeing many patients with the same illness. I first saw patients with silicone implant disease in 1989, but from 1992 to 1994, the number of cases I saw increased dramatically. I became ill in 1995, but I couldn't get my own implants removed until 1997 because I was so busy performing explant surgeries on my patients. To be eligible for settlement funds from a class action lawsuit against breast implant manufacturers, the injured women had to have their implants removed by December 1996 to prove that the implants had ruptured. Only after several hectic months of performing explant surgeries to satisfy this deadline was I finally able to get my own breast implants removed.

Unfortunately, my surgeons were only able to remove a portion of the scar capsules surrounding my implants because the scar tissue had adhered to my chest wall. Scar capsules form around implants, encasing them, and are often filled with the silicone that has leaked out of the implant. Removal of an intact capsule during surgery can keep the silicone somewhat contained, but if the capsule is opened or in some way breached during surgery, free silicone can be released into the chest cavity and wreak havoc on the immune system. Because so much silicone was released into my body, I got even sicker as a result of my surgery. I learned from experience the importance of removing the entire scar capsule. If explant surgery is not done correctly, patients can become very ill.

Typically, when the implant shell leaks or ruptures and the silicone gel is released into the body, health problems begin. Silicone, however, is only part of the problem. The chemicals used as solvents in the implant manufacturing process are also problematic. The symptoms of solvent toxicity (around thirty different chemicals are used in the production of implants) are very similar to the symptoms of breast implant disease, including fatigue, muscle aches, sinus disease, periodontal disease, numbness and/or tingling of extremities, hair falling out, and often endocrine, neurological, and immune problems. Because my surgeon, like so many others, did not remove the scar capsules completely, I was subjected to a large dose of silicone and chemical toxicity.

What my surgeons found when they took out the implants was that both were leaking, but the left one was the more severe. This explained why my neurological symptoms (such as the blurred vision and numbness and tingling) were primarily on the left side. Over the next six months, I started a rigorous detoxification program in order to get the silicone that was left in my body out of my system.

Before I had my silicone breast implants removed, I went into meditation and asked for guidance about whether I should get them replaced with saline implants. I was told, "This isn't over yet" and was guided to get saline implants. Ten years later, I began to manifest symptoms of mold toxicity that can occur after the saline implants have been in for eight to fifteen years.

What I learned through my years of healing myself is that there are four steps for women to follow if they have breast implant disease. The first is surgical: You need to get your implants out along with the capsules, any silicone in your chest wall, and any silicone-laden lymph nodes. Formerly, the standard practice was not to remove the capsules due to the myth that the capsule would dissolve, which turned out not to be true. There have been several peer-reviewed journal articles stating that the capsules are sources of problems and need to be removed. The second step is the detoxification of the chemicals, silicone, and biotoxins (harmful by-products of the infections that arise with implants). The third is addressing immune deficiencies through immune therapies, because the natural killer T cells are depressed as a result of toxicity associated with breast implant ruptures. The last step is to treat any infection. Because the implant is a foreign body, it can always get infected. There can be fungal and/or bacterial infections. Since leaking silicone that cannot be removed surgically travels all through the chest wall and probably throughout the body, infected foreign bodies present problems that require long-term treatment.

Holistic medicine, including functional medicine, teaches the concepts of detoxification and immune support and is the basis of the Silicone Immune Protocol, a detoxification program we developed in our clinic. To address the infections, I usually use conventional antibiotics and antifungals as well as holistic treatments. There are two main detoxification methods for getting the silicone, chemicals, and biotoxins out of the body: The first is the use of nutritional supplements and/or IVs targeting the detoxification of the substances; and the other utilizes devices such as infrared saunas and ionic and electrolysis foot baths that pull the substances out through the skin. The IV that I use most often is IV glutathione. This increases intracellular levels of glutathione used in phase 2 detoxification in the liver, and that is important, especially in eliminating biotoxins and chemical toxins, which can be very difficult to remove from the body.

Biotoxins are made by biological agents, in this case, usually fungi, molds, and yeast (including *Candida*). These by-products can be aldehydes and other biotoxins that are hydrophobic (lipid loving) and hide in cell walls, making them difficult to remove. The chemicals in the implants are primarily solvents, many of which are also hydrophobic and likewise hard to get out using conventional detoxification methods.

At this point, I have treated more than a thousand women with silicone implant disease and hundreds of women with saline implant disease. We don't know the total number of women who have breast implant problems, but we do know that all implants will eventually fail. The shell encasing the silicone or the saline contained in the implant will ultimately break down due to the body's lipolytic action, which seeks to break down any foreign object. The shell is virtually the same in all implants, and studies show that shells break down between eight and fifteen years after implant surgery. When the shell breaks down in a saline implant, the saline can become contaminated with bacteria and/or mold. In a silicone implant, the silicone gel leaks out and causes silicone and chemical toxicity. In 2006, silicone implants were returned to the market and it did not appear that any significant changes were made in the silicone shell envelope. In fact, some silicone implants were found to leak around the back plate sooner than in the older model implants.

It would seem that the FDA went against its own research when it approved silicone implants for release to the market in 2006. The FDA paid in part for a peer-reviewed study published in the *Journal of Rheumatology* (J Rheumatology 2001; 28: 996–1003), showing that patients with ruptured implant with extra-capsular silicone definitely have an increased risk of fibromyalgia and atypical connective tissue disease.

My book, *The Naked Truth about Breast Implants: From Harm to Healing*, reveals all the buried information about the health hazards of breast implants. For instance, a smoking gun in the breast implant controversy was the platinum issue. Platinum is used as a catalyst in the manufacture of the shell of some silicone and saline implants, and traces of this metal were found in the hair analysis of patients who were sick with this cluster of symptoms. Platinum toxicity may produce neurological symptoms, multiple lipomas, and rashes, and can cause new-onset, adult asthma. There is evidence, as well, that platinum can be passed to children of women with implants in utero or through breast milk, causing the same cluster of symptoms in the next generation. The FDA issued papers saying that the effects of platinum toxicity were not backed up by research. There are sound scientific studies, however, that indicate otherwise. The acknowledgment of platinum's generational problem—that it affects children—would, of course, create an even greater legal problem than did silicone. Platinum toxicity was just one of the medical issues buried in the controversy.

Women need to understand that they have to trust their intuition when making decisions that concern their health and not just trust outside authorities or experts. At this time in our evolution, corporate interests largely control the direction of conventional medicine. It's time for women to develop their inner powers of discernment and believe in their own wisdom. Either women are to be subjugated to men, listen to men, and obey men or women are to invoke the power of their inner knowing and bring in their whole history of knowledge of natural medicines—the midwife and the wisewoman—so they make their decisions based on more than just what someone else tells them to do. That, to me, is what the Goddess is about—reclaiming the power of the feminine, specifically the power of the intuitive feminine because women using their intuition have always known the right path to take.

The Path to Synthesis Medicine

When I got out of the military, I went into private practice in Atlanta with another surgeon. Two years into my practice, a patient who was clairvoyant and had been guided to find a surgeon named Susan called around to all the hospitals until she found me. She brought me a book, Barbara Brennan's *Hands of Light,* and said, "You're a spiritual healer and you need to get started." I went into meditation to find out what to do and I heard, "Quit your job." So I did. At the time I was making a lot of money, so the other surgeon in the practice couldn't understand why I would give up all that.

I was off for five months and I studied with a group of clairvoyants. There were seven of us, studying and meditating together. I meditated five to seven hours a day, became vegetarian, and did the spiritual exercises of yoga and tai chi to increase my awareness.

During this spiritual retreat, I developed my spiritual healing gifts more intensely and when I started practicing medicine again, I shifted to more of what I do today in practice, which is spiritual healing using medical intuition. A spiritual healer is someone who is guided to do healing work not just within this dimension. Spiritual healers are guided by feelings, spiritual hearing, visions, or knowing to help other people. Medical intuitives do not necessarily fall in this category because not all are healers; some are simply diagnosticians. The healer is a conduit for energy. In my case, I also receive intuitively information about the causes of disease. I ask for information about what a particular patient can do toward healing on all levels—not just the physical, but also the emotional, mental, and even spiritual levels.

After my spiritual hiatus ended, I started doing laying on of hands, and I began to receive information auditorily and visually in my surgical practice. Spiritual hearing is different from tuning in to your intuition. Intuitive information can be at a gut level, like when you walk down an alley and get a bad feeling in your gut (solar plexus chakra) that you better get out of there. It can be at a feeling level, where you merge with someone and feel their pain or feel what they're going through (heart chakra). Spiritual hearing is at the throat chakra level. You actually hear details about things, like very specific names, places, dates, and information that you couldn't possibly know. Spiritual seeing is when your third eye opens (brow chakra) and you actually see things. For example, I was driving to work one day and had a vision of doing surgery and seeing a hernia. When I got to work and started the scheduled surgery, there was a hernia right where I had seen it in the vision, and yet the patient had no history of prior surgery or any reason to have that hernia. The vision was protective, warning me that I was going to see something that I needed to avoid to prevent complications from cutting into the hernia and possibly injuring underlying structures during the surgery. After my spiritual retreat, I could see tumors more clearly. I would just look at patients and note where I saw metastatic disease using my spiritual sight, and then I'd go look at their scans and see if I was right. A lot of times I was.

People come to my clinic because of the range of holistic treatments that we offer. The most common health problem we see is breast implant problems because I have been the leader in that field of treatment for many years. I also see many patients with cancer, Gulf War syndrome, fibromyalgia, chronic fatigue syndrome, sick building syndrome, chemical toxicity, electromagnetic and chemical sensitivity, and Morgellons disease.

I had the opportunity to interview on my radio show, *Temple of Health,* the leaders in the treatment of these difficult diseases, the people who actually figured out how to treat them. I also interviewed most of the people who are the experts in the different areas of holistic and spiritual medicine as well as consciousness research. I've pulled all this information into my practice of what I call "synthesis medicine." I synthesize conventional medicine, alternative medicine, holistic medicine, and spiritual medicine.

My experience in synthesis medicine has taught me that doctors have to undergo spiritual transformations themselves in order to transform medicine. If you study the doctors or get to know the doctors who are in the American Holistic Medical Association, you find that many of them have had transformative experiences or have been personally challenged with very serious diseases and discovered that holistic medicine is the only path that helps. You can only be as evolved as you are. You can't just suddenly know everything about holistic medicine; you actually have to go through shifts yourself when you drop judgment, become more loving and more conscious. You actually have to do the spiritual work yourself before you can help your patients.

The Great Cycle

There is a balancing of powers now that is bringing the feminine back in to the picture whereas before the feminine was subjugated to the male energy. It's happening now because it's time. There are great cycles. Everything is a cycle in the manifested world. The spiritual cycle we're in is an upward cycle. What this shift means to me personally is more safety (another reason I can now release my book on the truth about breast implants) because there's less good-versus-evil in the world. We're coming more into the balancing of power. It's not all multinational corporations controlling everything and being able to do whatever they want with no consequences. The great institutions of medicine, law, politics, and religion are crumbling in many ways, and they're going to be rebuilt with a much better balance of power.

Victim consciousness implies that you don't have power and that you give away your power, whether it be to your husband, your preacher, your government, your friends, your family, or your doctor. I think that we all need to take whatever any of our advisors say and consider it, because after all, your doctor went to medical school, your attorney went to law school, and your politician presumably has some training in the area of politics. But in the end you're either a victim or you're not. Either you're going to blame somebody for everything that is not right with your life or you're going to say, "Hey, wait a minute, I have the ability to change this."

If you've been in spiritual studies for a while, you know that spiritual growth is all about becoming more conscious. As you become more conscious, you release things from your subconscious that no longer serve you and more of the subconscious material becomes conscious. So as we release victimhood, we actually empower ourselves to create the reality we want in terms of our health, our finances, and our relationships, including our relationship with God. One of the most important things is to have a healthy relationship with consciousness—Goddess, God, or whatever you want to call it—so that you understand how all this works. We're here to learn about ourselves in the context of the third dimension. What's exciting is that it is probably also the fourth and the fifth dimension because we're probably expanding into a higher dimensional awareness even now. Especially in the dream state and maybe in the meditative state, we're accessing higher dimensions. As we access higher dimensions, we also empower ourselves more, and we become conscious of more than just what is in the third dimension.

The return of the Goddess, the balancing of the male-female energies, is only part of what is going to be happening over the next few years to bring us back into balance and allow us to reach our full potential. The right brain–left brain polarity will be balanced as we bring logic and intuition together. We will bring all the races together and all the religions into oneness. Anything that separates people needs to be brought into oneness. This includes humans' separation from nature, which dissolves as we move into understanding that the Earth is a conscious being. The third dimension is the dimension of polarities, so every polarity can be brought together and the differences synthesized as we move into the higher dimensions.

As more people come into cosmic conscious awareness, many of the answers to our current problems—the energy problems, the political problems, the educational problems—will be brought into alignment. As Albert Einstein said, "No problem can be solved from the same level of consciousness that created it." Margaret Mead added to this in saying, "Never doubt that a small group of thoughtful committed citizens can change the world; indeed it is the only thing that ever has." We will use spiritual technologies to solve the problems we created when we were at a lower level of consciousness. The many more conscious beings on the planet have come here to help with this transition from separation to unity.

This is the essence of the Goddess Shift. As we approach the age of unity that has been predicted in virtually every religion, women must once again step forward to balance the masculine with feminine energy. In this time of transformation, we must develop our spiritual gifts (such as our inner knowing/intuition) and use them wisely. It is indeed an exciting time to be on the planet. Amid the rapid shifting of energy, old paradigms are falling away and new ones are emerging. We are at a turning point, a point of power.

Use your power joyfully. With your guidance showing you the way, follow your bliss and really enjoy what you came into the third dimension to create. And remember the old Chinese proverb: Those that say it cannot be done should not get in the way of those doing it.

Rossa Forbes blogs and writes about holistic approaches to schizophrenia recovery. She began sharing her observations about alternative treatments when she found Western medicine to be of little help to her son. His subsequent successes with some unusual interventions prompted her to work to change the way schizophrenia is understood and treated. She is writing a book about this journey, from the unique perspective of a mother who has undergone most of the therapies about which she writes. Rossa Forbes (pseudonym) is married and the mother of three sons. She lives and works in Europe. www.rossaforbes.com

CHAPTER THIRTY-FOUR

The Nerve to Diverge

Rossa Forbes

At the age of fifty, I was put to an extraordinary test. The test, which continued intensively for the next seven years, was how to help my son recover from schizophrenia. Chris was nineteen when we received this diagnosis of the downward spiral that had begun to claim him a couple of years before. Suddenly, everything I thought I knew, I didn't. And in the period that followed, as our family scrambled to get him the treatment he needed, everything I was supposed to trust, I began to distrust. After two years of searching for answers that Western medicine seemed unable to provide, I finally got it: I had to rely on myself. Nobody else was going to help me find the solution for Chris's healing that I knew in my heart was possible.

In time, I realized that I had the power to make something significant happen in a way that would change lives, but I had never used that power or even known it existed, though I had possessed it all my life. I am grateful for the wake-up that schizophrenia provided. I hope that someday my son feels this way too.

The Minority Camp

Though I didn't plan it that way, I ended up in the minority camp in the journey to heal my son. Though it was not a comfortable place to be, it was at least familiar. I have always been part of a minority. Growing up in a Presbyterian household in the 1950s in Montreal, Quebec, I was part of the English-speaking, non-Catholic minority. Montreal itself is an island, cut off from the mainland. Further, my family lived in a predominantly Jewish community within the overwhelmingly French Catholic presence on that island. The Montreal school system was divided along religious lines, like Northern Ireland. English-speaking Catholics and French-speaking Catholics were educated in the Catholic School Board; Protestants and Jews were educated in the Protestant School Board. When my family later moved forty-five miles south of Montreal to New York State, I found myself in the minority position again, amidst Catholics of French-Canadian descent. In fact, wherever I have moved since, I have found myself in a minority, at least according to linguistic, religious, and ethnic differences.

The Presbyterian influence in 1950s Montreal was actually a great training ground for what was to come. Although I hated going to church and mentally tuned out the sermons, never understanding where the minister was going with the message, I did internalize some things. The primary one was to think for myself. The Presbyterian Church encouraged me to question, and for that I am grateful. My family helped out there as well. On my father's side, the influence was Montreal Scottish and Irish Protestant. Irish Protestants, too, are a minority. These were tough, unsentimental people with a "no surrender" mentality exported from the Irish isle. In this community, there was little room for emotion and a lot of room for "who do you think you are?" They were suspicious of what they called the "overly educated," and viewed psychiatrists as strange people. Why would you need a psychiatrist, was the thinking, when, for better or worse, you have the family? That was also the thinking on my mother's Pennsylvania Mennonite side of the family.

I was true to my upbringing in that I made sure not to be flashy or draw attention to myself, not to brag, not to live beyond my means, and not to indulge in fantasies. Years later, I would work hard to overcome the strictures of this kind of thinking, but back then I submitted and my dreams for myself, such as to be an artist or a writer, or to have my own business, faded.

Instead, I got an art history degree, then worked for several years for a political party before going back to graduate school and getting an MBA. There I met my husband, Ian, who was completing his law degree. Within a year and a half of our getting married, Chris was born, followed two years later by Alex, then by Taylor.

We were a normal, happy family in suburbia. We took our boys hiking and camping; we went to church. With three sons and full-time jobs, life was busy. Chris seemed happy enough. Schizophrenia is not necessarily the result of an unhappy childhood, although people often try to make that connection because it can be an easy one to make. Schizophrenia usually goes deeper than that.

Of our three sons, Chris has always been the most intellectual and the quietest. He barely moved in the womb. He was born twenty-seven days overdue. He walked very late, at sixteen months. He spoke very early. By eighteen months, he could recite all his numbers and letters. He was a thinker; there was no doubt about it by the way he expressed himself verbally and the interest he showed in music and mythology. He had a problem, though, which was that he couldn't express preferences. "Would you like peas or carrots, Chris?" I would ask him. "Oh, I don't know," he would say. "You choose." Chris seemed to feel that he was not entitled to much in life. He was always apologizing for nothing. I used to say that Chris asked for permission to breathe. Knowing what I know now, he was slipping into fantasy, or probably he had never awoken from it. I felt at the time that Chris would eventually outgrow this maddening inability to choose and he would stop apologizing for being here in the first place.

When Chris was thirteen, our family moved to continental Europe when Ian joined an international organization. I quickly found employment (and became a member of yet another cultural and linguistic minority) and all three sons enrolled at an international school. Chris went from being a bright but undistinguished student to working hard for the first time. We bought him a guitar and he put together a band. He was busy, focused, and happy. He had a close-knit circle of friends, all academic achievers, and, by and large, only children. I think Chris identified with only children. They see themselves as special and their needs are met without having to jostle for position or ask. By his last year of high school, however, it had become clear that something was wrong. He began to lose focus, his marks slipped, and his face took on a waxy, strained look.

At university, Chris's behavior grew increasingly erratic. He grew a long scraggly beard and became intensely religious. He began to think that his mind knew the answers to complex mathematics and physics principles, so why take a course? He limped through his first year of university on academic probation and crashed partway through his second year. By then, he was lighting candles in his room, praying on a daily basis, and standing in the rain in the college courtyard for hours on end. He was hospitalized for three months, first in Canada where he was going to school, then for three months later that year in the European city where we live.

Ian and I were new to the game. We trusted the doctors and the latest medication to get Chris well. When, after two years, Chris was still an enigma to the doctors, I decided that Western medicine was not helping Chris and might even be harming him.

Standing Up

Though I didn't know it at the time, I had what I needed to deal with this crisis. My background of insecurity, which I had considered a hindrance, ended up serving me well. I naturally gravitated to the minority position and pitted my skepticism and my suspicion of psychiatrists (and now doctors) against the wider majority ideas regarding the proper way to treat schizophrenia, which is a lifetime of antipsychotic drugs, the individual as perpetual patient, the doctor as godlike authority, and acceptance that recovery from schizophrenia is only for the lucky few or the misdiagnosed.

I realized that my belief system had always been against what I perceived as the mainstream. Now, facing a diagnosis that condemned my son to live on the fringes of society, despite what is now touted as recovery, I had to stand up against the medical establishment and the entire "support" group of parents of schizophrenic youth that bought their model and helped perpetuate it. I had to ignore their dire warnings of the damage I would do my son by removing him from the "proper" treatment, and trust in Chris and myself.

Logically and biologically, the mother is the person who knows her child best, yet she is rarely consulted when it comes to treatment and, as far as I know, I may be the only mother writing a book about her child's schizophrenia, although I am not the only mother who blogs about it. The difference between me and the other blogging mothers is that I am particularly skeptical of the status quo and Chris and I have investigated some unusual therapies that helped him, about which I'm willing to write.

There are good reasons why you haven't heard from the mother. Although it is no longer acceptable to blame the parents for their child's schizophrenia (or autism), there are psychiatrists who hold the opinion (even if they don't express it) that the family environment has something to do with it. In my case, the insecurity bred from always being a minority made me take another look at myself, and that same status made me willing to diverge from mainstream advice regarding schizophrenia, both of which turned out to be vital for my son. When you diverge from the safety of the known to explore alternative therapies and ideas, it is also very important to suspend disbelief.

Diverging from the mainstream didn't happen overnight. For two years Chris was enrolled in a day program from 9 a.m. to 5 p.m. The program involved art therapy, light exercise, and weekly meetings with a psychiatrist. The problem with the program was that it treated all psychosis alike and everybody got the same medications. On this regimen, Chris didn't seem to be getting better, but the doctors continued to insist on the status quo. They would not entertain the idea that maybe drugs couldn't fix Chris's problems and might, in fact, compound them. I began to feel that the cause of Chris's problems was not necessarily biochemical. Once I arrived at that way of thinking, the stage was set for conflict. To today's doctors, it's strictly about the biochemistry. Chris's doctors were all very saddened about Chris, without being able to offer any practical advice about what to do to help him get well. I believe they didn't think he would ever get well. To a conventional doctor, schizophrenia is a very sad, lifelong condition. The prevailing medical attitude to schizophrenia is contagious. Many people accept this pessimism.

I wanted practical advice that was based on the premise that schizophrenia was curable, a definite departure from psychiatric convention, which tended to label such a desire "marked denial." This kind of practical advice was found only in implied advice or "hints." (Minorities are good at sensing the unspoken.) I came across two such hints, which were throwaway lines in something I was reading. (You don't find this kind of information without being alert.) The first was that doctors had noticed that people who recover often have parents who deny or hide their condition. The second was that they have parents who do not go along with what the doctor says. I said to myself, "I can do that."

Another Way

I embarked on a crash course of reading anything I could get my hands on that presented schizophrenia in a positive light. I had already read the leading authorities on schizophrenia, with their gloomy disease model of schizophrenia. Now I read what the critics had to say. The critics are the people who see schizophrenia more on the spiritual spectrum. Their opinions make for great reading. None of them were too controversial or too "out there" for me. I was prepared to listen to the message.

I turned to poetry and literature, too, because poets and writers understand schizophrenia. Hermann Hesse and Carlos Castaneda particularly drew me. Hesse believes that most of us are born "types," but a few individuals are given the chance to become "personalities." A personality is developed by undergoing revolutionary experiences and is the end result of a clash between the urge to create a life of one's own and the insistence by those around us that we conform.

My research led to trying new therapies. I entered into them alongside Chris. The main reasons why I, too, underwent the therapies were, one, it is easier to write about what you have personally experienced. I knew I wanted to write about our journey because once I got over my fear of schizophrenia and the fear of what it might reveal not just about Chris, but about me, I began to find it fascinating. Two, the more I read, the more convinced I became that schizophrenia has a basis in the family environment, which might be called the family energy field. Every case of schizophrenia has a cause, and probably more than one. I looked for Chris's causes and kept digging. A mother is especially well suited to this kind of detective work because, as I said, she is the one who knows her child best.

I found that the mother does play a role in her child's schizophrenia. I learned that if a mother has insecurities and the fetus is sensitive, it is possible that the child will pick up the resonance of these emotions while in the womb. The mother is only part of the picture; the fetus may pick up other disturbances in the environment. I also learned about resonance and cellular memory, and how the family energy field can become misaligned. There is much to learn about how these factors can contribute to schizophrenia.

The common factor in nearly all the therapies we undertook is the use of vibrational energy and emotions to heal. After establishing an orthomolecular (vitamins and diet) regimen for Chris, which I consider a base and a constant, one of the most profound therapies our family undertook was Family Constellation Work, which helps restore the balance of the family energy field. It is based on the premise that all members of a family, living and dead, have the right to their place in the family tree. If someone is denied this right to belong through an untimely death, imprisonment, or perhaps being the family "black sheep," another family member will (usually unknowingly and often generations later) exclude him or herself as an act of atonement for the injustice. People with schizophrenia are particularly susceptible to acts of atonement. In the course of several Family Constellation sessions, I realized on an emotional level how the death of my grandmother when my mother was four left a nervous energy on the generations that followed. The therapist told Chris that he no longer had to carry this burden.

This and other therapies moved Chris forward in incremental steps. We noticed improvements, while the doctors continued to advise against my methods. After a while, I stopped telling them what I was doing. They knew no more than I did in this new area of endeavor and would only try to put a stop to what they failed to understand.

There were many discouraging days and many sleepless nights, but I never became discouraged for long. I recognized in me a strong minority tendency to be discouraged or negative and I told myself, "No, that's not going to happen this time." I only read the good news, even if it meant reading and rereading the same small sliver of hope that someone had written somewhere. I always felt empowered after reading small slivers of hope.

Some nights I would wake up to a split second of blessed nothing and then I would remember why I had woken up in the first place. All my anxiety and sadness over Chris would come flooding back. My solution to this was to tap into the universal mind, which many call God, but you can call it the Akashic field or whatever you want. I would whisper, "I am here, Lord, I am listening." I was asking God for an idea, something I hadn't thought of to help heal Chris. For once, I was really listening. The words were barely past my lips before I began to feel better. I usually got an answer by the next day, pointing me to the next action to take. It was always the right answer, by the way. I began to trust myself because I came to see that I had the tools. I just needed to trust in myself and use them.

I discovered that the "who do you think you are?" mind-set from my childhood could be helpful. When Chris's doctors waved pictures of the damaged schizophrenic brain at me as proof positive that there was something wrong with my son's brain, I protected him and me by thinking, "Oh yeah, says who?" Of course, I had already done my homework to know that there are psychiatrists and doctors who refute this kind of evidence. When Chris's doctors tried to scare me into increasing his medication, I had to summon all my reserves against both the doctor and the institutional program in which Chris was enrolled.

Another challenge was that my husband and I often disagreed on what was best for Chris, especially when it came to the medications. He was willing to trust the doctors more than I was. Though we had no ready answer to resolving the disagreements, we took up yoga and meditation to relieve the stress of the whole situation with Chris. I suspect that our energies were subtly realigned in the process. We eventually moved into synch about Chris.

I would love to say that Chris has now picked up where he left off and is back in university and focused on a career goal, but this has not happened and may never happen exactly as I would like to see it, not because Chris isn't capable, but because Chris may be on a different life path. He is becoming a personality. To our astonishment, he began voice lessons and by all accounts is an excellent singer. We always knew he was a good musician. He is also an expressive writer, which is a new development.

Recently, my husband and I got a lesson in patience. Chris was doing so well that we were pushing him to go back to university away from home. We were still thinking in terms of "type." He had a relapse and spent time in hospital. Yet, with him having become a much stronger, more evolved personality, this was more of a pause than a regression. His sense of self is developing nicely.

The Unity of All Things

It has become clear to me that the label "schizophrenia" is a stumbling block. What my son really has is a profound awareness and is undergoing a struggle to lead a life that is meaningful. A person going through schizophrenia is highly sensitive and creative, and open to communicating with others at a lofty level of abstract thought. I had to be worthy of him, so I, too, wised up. I ask what this experience can teach me. I realize my son is my teacher. He is telling me that there is more to life than meets the eye. He is coaxing me along a road to enlightenment. I, in turn, am helping him to live in this world.

Many people could say I am in denial about his diagnosis. Well, here's to denial. Had I accepted Chris's diagnosis, I am convinced he would not have succeeded as far as he has and will continue to do. I am once again a minority, because the naysayers are all around.

I am using my minority viewpoint about healing to encourage recovery in others. My message is that schizophrenia is not a pathological disease. It lives within most of us to one degree or another and is a familiar presence if we care enough to pay attention.

The experience with Chris has helped me to see that we are all connected; we are one. Understanding each other is our healing. This revolutionary process called schizophrenia, properly understood and handled, gives those of us who care a chance to break away to lead a more fulfilling life.

The only difference between me and others in my situation is in attitude.

You don't have to be a different kind of person to empower healing; you just have to trust yourself enough to realize that you have what it takes to help yourself or your relative. It doesn't matter what other people say or think. It is important to remember in the case of schizophrenia that even doctors will admit that those who eventually do well are not usually good patients. There is a lesson for everyone in this, no matter what health or other challenge you are facing. Listen to what you know inside of you, and stand up, speak up, and have the nerve to diverge in a way that might just lead you to exactly where you need to go.

Pamela Wible, MD, is a board-certified family physician and nationally recognized innovator in patient-centered care. She was born into a family of physicians, but her parents warned her not to pursue medicine. She followed her heart, however, only to discover that to heal her patients she had first to heal her profession. With this in mind, she pioneered the community-designed ideal medical practice in Oregon. In this model, designed to heal health care, she inspired ordinary citizens to define ideal care and then design their own clinic. www.idealmedicalpractice.org

CHAPTER THIRTY-FIVE

Love Uncontained

Pamela Wible

I could never control my curly red hair. My parents tried everything. I screamed as Mom sprayed me with "no more tears" detangler. When her yanking and pulling failed, Dad stepped in and turned my plight into a neighborhood competition, complete with prizes. He'd give a dollar to any kid on the block who could comb through my matted locks. When older, I'd straighten my hair by blow-drying it for so long that one time I melted the bristles right off my brush into my freshly singed bangs. I'm wiser now. I've stopped trying to beat my hair into submission. Let it fly where it will. Like me, it cannot be restrained.

Now I'm all grown up and a physician, but certain concerned friends and relatives still try to get me to comply with social norms. They recommend a professional hairstyle and a nice home in an upscale community of the well-to-do. I'm not supposed to have untamed hair or live in a plain, old, small house in some average neighborhood.

Society divides us from each other and from ourselves, constricting and confining individual identity with rules and codes of conduct designed to keep life orderly, safe, and predictable. I'm not interested in an orderly, safe, predictable life. I believe in feeling my way through each moment with an open heart, in living my dreams fearlessly.

But my love is unwelcome in the medical profession. When I was in conventional practice, I was inundated with guidelines and policies in conflict with my values. I was supposed to observe professional distance, but why would I want to learn how to dissociate from myself or from those I care for? Why would I pretend to be reserved, restrained, and aloof when I'm naturally warm, affectionate, and friendly?

On Valentine's Day at my first job, I admitted a colleague's patient, an elderly man dying of heart disease. His wife, unable to bear the pain of watching him die, left his side. I could have left too, but it didn't seem right to let this guy die alone on this romantic day, so I sat with him, held his hand, and cried. A cardiologist, startled by my emotion, said, "You must be a new doctor," then he disappeared down the hall. Maybe experienced doctors don't cry, but I didn't want to close my heart to the world. Why is it unprofessional to love patients? Maybe love isn't valued in a traditionally male-dominated profession. After all, love is not easily measured or reimbursed. Love is hard to control.

I used to hide in a world hostile to women—the "good-old-boys" medical school and patriarchal health-care system I joined in order to be a doctor—until one day I decided to celebrate my life without shame. On that day, I fell in love with myself and I gave myself permission to fall in love with my patients, to hug and kiss them, to sing and laugh with them, and to look deep into their eyes, cry, and allow our tears to flow together.

Grandmothers of Medicine

I admire the courageous women doctors who came before me. My foremothers in the field bore the brunt of the prejudice and abuse from medical men intimidated by women's strength and transcendent love for humanity. One hundred and fifty years ago in Philadelphia, the birthplace of American medicine, "lady doctors" with freshly spit tobacco juice dripping from their hair, were pelted with rocks as they walked into hospitals and lecture halls. Some passed for men to avoid the humiliation. Most walked through the pain—for they too would no longer be contained.

Last year I made a pilgrimage to my matrilineal ancestral home in the City of Brotherly Love. Housed in the basement of Drexel University College of Medicine Library are the archives of the first medical school dedicated to women, Woman's Medical College of Pennsylvania, a safe haven for female physicians. There I convened a private ceremony with my foremothers amid the remnants of their lives. I read aloud letters, poems, and commencement speeches, and I honored the first class of eight graduates by reciting the 1852 valedictory address. In that class was Ann Preston, the grandmother of American medicine.

Dr. Preston paved the way for all women physicians. Undeterred by rejections from male medical schools, she founded an all-women's teaching hospital. Upon graduation, she was appointed professor of physiology, and in 1866 became the dean, the first woman in America to hold such a position. She nurtured the initial wave of female physicians in the United States, including the first African-American and Native-American physicians. On her death, she bequeathed her estate to scholarships for future generations of women physicians.

I discovered Ann's box of letters and read them all. Underneath the letters were her anatomy textbook and her bible, the most enormous I'd ever seen, perfect for a woman with such faith in humanity. Holding her anatomy book, pages torn and spine fractured, I was imbued with her unbroken spirit. She stands ever tall in me and I carry the torch of her unfulfilled aspirations for the good of all.

America has matured now and it is time to celebrate and honor women physicians for their feminine strength in the realm of medicine. It is time to unabashedly welcome women's nurturing hearts, brilliant minds, and tender souls. I believe it is women who will heal health care in America.

We need more unrestrained women in medicine—women who aren't afraid to love. Women tend to provide more empathic, holistic care. Patients know this; they ask for women doctors because women doctors spend more time with them. Studies reveal that female physicians care for more complicated cases, more uninsured patients, and more vulnerable populations. How different health care would be in America had it been designed by our grandmothers.

Before Dr. Ann Preston's influence on medical history, there was only one female physician in the United States, Elizabeth Blackwell. By 1860 there were two hundred, and by 1911 there were more than seven thousand, according to the American Medical Association. In 1965 my mother, Judith Wible, received her medical degree from the University of Texas Medical Branch in Galveston. Of 160 graduates, eight were female. The dean and fellow classmates reminded the "girls" in the class that they were "taking a man's seat" and they'd never use their degrees. Even the anatomy professor refused to accept female anatomy and persisted in addressing the women as men. Despite her protests, my mother remained "Mr. Wible." Women were excluded from urology—from palpating penises and prostates—while men dominated obstetrics and gynecology. Daily the women were exposed to filthy jokes that demeaned female patients, and in the evenings they slept in cramped nursing quarters while the guys had fraternities complete with maids, cooks, parties, and last year's exams.

Bambi Syndrome

Two years after my mother graduated from medical school, and nearly a century after Ann Preston's death, I was born. At the time of my delivery, Dad was teaching anatomic pathology at the Woman's Medical College of Pennsylvania. He interrupted the class to announce my arrival, and then polled the students for a name. They voted "Pamela." Thus I was inducted into a community of female physicians at birth, then spent my childhood wandering the hospital halls alongside Dad, peeking in on autopsies, and examining gross anatomy specimens while most girls my age were playing with Barbies.

In 1993 I followed in my mother's footsteps and received my medical degree from the University of Texas Medical Branch in Galveston. Times had changed—sort of. Half the students were women, but the raucous frat party ambience prevailed. Having graduated from Wellesley, a progressive all-women's college, I was unaccustomed to a male life of hunting, womanizing, and drinking. At Wellesley, I had never seen men jump off rooftops through rings of fire or drive cars decorated with "Trust me I'm a doctor" painted over naked silhouettes of women. And I had certainly never been exposed to the mass murder of dogs as part of the curriculum. It wasn't exactly safe to let my hair down, but I did open my mouth, start petitions, and protest live-animal labs. Undeterred by intimidation tactics, I landed in the dean's office. There I was diagnosed with "Bambi syndrome" and exempted from the barbaric experiments. Though ridiculed for my compassion, I graduated without sacrificing innocent life, my ethics intact.

After graduation, I continued to feel spiritually and psychologically demeaned by my profession, a profession devoted to healing. Kahlil Gibran wrote, "Work is love made visible." I wanted to be free to express my love through my work, but doctoring had been dumbed down to a numbers game with cookbook protocols and computerized flow sheets. My soul was considered irrelevant; it slowed down the production line. When a nurse and I transformed our corner of the clinic into a "happy triangle" where we smiled and behaved lovingly with everyone in spite of our inhumane working conditions, we were reprimanded for being "too happy."

After six jobs in ten years, I was tired of the abuse. I was tired of interrupting panicked patients who were crying to say, "Sorry, we're out of time." I was tired of being rude to patients and neglecting myself, all in the name of health care, when what I wanted to do was smile and ask, "How can I help you?" I dreamed of returning to my college waitressing job just so I could be nice to people again.

Dreaming the Ideal Medical Clinic

There came a point when I refused to hold Americans hostage to a loveless health-care system. I knew that health care begins with a complete human relationship founded on unconditional love. I believed it's what Americans desperately want, so I left my job and invited my community to join me on an adventure.

Our journey began on January 20, 2005, when I held the first of nine town hall meetings in Lane County, Oregon, where I lived. I publicized this and the subsequent meetings by e-mail, in the newspaper, and with handmade flyers posted around town. From living rooms and Main Street cafes to neighborhood centers and all venues in between, I invited ordinary citizens to do something extraordinary: create the medical clinic of their dreams. Activists, teachers, psychologists, health-care workers, college students, and folks of all ages joined together to design a new model, a template for the nation.

The process was simple. Each participant received a piece of paper on which was one sentence: "Create an ideal medical prac-tice—please take time to imagine what it would be like to walk into an ideal medical clinic in an optimal health-care system." The rest of the paper was blank.

What if Americans were free to dream their highest vision of healing and health care? And what if a physician promised to bring those dreams to life? Imagine what it would look like, sound like, and feel like to enter an ideal clinic designed by the Ameri-can people. No lobbyists or experts. No government officials. No hidden agenda. Just an open-minded doctor with an open-ended request that had never been posed before: Describe the clinic of your dreams...

After a brief introduction, I witnessed history in the making. The room was abuzz with excitement as people wrote their fantasies. Then we sat in a circle and shared. A free-spirited mother of two read, "An ideal clinic is a sanctuary, a safe place, a place of wisdom where we can learn to live harmlessly, listen with empathy, observe without judgment. It's a place where a revolution starts, where we rediscover our priorities."

A Chinese woman with an Australian accent requested, "No front counters separating people from people, a lounge of sorts with sofas...complimentary massage while waiting...fun surgical gowns."

Then a soft-spoken young man with dreadlocks asked for "intriguing magazines" and a "pet cat that greets people at the door."

A disabled elder defined the doctor as "so mature and integrated in psychological, spiritual, physical, East-West medicine that he or she is able to guide with affirmations supportively into the spiritual truth of the moment and help patients come to terms with fears, anger, pain, and rejection."

A local contractor offered, "The doctor knows everyone by their first name, knows the patients in a social context."

The community mandate was clear: "The doctor has a big heart and a great love for people and service, and is someone whose presence itself is enough to cheer a patient."

But most important, a shy East Indian girl read, "Patients leave feeling warm, nurtured, loved, and important."

The word "doctor" is derived from the Latin word *docere,* meaning "to show or teach." I came to understand my responsibility as a physician when a bearded man in the back of the room raised his hand and asked, "Is it possible to find a doctor who's happy?" In a world fraught with despair, people need happy doctors. Naturally, I accepted the position.

From nearly a hundred pages of submitted testimony, in poetry and prose, complete with doodles and floor plans, I incorporated 90 percent of public input and with no outside funding opened our community clinic one month later. For the first time, my job description had been written by the patients and community I served. It was health care of, by, and for the people.

Love Triumphant

Can health care really be overhauled in a month? Yes.

In less than thirty days, we successfully redesigned production-driven medicine into a relationship-driven model—a community clinic where patients are in charge and the doctor answers the phone, says "Come right over," and is waiting when the patient arrives.

Our clinic is housed in a wellness center tucked into a wooded residential area and features yoga, massage therapy, and counseling, plus a solar-heated, wheelchair-accessible, indoor therapy pool and hot tub. A covered walkway connects the pool to the medical office. Patients can relax in the hot tub instead of a waiting room. Then they enjoy a short walk into the office, which feels more like a living room filled with overstuffed chairs and pillows.

With no administrators or staff at the clinic, patients enjoy 24/7 direct access to their family doctor by phone or e-mail. Appointments are thirty to sixty minutes scheduled on weekday afternoons and evenings with same-day and weekend visits available. Leisurely appointments begin on time—guaranteed—or patients choose a present from the gift basket. Additional prizes are awarded for healthy behavior. Uninsured folks can trade services such as massage or donate handmade items to the community gift basket for their medical care. Nobody is ever turned away for lack of money.

I'm a board-certified family physician. I do all the things doctors do, but health care is so much more than touching the surface of physical ailments. It's acknowledging the lack of meaning in people's lives—their real pain—and it's addressing our national epidemic of loneliness and despair.

One afternoon I hired a patient, a massage therapy student, to work on my high-needs psychiatric clients during their medical appointments. All enjoyed free footbaths and hand massages. Not one had ever received massage; most had never experienced safe, loving touch in their lives. Now they require less medication.

A new patient limped in one day with heel pain. We chatted and joked around for the entire visit, like girlfriends at a slumber party. I laughed so hard I nearly inhaled the navy-blue sock lint between her toes, her naked foot resting inches from my nostrils. When she left, I realized I had not examined her foot! Immediately, I called to apologize and offer another appointment free of charge, but she told me her pain had disappeared.

On random "patient appreciation days," I shower my clients with extra affection, chocolates, and Mylar smiley-faced balloons when they enter the office. This is in addition to the gifts many receive for meeting their health goals. Sitting on the couch next to her balloon, treats piled high in her lap, a woman claimed, "This is like going to Grandma's!"

One of my sweetest patients is John, a man in his fifties with debilitating arthritis. He's a fast-talking anxious fellow who returned for some advice. He told me he wanted to stay active and volunteer, and was ready for the companionship of a good woman. His blood pressure was higher than usual. I wrote two prescriptions. The first was a small dose of a beta-blocker for blood pressure and anxiety. The second prescription read: "John is a great guy. He needs a wonderful woman in his life. I highly recommend him." As I reviewed his instructions, he jumped up from the sofa and hugged me. I guess I'm old-fashioned. I still handwrite my prescriptions because what patients really need can never be prescribed electronically.

During my pediatric rotation in medical school, I used to stay up late at night in the hospital, holding sick and dying children. I'd lift them from their cribs and sing to them, rocking them back and forth. One day the head of the department gave me a compliment

I'll never forget. He said that I was a doctor when my patients needed a doctor and a mother when they needed a mother. Eventually, I allowed patients to reciprocate—to mother me, to love me, to dream with me. And I discovered that the greatest healing takes place when we are willing to transcend artificial boundaries, love freely, and embrace each other's dreams as our own.

Cynthia Lubow, MS, MFT, a licensed marriage and family therapist, consultant, teacher, and poet, has specialized in psychotherapy with women for twenty-five years. She has worked with hundreds of women to resolve their depression, and the self-esteem, anxiety, trauma, grief, relationship, and other issues that can drive depression. Cynthia is the author of two full-length e-workbooks, *Ending the Blues: A Psychotherapist's Guide to Living Depression-Free,* and *Higher Power for Recovering Cynics: Developing a Unique, Personalized Spiritual Life Without all the B#*$#t.* www.WomensPsychotherapy.com

CHAPTER THIRTY-SIX

Transforming Depression into Empowerment

Cynthia Lubow

Depression shuts us down like a flipped circuit breaker, leaching energy from our muscles and draining our mechanisms for motivation, confidence, hope, and love. Power is shut off for the normally effortless process of forming and pursuing a simple desire such as cooking a meal or even curving the corners of our lips up into a smile.

As many as one in three women in the United States suffer from depression at some point in their lives. Nearly three-quarters of the prescriptions written for women are for antidepressants. Yet depression in women often goes untreated or is undertreated by doctors and other professionals not trained as mental health practitioners. A major factor in the incidence of depression in adult women is having survived abuse as a child. Depression is also overrepresented in women who have the least power in our culture by virtue, for example, of their race, income, or education. Depression can be one of the most severely or insidiously disabling conditions we face in life.

How, then, is it possible to transform this experience of such utter disempowerment into empowerment? Whereas a medical model might suggest we try to conquer, amputate, or fix depression,

I have found in both my clinical work and my own personal journey that the answer lies in relationships. Perhaps surprisingly, recovery can begin with developing a relationship with depression itself. For most women, this means understanding how depression tries to protect and inform us. For those who grapple with long-term or multiple, intense episodes of depression, the relationship is more complicated. Using the relationship with depression to guide the process, it is another relationship, a personal or professional one with a consistently empathic human being, that empowers women emotionally.

If Depression Knocks at Your Door, Invite It in for Tea

In the most common scenario, depression operates somewhat like physical pain. It protects us first by getting our attention. Just as we can seriously burn a hand on a hot stove if pain doesn't tell us to pull it off, we can go on enduring hurtful emotional situations if depression doesn't warn us to stop. Although depression usually descends as a result of an event, situation, or history, it can also be initiated in part or entirely by a brain chemistry imbalance. Regardless of the source, depression alerts us that something needs to change.

Sapping our energy, motivation, and ability to function is a crude, sweeping, and disabling tool, but it can also serve to protect us. Without physical and emotional energy, we usually have to limit or stop doing what we normally do, hopefully including whatever we're doing that is hurting us. For example, when we chronically take care of other people and not ourselves, depression often intervenes, pulling in our resources and leaving us no energy left to give. It forces rest when we refuse to give ourselves rest. It leaves us little choice but to focus our attention on our own starved needs.

Perhaps most important, depression ups the ante on attending to our emotional health, much like diabetes and heart disease do for physical health. Having any of these conditions means we cannot ignore daily healthy self-care, without potentially serious consequences. Having a relationship with depression, then, includes translating its symptoms into messages about self-protection and self-care.

Depression Is My Companion, Dog, Grandmother

For most women, depression comes and goes, visiting briefly once, or occasionally. For others, depression moves in and refuses to leave for long periods. If we can evict our unwelcome roommate, then problem solved. But if we can't evict it, our best option is to develop a relationship with it. A relationship with this long-term roommate goes beyond merely listening to its communications about self-protection and self-care.

This next level of relationship with depression is difficult to describe. I suspect that it is this type of relationship that has inspired the work of certain artists, philosophers, spiritual guides, and psychotherapists. The best way for me to explain it is to describe my own personal experience in developing a relationship with the depression that plagued me during my first three decades of life.

By the time I reached my mid thirties, I had benefited from many years of excellent psychotherapy and had developed a reverence for self-care. I have not had to grapple with disabling depression since. However, the relationship I formed with depression in my youth remained a part of me. Now it feels something like a fond, trusting relationship with a wise elder, close companion, or perhaps a loyal dog.

As I was developing this relationship, many years ago, it felt like this: Even if I was alone, depression was there. It pulled a dark blanket around me and held me inside. It was family—pain-in-the-ass family, but familiar and enduring family, nonetheless. Depression gave me permission to push my own limitations and consider uncensored possibilities outside any boxes. This led me to the true nature of what I wanted and who I was. I could seriously consider dying and, in doing so, recognize the simple truths of why I wanted to live. I could consider leaving my life or changing it completely and, in doing so, open my mind to every potential choice.

When I was at points of complete enclosure in the blanket, I had nothing to lose. If I took no pleasure in the world, I knew I could leave it. If I was getting nothing from the world, I could take liberties with it. If I acknowledged I had control over how long I would live, I was free to do almost anything in my remaining time. In those moments, I did not have to worry about old age, disease, poverty, or most of what scared me. I found that I could write a mock suicide note and discover feelings I didn't know I had, until the freedom of leaving life forever felt palpable. I had no obstacles to making each moment count, knowing I was *choosing* to live each one. Opening to the entire world of possibilities informed me about what was missing in my life, where I was not being true to myself, or what I secretly yearned for but denied myself—until depression made space for me to acknowledge it.

Depression made me quiet, introspective, and ultimately more conscious. It inspired me to look for meaning in life, to question my assumptions. Like meditation, it focused my attention and filtered out much of the world. It made me rest when I'd overextended myself. It set limits on what I could do, when I tried to give too much. It demanded I give *myself* attention. The fact that it limited me forced me to clarify my real priorities and what I truly valued. It took me out of the world, so I could have perspective on my life, and life in general, rather than just surviving with tunnel vision. Depression gave me a deep, rich inner life and made me comfortable with others' depths. It made me most comfortable with diving past superficiality and connecting honestly, deeply, and intimately. It made me very attuned to other people. Some of these benefits didn't appear during the most intense periods of my depression, but were planted then and grew out of those dark times. Ultimately, this relationship made me a better person and a better psychotherapist.

My Calling to the Huge Vat of Soup

Now, having this intimate relationship with depression without actually being depressed is like lounging on a deck around a huge vat of thick, murky soup. I am not afraid of anything in the soup. I am at home there. I am totally comfortable, even in the deep and dark parts, because I have thoroughly explored every bit of it. I don't see it as a monster, or a growth that must be removed. I don't swim in the soup anymore, but I remember and, occasionally, I get a quick, familiar splash.

When women who've fallen into the vat pull themselves over to me, they are swimming with my oldest friend. I have no judgments about it, only interest. Though I am lounging on the deck, I am deeply connected to them. We share a soup. I don't need them to get out. I don't need them to stay in. I don't let them drown, but I don't need to rush in like a lifeguard and drag them out. I let them find their own way and pace of change. They peer into the soup, unable to see its bottom. We look together at everything blocking the view, until we can see more clearly. We look carefully in the deep and dark for their sorrow, traumas, fears, and self-attack. I am not shocked by anything, because I've experienced it all myself. I am not scared of their depression, emotional pain, or talk of death. They reveal their painful feelings and thoughts because they see that I can't be scared away. I am comfortable enough with the soup that I can just stay close, offer my heart and guidance until they are ready to grab my hand and climb out.

The most profound gift of having a relationship with depression is that this relationship bathes me in soothing humility. While providing psychotherapy is emotionally challenging, I find that this infusion of humility offers me perspective and support more than I have found from any other source. Feeling utterly equal with other beings makes it easy and natural to be calm, to have no negative judgments, and to help them find meaning in painful feelings. While I value my professional skills, knowledge, and experience, I live my life and do my work every day as just one of all human beings, one who knows firsthand the deep and extensive emotional pain human beings can suffer.

From Woman-Style Depression
to Woman-Style Empowerment

Although most of my patients come to me because they are depressed, depression is usually only the bus that brings them in. Once there, we work on every issue imaginable, because any emotional or relationship problem can cause depression. The most common issue I see fueling depression in women, and probably the most disempowering, is self-attack. It's like breathing—women often don't even know they are doing it, because they do it so much and have done it for so long. This is an example of the kind of self-attack that goes on in depressed women's thoughts each day:

Ugh, my hair looks like shit today... I look terrible in these pants; I wish I had a body like_____... I can't believe I spilled my coffee on myself; I'm such a stupid idiot... I should be doing my job better; if everyone knew how little I know about how to do my job right, I'd be fired; maybe I should be; I can't do anything right... Everyone must think I'm a loser because I'm not married... I should be more financially secure by now... Nobody's ever really going to love me; I have to be really, really nice for anyone to want to hang out with me... My friends have it so much more together than I do... I should go to the gym but I'm too lazy... No matter what I do, I get nowhere... I'm so far behind in everything... I'll never amount to anything... I'm a worthless loser!

How can women feel powerful with this going on inside of them? How can they love, parent, succeed, or take care of their physical and mental health when they hear their own voice all day telling them they're unlovable, incompetent, unattractive, worthless, and a fake?

To shift self-sabotage, women need a relationship with some-one who is fluent in the language of feelings. Emotionally fluent people are able compassionately to access and express their own feelings and the feelings of others. When children are raised by caretakers who have this fluency, the children have some immu-nity to depression. But when women have not had the instruction, role models, and permission to identify and express their feelings, they are less likely to find friends and partners who can offer this later. A professional therapeutic relationship, then, can provide the emotionally fluent interactions that heal.

Psychotherapists use empathy to help women develop fluen-cy with feelings. We listen and strive for a deep understanding, reading words, tone, face, body, and other nuances. We receive our patients' feelings and needs like they are newborn babies, so they can breathe in the oxygen of being understood and valued—essential needs we all have. We verbalize what we perceive in or-der to help women understand how to express what they are feel-ing. We sift through the undifferentiated pain of depression to find the individual emotional strands fueling it.

To understand this differentiation process, imagine that when a woman was a child, her mother regularly told her she was ugly and stupid. She may experience depression as an adult but not be able to identify its emotional components. This is analogous to feeling physical pain but not knowing where the pain is, what's causing it, or specifics about the sensations of pain. In contrast, being able to say the pain is in the left palm, feels sharp, electri-cal, and intense, and comes from the site of a bee sting would be parallel to being able to talk about the hurt, anger, and shame she felt when her mother criticized her. With depression, unlike pain, just feeling and being able to express those feelings to an empathic listener can be enough to relieve the depression.

A former patient of mine who came to me depressed needed this differentiation. Part of her experience of depression was feel-ing like her arms were so heavy when she was at work that she could barely lift them. She felt horrible, but it was not clear where the problem was. As we worked together, she realized that she was very angry at her boss because the way he acted reminded her of her father's abuse. Some unconscious, young part of her that felt all this anger wanted to punch him, and holding that anger back made her arms feel heavy, protecting her from the potential consequences. Feeling depressed at the same time warned her not just to endure the heavy arms but to get help. Identifying the anger and expressing it in therapy allowed her to find a more effective way of dealing with her boss, and she no longer had heavy arms.

Such work in therapy fertilizes the soil for emotional growth and leads to the healing of women's relationships with themselves and with others. With compassion replacing self-attack, women feel more self-confident. Armed with emotional fluency and practiced at good self-care, women leave therapy feeling more powerful, and go on to lead effectively in whatever their arena may be. We now know that the most successful leaders are those who are emotionally fluent.

Women who bring more emotional fluency to management are better able to inspire people to be loyal, to work hard, to be creative, to cooperate, and to feel good about what they are doing. These women are also likely to parent with the empathy children need to be healthy and empowered. Working through disempowering emotional blocks in therapy can give artists better access to their creativity and ability to produce their art, writing, music, dance, or other creative expression. Some of these women will want to become psychotherapists and help other women develop self-love.

Depression is a many-headed beast. Probably nothing can be said about it that applies to everyone who has ever experienced depression. There are also many treatments for it. Nothing works for everyone, and something works for most people. However, most of the time, developing a constructive relationship with depression and one with an emotionally fluent human being will help guide the sufferer to the sources of the pain and, ultimately, to sources of healing and empowerment. Of all the ways we can support the empowerment of women, my best contribution is one woman at a time, from the inside out.

Janine Talty, DO, MPH, is an osteopathic physician, medical director of the Wellness and Rehabilitation Center in Watsonville, California, and assistant clinical professor in the Department of Manual Medicine at Michigan State University, College of Osteopathic Medicine, in East Lansing. Her practice focuses on diagnosing and treating musculoskeletal diagnostic dilemmas of the spine and extremities, sports medicine, pain management, Lyme disease, and natural hormone balance for women and men. Having had unusual artistic and healing talents since childhood, she discovered she is an "Indigo" and wrote the book *Indigo Awakening: A Doctor's Memoir of Forging an Authentic Life in a Turbulent World*.

The Power of Perception
Janine Talty

Mari, my receptionist, tossed the new-patient chart on the broad desk in my office and set right next to it an eight-inch stack of medical records—all imaging studies and consultation reports for my next patient. My morning had been filled with seeing chronic spinal pain patients, many of whom had consulted more than a dozen doctors, usually including a psychiatrist or two, before showing up at my door. Janet was a new referral from a colleague, a pain physician who practices in San Francisco, a ninety-mile drive north of the California coastal town where my clinic is located. He is widely considered the best in the United States in interventional pain management, and when even his injection treatments cannot alleviate chronic back or neck pain, he often sends the patient to me. My task is to unearth the proper diagnosis, the one missed by the gauntlet of referral doctors the patient has seen. Those physicians rely on the left-brain-dominant, masculine paradigm we are all taught in medical school. In the case of pain patients, this paradigm mainly offers technologically advanced imaging studies along with a cursory neurologic exam. For the toughest pain conditions, this is rarely enough.

After a quick look at the paperwork, I tapped on the examining room door and entered to meet Janet. She was an attractive woman in her early fifties, but her eyes showed the sullen, tired look of someone once again trying to muster up hope but by now all but resigned to disappointment. She sat stiffly in her chair, trying to manage the continuous pain in her mid-thoracic spine that had driven her from one doctor's office to another in search of relief. I introduced myself, extending my hand to make first contact, and sat down with her to spend the next thirty minutes taking her history.

My new-patient intake sessions have evolved during my thirteen years of practice into a multichanneled, multisensory process. With my training in sports medicine, osteopathic manual medicine, family practice, orthopedics, and clinical biomechanics, I approach a musculoskeletal diagnostic dilemma by first examining the entire neuromusculoskeletal system through the eyes of osteopathic manual medicine, a hands-on field now largely marginalized by the current trends in medicine toward seven-and-a-half-minute appointments, lab tests, and reimbursements based on passing out prescriptions. I begin to ask questions that allow me to piece together a strong impression of what I will likely find on the physical exam that follows. What I also find myself doing during these sessions is deeply listening and tuning into my body's energetic system as I sit in the patient's presence and am exposed to all that he or she is saying not with words. I feel the interview with my whole being, rather than simply hear the information.

As the interview progresses, I remain tuned into how I am feeling. Are we making eye contact and is there energy flowing between us? Am I feeling uplifted or drained by the patient's mood? I also assess where the information is coming in. Is it my forehead, throat, chest, abdomen, or pelvis? Each location tells me something about where the patient's energetic focus lies. As he or she describes how the injury took place, my brain's right hemisphere is creating a three-dimensional picture of the tissues and structures that are probably involved, as well as the direction and intensity of the force sustained to create the injury or degeneration.

Something else is going on as well. I am receiving intuitive information through the top of my head that assists me in knowing what treatments are needed and in what sequence to do them. This is the language of intuitive medicine, which, in my opinion, all human beings, including physicians, possess. Unfortunately, it is not mentioned in modern medical training.

I stepped out of the room while Janet changed into a cloth gown. When I returned, I consciously cleared my mind of everything she just told me and slipped into a familiar mental space where my entire being becomes a receiver of all the information that a patient's somatic system is willing to share.

Applying the laws of physics to the body, I observed her as I was taught as an osteopathic physician to "see" the anatomy with my hands, a skill that is threatened with extinction in medical training today. I palpated her system while it was in various positions, determining how her pelvis, sacrum, extremities, cranium, and each vertebral segment of her spine responded to different gravitational loads, stresses, strain patterns, and vectors in both the standing and lying positions. I assessed all of the muscle firing patterns and looked for the typical muscular tight/loose relationships that begin to emerge in all of us by the age of six and are exacerbated in chronic pain disorders. As I went through this exhaustive process, palpating the tissues, visualizing the deep and superficial tissues in my mind through my hands, the story that eluded the other physicians gradually began to tell itself.

The body's patterns of compensatory mechanisms always tell the history of the injury or degenerative process for an observer perceptive enough to hear it. Treating each restriction using osteopathic manual medicine techniques reveals the next sedimentary layer of adaptation the body employed so it could keep performing under mounting restrictive challenges. Treating each subsequent area of greatest restriction while listening to the body's story

reveals an account of the forces that caused injuries in car accidents, at work, during sports activities, or simply through the re-
petitive strain of daily life.

While removing restrictions, I also reset the neurologic motor
control mechanisms at the spinal cord and cortical levels, restoring normal tissue tension and range of motion permanently. What
results is often nothing short of remarkable. Patients who have
had pain for years, sometimes decades, frequently feel immedi-
ate improvement, restored to a sense of lightness, flexibility, and
strength. Many confide to my receptionist as they leave the clinic
that their osteopathic biomechanical exam transcended all previous experiences they have had with the medical system. A surprising number add that they feel as though their soul has undergone
an unusual contact experience.

The Missing Touch

Part of what makes this method of clinical examination and
treatment so different is the key element of touch. What happens
when a healer touches a patient? Healing touch unconsciously reminds us of what we felt when we were lovingly touched as infants
and children. We felt safe and cared for; we felt seen, validated,
and nurtured. Touch is our first mode of communication. It is also
our richest source of perception and our most subtle yet powerful
means of expression.

Sadly, in today's medical schools, touch is discussed only in the
context of how to stay out of trouble with disgruntled patients and
their attorneys. There is "clinical touch," appropriate when a physician is examining a patient. Especially before performing a pelvic
or genital exam, we are trained to tell the patient what we are
going to do before we do it and to perform a "warning touch" in a
less personal but nearby area of the body so the patient doesn't feel
invaded or get the wrong impression. There is also "social touch,"
as in a handshake or when the physician puts a steadying hand on
the shoulder of a trembling patient.

I call the type of touch I use in my practice "unconditional touch," a safe, inquisitive, nurturing contact that communicates deep concern to seek out and understand what is ailing the body. There is a lot of physical contact during this kind of examination and treatment. It has to be this way not only to diagnose but also to treat each restriction in the body. Patients do not misconstrue this kind of touch, however, but clearly recognize it as unconditional love expressed through the healing hand.

The physical body, in my view, is a biological computer that holds and stores "data" in specific places. It "remembers" when it was improperly touched or when it sustained any sort of trauma. During an exam, the energetic communication through touch between doctor and patient is profound, as if an electrical circuit is created through which energy and intuitive information can be received and transmitted one to the other. Opening up this level of soulfully honest nonverbal communication allows the patient and his or her body to feel safe on a subconscious level and begin to let go of the hurt, anxiety, and trauma that always surround a pain experience.

Free of Pain

As Janet's session drew to a close, I asked her to sit up and then to move in the ways that an hour earlier would have caused her severe thoracic spinal pain. Almost in disbelief, she discovered that the pain was gone. Reevaluating her in a standing position, I had her stand in shoes with arch supports. Now that her restrictions had been identified and treated, her somatic system revealed the primary problem. Her fallen arches in both feet, the left worse than right, were placing an asymmetric tibial torsion on the ankle and knee, creating a virtual leg-length discrepancy on the left that unleveled her pelvis, side-bending it to the left, creating a compensatory scoliosis of her spine along with pelvic and sacral rotational restrictions. With support under the arches of both feet, the leg lengths became equal and all of the asymmetry and mechanical stress resolved.

But this was not all that happened during Janet's treatment. After I had restored her pelvis, lumbar spine, and sacrum to neutral position, I asked her to sit up so I could work on her thoracic spine. Palpating down her back, one vertebral segment at a time, I noted how hard her fourth and fifth thoracic segments were. They felt more like concrete than living tissue. As my hands paused on the transverse processes of her fourth thoracic segment, I began to experience what I can only describe as an electrical surge that came in through the back of my head and down my spine, circulating through my arms and hands into her. It lasted only seconds.

This now familiar but still curious electrical current often causes all kinds of strange things to occur. At that moment, Janet broke into tears, and through her deep sobs, she shared that her only son had died in a car accident eight years before, when he was a senior in high school. As the barrage of emotion poured forth, she and I relived some of the events that had impacted her during that time and the guilt she never expressed to her family and friends, thinking they would somehow blame her for her son's decision to drink and drive. It seemed that she had been holding the "data" of this unresolved trauma and grief in the segments of her mid-thoracic spine, right behind her heart. Energetically, the mid-thoracic segments contain the heart chakra, the energy center of the body that stores information regarding emotion, love, and forgiveness. It is also a natural transition area for the mechanical forces moving through the spine in a scoliosis condition. With her fallen arches creating a functional scoliosis and binding the tissues in this particular area, she was unable to process and forgive herself for the death of her son.

Janet was pain-free after her first visit, but she returned for two additional appointments, still not quite believing that it could really have been this simple. No needles, scalpels, drugs, or even electricity—just a physician who combines the ancient art of soul healing with a technologically advanced, outcome-based medical tradition that uses touch. I recommended that she use arch supports to prevent the mechanical pattern from reestablishing itself, and she also followed up with a spiritually oriented grief counselor. After all the procedures that she had been through over the years, not to mention the thousands of dollars spent, she was finally free of the medical system.

The Surge

I first experienced the "surge," as I now call what came through me into Janet's fourth vertebra and then through her body, ten years ago when I was treating a colleague scheduled to undergo an open heart procedure the next day. This current blasted through me and into him, leaving us both startled and conveying to him a profound reassurance that his operation would be a success and he would be safe.

It began happening with a few other patients, usually when I had my hands on their temporal bones while finishing their treatments with craniosacral therapy. As I cleared my mind of all thought, a very physical surge of electrical current would come crashing down through the back of my head and circulate through my nervous system, jettisoning down my spinal cord, down my legs and back up, then exploding out my chest and through my arms and hands into the patient, who was lying face up on the table. Feeling it, patients began asking what it was. I would tell them I wished I knew. They described all kinds of physical, emotional, or spiritual experiences that occurred for them during the surge. These experiences were consistently healing and positive, so I remained merely curious as they continued and simply noted them in the patients' charts. Early on, when I was first adjusting to this phenomenon, I would occasionally see imagery in my head with my eyes closed that would turn out to be some part of the patient's story that he or she had been unable to share consciously at the moment.

Over the years, I have worked with this phenomenon, manipulating my intention, body position, and physiology to become a clearer channel for bringing it through. Gradually, I learned how to initiate it by what feels like voluntarily contracting my optic nerves down into my brain stem, creating what feels like a vortex in the middle of my skull between my ears and eyes that then turns into a sort of funnel, drawing the energy down through my spinal cord, back, and legs, then circulating back up and careening out my chest, arms, and hands into the patient. Its occurrence seems to depend on the electrical resonance among the three components: the patient, the surge, and myself. Just like tuning into a radio signal, the frequencies must be of the same magnitude and character. I am simply the resonant conduit through which the surge passes. If the person's (the receiver's) electrical frequency does not match that of the surge (the transmitter), the signal fades away in my hands, never entering the patient's system.

My curiosity about this phenomenon—what it was, what it meant, and why it was happening to me—set me off on a personal odyssey across the globe to visit sacred sites, ley lines, and indigenous healers in search of an explanation. That journey led me to the discovery that I am what is called an Indigo Adult, and that I am not the only one.

The Evolutionary Healer

"Indigo children" is a term for special, oft-considered challenging children, the common characteristics of which teachers, parents, and psychologists first identified in the mid-1980s. Ancient prophesy foretold their arrival, however, as a new generation of people with unusual talents and abilities, the next evolution of the human species. Indigos seem to arrive on the planet already hardwired with advanced ancient knowledge and skills. Often, they already know what the conventional school systems are teaching, so they became bored in class and may begin to get fidgety and act out. They learn differently, detest authority of any kind, and frequently begin changing the systems to which they are expected to conform. Psychic by nature, with the ability to manipulate energy and access knowledge they have not been taught, they stand out, which is sometimes unsettling to the adults who care for them. Altruistic, honest, and with high moral standards, they seem to be on a mission to change and improve society's systems and ways of doing things that are no longer serving us. Some say that they are here to shake everything up. And currently they are not all children. In fact, an estimated 50 percent of all people born in 1970 are of this persuasion, as are an estimated 12 percent of those who are now sixty years and older.

Unaware of Indigos until I was in my early forties, I recognized my own life story as I read about them. As a child, I was on a relentless quest, beyond all odds, to become the doctor I knew I was. Considered mentally retarded until sixth grade because my brain worked differently, I could not grasp reading, writing, or arithmetic. I exhibited other curious traits and characteristics that seemed unacceptable to the world around me. I could communicate telepathically with animals and some adults, I was psychic and had clear images of what I later understood were past life events, and I thought in pictures and in three dimensions, to name but a few. I was alone in my struggle, all the while aware that it served a purpose in the grooming process I sensed was afoot. I needed to experience the full spectrum of human emotion, including disappointment, pain, and despair, so I could one day in my work with others draw on what it taught me.

The small but increasing number of doctors who seem to be Indigos utilize their inherent intuitive skills to read and manipulate energy when diagnosing and treating their patients. Few discuss it openly, and many are not even aware they are doing it. Some whom I have gotten to know rely on these skills as their first mode of diagnosis, despite what the objective medical data might show. One female internist simply passes her hand over a sick patient's abdomen, sensing with her palm the energetic shifts, best described as variable intensities of tingling, while visualizing the tissues and organs that lie beneath.

This way of doing medicine is difficult to quantify; it does not lend itself to well-designed double-blind studies to prove its effectiveness. It uses feminine qualities of intuitive, kinesthetic, and sensory awareness that are the domain of the brain's right hemisphere. Yet accessing this level of awareness is not dependent on the physician's gender. It is simply a softer, gentler way of perceiving that allows profound levels of communication to occur. One male surgeon friend of mine says he sees with his hand and mind the cancer hiding deep in the tissue even if the CT scan looks normal. He admits to taking patients to the operating room despite the hard objective data and reports that he has saved many lives this way.

What effect might the presence of this kind of physician have on our medical delivery system? Today's health-care system is failing all of us—physician and patient alike. The highly advanced technology and services now available are too expensive to be made available to all who need them. The for-profit health insurance system and its focus on the bottom line is driving patients' and their physicians' choices, instead of choices being made for health. The need to keep costs down through efficiency has pushed the human-centered healing professions toward an industrial model that dabbles in dehumanization. With premiums rising yearly while services and physician reimbursements decrease, many doctors can no longer afford to practice privately and must join large groups or become employees of health-care corporations.

The change we seek may or may not come by revamping the currently broken and corrupt system, where special interests have a stranglehold. I personally believe it will come with changes in the practitioners. The physicians with Indigo gifts who are already in practice are here to help midwife the delivery of this new way of being in medicine. It is challenging to live in a time between worlds, when an old paradigm is being dismantled and the new one is not quite born. Yet I hold out the hope that one day health care and the deliverers of it will bring the elements

of true soul connection to medicine, utilizing whole-being listening, intuitive guidance, unconditional touch, and the power
of perception.

Debra Greene, PhD, is an energy health specialist who has worked with thousands of clients and has taught hundreds of workshops. She is recognized for her ability to get to the core of energy imbalances and facilitate lasting improvement. Author of *Endless Energy: The Essential Guide to Energy Health*, Debra is also the founder of Inner Clarity (IC), an integrative balancing method that uses energy kinesiology to pinpoint hidden limiting beliefs and a variety of energy based techniques to facilitate conscious transformation. www.InnerClarity.us

CHAPTER THIRTY-EIGHT

Energy Health and Hygiene— The Personal Is Planetary

Debra Greene

Whenever I teach a personal growth workshop, give a talk, or offer an Inner Clarity (IC) training, the majority of participants are women. In graduate level courses I've taught in holistic health and consciousness studies, 87 percent of the students were women. Colleagues who teach yoga, self-help, and meditation report mostly women in their classes. Among friends, women are the ones who lead men (sometimes willingly, sometimes kicking and screaming) into the new medicine. Indeed, the vast majority of clients in my practice are women.

Why is this? It's because women are natural healers. One of the main ways we accomplish this is through our sophisticated sensitivities to subtle energies. Maybe we are the products of socialization, perhaps it's genetically determined, maybe it's our collective karma, or it could be due to latent maternal instincts or good old-fashioned women's intuition. All I know is women have the ability and desire to tune in and take seriously the energetic realms. That's why women are perfectly poised to save the planet.

It's a good thing they are because when it comes to health care, we cannot rely on government to help us. Those wheels just turn too slowly, and sometimes even in the wrong direction! Any significant advances in the day-to-day health of families, relatives, lovers, friends, and even foes will happen, as it probably always has, at the insistence of women.

When I was a young woman, "the personal is political" was the resounding anthem of the times. Women all over the country were meeting in groups and talking to each other about their personal lives, a simple act that had widespread ramifications. The phrase was popularized by Carol Hanish in 1969 when she wrote an essay claiming that women's consciousness raising groups were not therapy groups, they were political action groups.

While honoring the importance of the original concept, I'd like to take it a step further. I'd like to suggest that *the personal is planetary*. I'm not talking about global warming, going green, or voting with your dollars (all important things). I'm talking about the seamless, uninterrupted continuum of energy that connects our most private inner thoughts and feelings with the totality of manifested existence, to the extent that we impact that totality on an ongoing basis by every thought we think, every word we utter, and every action we take (or choose not to take). I want to talk about this in terms of human health and the health of the planet because, in the new medicine, they cannot be separated.

The Energy Bodies

Simply put, everything is energy. All matter is condensed energy, including us. This energy takes different forms. In the case of humans, it takes the form of four distinct but overlapping levels of experience, or energy bodies. These are the physical, emotional, mental, and universal bodies. We humans exist on these four planes of experience simultaneously.

An example of what I'm talking about can be found in just about any situation. Let's say you're drinking a glass of water. You can experience this simple act on various levels at the same time. There is the physical sensation of the water in your mouth (its taste, texture, and temperature); there is the emotional aspect, meaning, how you feel while drinking (anxious, disappointed, irritated, joyous, etc.); and there are your thoughts (the mental stuff of ideas, memories, fantasies, criticisms). Your water drinking may even inspire a spiritual epiphany (what I call the universal level of experience). My point is, these various levels of experience are distinct, yet they overlap. Any one of them, or all of them, is available to you at any time. I'd like to talk about each of your four bodies—the vehicles through which you have these experiences—in a bit more detail, with particular focus on their health and hygiene.

Your four bodies represent an energy continuum ranging from the lowest, or slowest, vibratory frequency (the dense physical) to the highest, fastest, frequency (the enigmatic universal). As the bodies go up in frequency, they become more potent and have a greater impact on the lower frequency, denser bodies (think of the tone that shatters a glass). An example of this happens during dreamtime. If you're sleeping and dream you are being chased by a tiger, your emotional body reacts with fear, while your physical body responds with the accompanying increased heart rate and rapid breathing, even though the ordeal is only happening in your mind (mental body). Although there are factors that mitigate this, ultimately, the physical body has to obey the energetic commands of the higher frequency bodies—a key to energy health.

One of the ways it does this is through its etheric layer. Your physical body is not just physical. If it were, you would be lifeless and inanimate. There is a force that powers your physical body, enabling it to move and be vitalized. I refer to this energetic component as the *vital body*. It is woven into the physical through a series of energy capillaries, distribution channels, and power centers (sometimes referred to as the chakra and meridian systems). The physical and vital bodies are so intertwined that they must be understood as two sides of the same coin; you have a vital/physical body.

Energy Health for Your Vital/Physical Body

The intricate energy webs of the vital body are susceptible to subtle influences and require care and attention to maintain them—what amounts to vital body hygiene. An important first step in the hygiene process involves protecting yourself from electromagnetic radiation (EMR), an ever-increasing energy menace. The recent explosion in the use of cell phones and other wireless technologies means EMR is rapidly on the rise. This carries with it important energy health concerns not only for humans but for plants and animals too, as no living thing is exempt from the invisible radiation field that is slowly blanketing the Earth.

Because we spend, on average, seven hours per night in bed, one simple home hygiene technique is to create a three-foot safety zone around the beds in your home. This means removing all electronic and wireless devices within a three-foot radius (especially baby monitors, many of which operate on carrier signals in the microwave frequency range). Due to their developmental stages, children are especially susceptible to EMR, and they require special energy health care. For example, children should not use cell phones. Well, adults shouldn't either, for that matter, but if you plan to continue cell phone use, consider following some simple Safe Cell methods, outlined here.

- **The cell is not for kids.** No matter what advertisers may say, do not allow children (ideally to age fifteen, but especially through age seven) to use a cell phone, except for emergencies. Not only are children more susceptible to EMR, the health effects of long-term, cumulative use are of particular concern. Do not put a wireless baby monitor near your child's bed and don't use a cell phone if you are pregnant.

- **Limit cell use.** Don't use a cell phone for more than a few minutes at a time. Turn it on only to establish contact, then turn it off. Use a landline with a corded phone for longer conversations.

- **Keep the cell off your body.** Don't keep your cell phone in your pocket, in your bra, on your belt, or in your bed. Keep it as far away from your body as possible and transport it in a bag or briefcase.
- **Use speaker mode.** If you can't use the speaker mode, wait until your party has picked up before putting the phone to your ear. Switch ears regularly to spread out your exposure.
- **Text message instead of call.** This keeps the phone away from your body mass. Put the phone down after sending as it emits radiation/signals even when texting.
- **Avoid others' cells.** Keep a safe distance from other people's cell phones and avoid using yours in places where you expose others to secondhand radiation/signals.
- **No cell in the car.** Don't use a cell phone inside a car (or other enclosed metal space) because the metal traps the microwave signals inside, potentially turning your car into a mobile microwave oven with you inside.
- **Keep the cell turned off** (or in offline mode) until you need to use it. Make calls and access all your voicemails, e-mails, and texts at once, then turn it off again.
- **Use a safe cell position.** If you must carry a cell phone on you, position the phone so the keypad is facing toward your body and the back of the phone is facing outward. This may help the frequencies to flow away from, rather than through, your body.
- **Beware of movement.** Don't use a cell phone when moving at high speed (i.e., in a car or subway). This will cause it to ramp up in power, producing more radiation, as it repeatedly searches for new relay towers.
- **Beware of SAR.** Don't mistake a low SAR (specific absorption rate) rating for cell phone safety. The FCC and mainstream science do not recognize the existence of the

vital body, thus, SAR ratings are meaningless in terms of energy health.

Energy Health for Your Emotional Body

In addition to your vital body, let's take a look at another aspect of your energy constitution, your emotional body. One important thing to know about your emotional body is that it is prone to being either overweight or underweight. Of course, since it is an energy body and has no actual weight, I am speaking metaphorically. But the idea of an over- or underweight emotional body is helpful in understanding emotional body hygiene.

Feelings are food for the emotional body and if yours tends to be overweight, you will experience roller-coaster rides of emotional intensity; in other words, lots of drama. In contrast, the underweight body is starved of emotional energy. In its emaciated state, it lacks emotional expression and tends to display the same hollow feeling (i.e., the plastic smile, the predictable grumpiness) no matter what the situation.

If your emotional body is obese, consider putting it on a diet. Take a break from emotional body junk foods like fear, anger, gossip, and irritation. Although this may be easier said than done, like most diets, a little awareness and a good dose of willpower can go a long way. Pay attention to what you are feeding your emotional body. Try keeping a journal to track your emotional diet. If you find yourself frequently indulging in the "high calorie" emotional junk foods, consciously choose out of those feeling states. I'm not talking about denying or suppressing emotions; I'm just suggesting that you not overindulge them if you want a fit and healthy emotional body.

Awareness can help an underweight condition as well, but in a different way. If your emotional body is undernourished, remind yourself, on a daily basis, to feed this body by bringing awareness to your feelings. Ask yourself what you are feeling in any given situation and name your feelings in words (i.e., I feel disappointed, happy, anxious, frustrated). When making decisions, balance out rational analysis by allowing your feelings, and those of others, to have a place in your process.

Regardless of your emotional body type, it will benefit from compassion. Compassion is a high vibration energy that has the capacity to restore and sustain the emotional body, constituting a good energy hygiene practice. Imagine you are walking down a sidewalk when someone steps sharply on your foot from behind. Angered, you turn around to give the culprit a piece of your mind only to find that it's an elderly woman struggling with a cane. You move from anger to compassion in less than a nanosecond. There's no need to process the anger, no need to release it, no need to talk about it. That choice is always yours. You can shift into compassion at any time and, in so doing, recalibrate your energy system to a higher, healthier frequency.

Ammachi, the hugging saint who so readily embodies the divine mother, points out there are two kinds of poverty—material poverty and emotional poverty. She says emotional poverty is more crucial, for if we address emotional poverty by teaching compassion, the material poverty will be taken care of; when there is compassion we automatically want to give to others. Born into a poor family in southern India with no formal schooling past age nine, Amma is a living example of the power of compassion. She has personally, physically embraced more than twenty-seven million people and, through her organization, has donated tens of million dollars to help the disadvantaged on a global basis. It all started with a hug.

Energy Health for Your Mental Body

The next higher vibratory level of your energy constitution is your mental body, the domain of thoughts. Because your mental body is calibrated toward the higher end of the frequency spectrum, its effects are particularly potent. Most of us don't realize this and so we allow a constant stream of random thoughts to run endlessly through our minds without discrimination. From the perspective of energy health, thoughts are things. They have certain properties and carry specific frequencies that can significantly impact our health.

Good mental hygiene requires vigilance and self-discipline to eradicate unwanted thought-forms. Concentration is the hallmark of a healthy mental body. A beneficial practice is to become aware of your thoughts on an ongoing basis, not just when you can't seem to shut them off. Pay particular attention to the overall quality of your thoughts: Do they tend to be optimistic, uplifting, and inspirational or opinionated, judgmental, and limiting? If your thoughts offend you, instead of attempting to cut them off, try replacing them with more desirable thoughts. Directing energy into controlling your own thoughts is much healthier than wasting energy trying to change or avoid other people.

Our brains are like antennas that broadcast and receive thought-forms. The thought-forms act as mobile magnets and attract corresponding energies as they travel to their recipients. For most women, this comes as little surprise because we so readily pick up on the thoughts of others, especially our children and husbands (much to their dismay)! But knowledge of the subtle world carries with it responsibility. Our private thoughts are not our own. They energetically affect others in invisible yet powerful ways that call forth a new level of ethics and awareness. We must extend the ethic of care that psychologist Carol Gilligan so insightfully identified as the domain of the feminine. We must be careful (full of care) with what we think.

The goal is to have every thought a consciously chosen thought, every action a consciously chosen action. This doesn't mean losing spontaneity and becoming rigid; it simply means an end to automatic reactions, programmed patterns, and unconscious behaviors. This brings us to the next higher frequency body of your subtle energy constitution—the universal body.

Energy Health for Your Universal Body

If the substance of your vital body is vitality, the substance of your emotional body is feelings, and the substance of your mental body is thoughts, what, then, is the substance of your universal body? It can't be vitality, emotions, or thoughts because when you are not moving, feeling, or thinking, you still exist. There is something more to you. What occupies the space between thoughts? What is the singular, constant backdrop upon which everything plays out and from which everything emerges? Yes, consciousness. It is the highest, fastest frequency domain of your energy makeup.

Essentially unitive in nature, consciousness is the great mediator, the "glue" that holds your energy bodies together so that you act as a coherent whole and can connect the dots of your multitudinous experiences. It is also the high-powered energy that connects all of us together, allowing for the palpable experience of unity consciousness.

Similar to your entire energy constitution, consciousness is a continuum. It ranges from selective consciousness (wherever you choose to direct your attention) on one end of the spectrum to unity consciousness (the oneness of all) on the other end. This means your personal attention span is an offshoot of unity consciousness! Therefore, use and care of the universal body involves becoming aware of what you choose to pay attention to in any given moment, knowing that your choice is contributing to the entirety of consciousness, simultaneously affecting everyone everywhere.

Consciousness is a dynamic field of all awareness that we constantly participate in. When choices are of a lower vibration, we pull the collective down, but the converse is also true. As in the proverbial hundredth monkey, we can actively contribute to the tipping point, to the quickening of critical mass. The more we transform and shift, the more we help uplift.

Women invented the personal growth movement. Women have continued to embrace it, to advance it, and to demand that it extend to its logical conclusion—the universal level. Our overwhelming participation in personal growth is exponentially accelerating the collective consciousness, raising the mass vibration. By doing the inner work, becoming energy healthy, women are powerfully saving the planet, one person at a time.

> As you work with your own energy
> Any expansion of consciousness you may achieve
> No matter how small it may seem to be
> Helps to uplift all of humanity

Part VIII:
Living Goddess Wisdom

Maya Angelou is a poet, writer, performer, teacher, director, and life-time African American activist. Among her many published works are a five-volume autobiography, which began in 1970 with *I Know Why the Caged Bird Sings,* and the collections of verse *And Still I Rise* and *Just Give Me a Cool Drink of Water 'Fore I Die*. In 1993, she wrote and read the poem *On the Pulse of Morning* at Bill Clinton's presidential inauguration, at his request. It was only the second time a poet had been asked to read at an inauguration, the first being Robert Frost at the inauguration of John F. Kennedy.

Letter to My Daughter
Maya Angelou

Dear Daughter,

This letter has taken an extraordinary time getting itself together. I have all along known that I wanted to tell you directly of some lessons I have learned and under what conditions I have learned them.

My life has been long, and believing that life loves the liver of it, I have dared to try many things, sometimes trembling, but daring, still.

There have been people in my life who meant me well, taught me valuable lessons, and others who have meant me ill, and have given me ample notification that my world is not meant to be all peaches and cream.

I have made many mistakes and no doubt will make more before I die. When I have seen pain, when I have found that my ineptness has caused displeasure, I have learned to accept my responsibility and to forgive myself first, then to apologize to anyone injured by my misreckoning. Since I cannot un-live history, and repentance is all I can offer God, I have hopes that my sincere apologies were accepted.

You may not control all the events that happen to you, but you can decide not to be reduced by them. Try to be a rainbow in someone's cloud. Do not complain. Make every effort to change things you do not like. If you cannot make a change, change the way you have been thinking. You might find a new solution.

Never whine. Whining lets a brute know that a victim is in the neighborhood.

Be certain that you do not die without having done something wonderful for humanity.

I gave birth to one child, a son, but I have thousands of daughters. You are Black and White, Jewish and Muslim, Asian, Spanish-speaking, Native American and Aleut. You are fat and thin and pretty and plain, gay and straight, educated and unlettered, and I am speaking to you all. Here is my offering to you.

*   *   *   *   *

Keep the Faith

Many things continue to amaze me, even well into my seventh decade. I'm startled or at least taken aback when people walk up to me and without being questioned inform me that they are Christians. My first response is the question "Already?"

It seems to me that becoming a Christian is a lifelong endeavor. I believe that is also true for one wanting to become a Buddhist, or a Muslim, a Jew, Jainist, or a Taoist. The persons striving to live their religious beliefs know that the idyllic condition cannot be arrived at and held on to eternally. It is in the search itself that one finds the ecstasy.

The Depression, which was so difficult for everyone to survive, was especially so for a single black woman in the Southern states tending her crippled adult son and raising two small grandchildren.

One of my earliest memories of my grandmother, who was called "Mamma," is a glimpse of that tall, cinnamon-colored woman with a deep, soft voice, standing thousands of feet up in the air with nothing visible beneath her.

Whenever she confronted a challenge, Mamma would clasp her hands behind her back, look up as if she could will herself into the heavens, and draw herself up to her full six-foot height. She would tell her family in particular, and the world in general, "I don't know how to find the things we need, but I will step out on the word of God. I am trying to be a Christian and I will just step out on the word of God." Immediately I could see her flung into space, moons at her feet and stars at her head, comets swirling around her shoulders. Naturally, since she was over six feet tall, and stood out on the word of God, she was a giant in heaven. It wasn't difficult for me to see Mamma as powerful, because she had the word of God beneath her feet.

Thinking of my grandmother years later, I wrote a gospel song that has been sung rousingly by the Mississippi Mass choir.

You said to lean on your arm
And I am leaning
You said to trust in your love
And I am trusting
You said to call on your name
And I am calling
I'm stepping out on your word.

Whenever I began to question whether God exists, I looked up to the sky and surely there, right there, between the sun and moon, stands my grandmother, singing a long meter hymn, a song somewhere between a moan and a lullaby and I know faith is the evidence of things unseen.

And all I have to do is continue trying to be a Christian.

Olympia Dukakis, actor, director, producer, teacher, and activist, was born to Greek immigrant parents in Massachusetts. She has been on stage and screen for more than forty years (fifty on the stage), earning myriad awards and accolades. With husband Louis Zorich, she founded the Whole Theatre Company in Montclair, New Jersey, and ran it for fifteen years, producing, directing, and acting in a range of theatrical classics. She describes the not-for-profit venue as "a collaborative venture of actors and directors and designers." Among her many films are *Steel Magnolias*, *In the Land of Women*, and *Moonstruck* (in which the role of Rose won her Academy, Golden Globe, and BAFTA awards). A close friend of archaeologist Marija Gimbutas, she narrated *Signs Out of Time*, a documentary on her life and work.

Celebrate Her

Olympia Dukakis

I went into rehearsal at the Whole Theatre for *The Trojan Women,* by the great Greek playwright Euripides, directed by my brother, Apollo. I was to play Hecuba, the queen of Troy. As her beloved city burns around her, Hecuba survives the loss of her husband and son, and now must watch as her daughters become slaves. She herself will become the slave of her conqueror, Odysseus. There is a moment late in the play when Hecuba falls to her knees and beats the ground with her fists, crying, "Do you see? Do you hear? Do you know?" I was puzzled. "Who is she talking to? What is she trying to make happen?" Apollo suggested that perhaps she's appealing to her ancestors. Now I was completely intrigued.

A week later, I went to my favorite used bookstore in Montclair to buy token opening-night gifts for the cast and crew. I could always find treasures within my budget at the aptly named Yesterday's Books. From a box in the back of the store, I pulled out a small book called *Perseus and the Gorgon,* by Cornelia Steketee Hulst, an archaeologist who wrote about a 1911 dig on the island of Corfu. The book was dedicated to Gorgo, a goddess figure from Greek mythology—she with the hair of writhing snakes—so terrifying that anyone who gazed at her would turn to stone. According to Hulst, the Gorgon of Corfu had once been the goddess Ashirat (which means happiness, energy, and joy). When the island was overrun by Perseus (whose name means "to lay waste"), he cut off her head and sacked her temple. He also decided that her name should be stricken from all written records and that henceforth she should only be known as Gorgon, the snake goddess. In describing what Perseus had done, Hulst wrote that he had "buried in oblivion and covered with silence the teachings of the Great Mother." This line struck me with so much resonance. What teachings was Hulst talking about? Who was the Great Mother? I bought the book for two dollars, but instead of giving it as a gift, I kept it for myself and continued reading.

Finding Hulst's book marked the beginning of an extraordinary time of reading and discovery for me. I wanted to know who the Great Mother was and why her teachings had been buried in oblivion. I began to look for information about this history—or, rather, this prehistory—wherever I could find it. Information and material on this subject began to find its way to me in extraordinarily serendipitous ways. For example, just a few weeks after coming across Hulst's book, I wandered into a Buddhist bookshop in the East Village and a book fell off the shelf, landing at my feet. The book was called *When God Was a Woman,* by Merlin Stone. She had used archaeological evidence and historical documents to piece together a compelling portrait of the Goddess religion that predated the Judeo-Christian legend of Adam and Eve. Merlin Stone was the beginning of my passionate interest in prehistory. The phrase "buried in oblivion, covered in silence" stirred my heart. Merlin Stone's book opened my eyes.

Then I went to school. I read everything I could find. I'd read one book, check the bibliography, and find other authors to read. Esther Harding's *Women's Mysteries,* Barbara G. Walker's *Woman's Encyclopedia of Myths and Secrets* and her *Woman's Dictionary of Symbols and Sacred Objects.* And on and on. I began to understand that there was a time when the feminine was celebrated. When men and women worshiped a Goddess who was revered as the wise creator and the source for universal order and harmony. It wasn't until the ascension of Greek male-oriented culture, when the Goddess began to be perceived as threatening, that these matrifocal cultures were dismantled and even erased from the historical record. I became a sponge for any information I could find about the Goddess and prehistorical culture. I felt I had found something of incalculable value that I had somehow lost or misplaced. I kept reading.

Then something inexplicable happened to me. I was lying on a massage table, and while the masseuse was working on me, I slowly became aware that there was someone—something?—else in the room. I opened my eyes and there was nothing there. When I closed them, the sensation came back. I sensed a large, androgynous presence in the room. From the back of my head I heard a voice say, "Celebrate Her. Celebrate Her."

I got frightened and started to cry. The masseuse asked what was the matter with me. I was very reluctant to admit what I just experienced. I was afraid she'd think I had lost it—I was wondering if I had lost it—but I finally told her about the presence and the voice. She said, "Well, say something back." I started to cry even harder. "I don't know how. I don't know how to celebrate Her. I know how to suffer, but not how to celebrate." Then the voice spoke again. "You are of Her. You will know how to celebrate Her."

I asked the masseuse never to tell anyone what had happened. On the way home, I decided it was some aural hallucination brought on by stress. I kept it completely to myself.

The next time it happened, I'd just gotten off the N train at Forty-second Street and was angrily pushing my way through the rush-hour crowd on the ramp, trying to make the five-thirty bus. I was late as usual. Everyone was moving so slowly, my patience was at an end. I couldn't bear the thought of having to wait another thirty minutes if I missed the bus. I had to get home and make dinner for the kids.

Then I heard a voice, as if it were coming through a loudspeaker, saying, "Turn around, turn around." This time I wasn't scared, I just turned around. Below me on the ramp and the platform was a sea of people. I heard the voice say, "She loves everyone."

Call it aural hallucination. Call it inner perception. Or even a spiritual experience. Whether it comes from a female essence of a male essence, the message is, we are loved.

I received a script from a Greek-American screenwriter who I agreed to meet with. During the course of our meeting, it turned out she had worked as a translator for the controversial archaeologist Marija Gimbutas [see Chapter 5]. I asked that she introduce me.

Marija Gimbutas was a feisty, clear-headed, and brilliant woman. She was an impeccable scholar with a sense of humor and a reverential respect for the mystical. When we first met, she was skeptical about me: after all, I was a movie actress. But she soon realized that my interest was genuine, that I wanted to learn more about her and her work.

Marija's book *Goddesses and Gods of Old Europe* is considered a classic text, spearheading the study of Goddess cultures and prehistory as a legitimate discipline. Through her scholarship, Marija created a portrait of life during prehistory. She showed that in Goddess cultures there was no separation between the secular and the sacred, and that societies were built around the realities of the cyclical nature of life: the processes of birth, death, and regeneration. These civilizations enjoyed a long period (several thousand years) of uninterrupted peaceful living, and they predate the ages of weaponry and male-established hierarchical systems. What first struck Marija was how no weapons were ever found from earlier cultures, which were highly sophisticated and productive. They were built on patterns of sexual equality and nonviolence. Central to these cultures was a queen or priestess who encouraged and promoted unity and an understanding of the divinity within all living things. Her work had a major influence on my thinking, and meeting her turned out to be one of the most important encounters of my life.

I worked, between projects at the theater, compiling material, hoping to create something related to the Goddess culture for the stage.

The Goddess Project moved forward. I elected a director, and together with the writer we structured an evening in two parts. Part One was "Women's Passages," about the three stages of a woman's life central to Goddess worship and culture: Virgin, Mother, and Crone. In Part Two, we dramatized a version of the Sumerian myth of Inanna. In this story, the goddess Inanna, who reigns supreme in the world above, descends into the underworld to visit her exiled sister, Ereshkigal, who reigns over the world below.

One interpretation of the Sumerian myth is that Inanna and Ereshkigal represent two aspects of the female essence, one that is "acceptable" and therefore can live aboveground, and one that is "unacceptable" and must reside belowground. For me, Ereshkigal exemplifies that aspect of woman that is "buried in oblivion and covered in silence." As we enact it, the two sisters are given an opportunity to see and know each other, becoming a tale of rebirth and regeneration. Our first performance was at the Whole Theatre; it was a physical, exhausting, exhilarating evening. At the end, the audience jumped to their feet and I went to find my mother. She looked at me in wonder and said, "I never thought I'd live to see anything like this." My satisfaction in making this happen for her was profound.

Oprah Winfrey may be the best-known woman in the world. In addition to her long-running talk show, her media empire extends into movies, books, and magazines. The *Oprah Winfrey* show is broadcast in more than one hundred countries, and including her magazines and other media, Oprah reaches hundreds of millions of people each week. She is on the *Time* list of "100 people who most influenced the twentieth century" and has been on the magazine's annual list of "the most influential people" for the past five years running. A model for overcoming adversity, she is famously known for helping others do the same, through her show, her nonprofit Angel Network, and her personal philanthropy. www.Oprah.com
Disclaimer: This chapter has not been prepared, endorsed, or licensed by Oprah Winfrey or any person or entity affiliated with Oprah Winfrey, Harpo Productions, Inc., or related properties.

CHAPTER FORTY-ONE

Living the Church Inside
Oprah Winfrey

Oprah is the first African-American woman to become a billionaire, and she did so without pillaging her competitors or exploiting the planet. In all the projects and ventures she offers to the world, she demonstrates compassion and integrity. Thus she is one of those who are modeling the new leadership—embodying the Goddess Shift—on a grand scale. The fact that she is one of our cultural icons is a sign of our growing health as a species, that more and more we are choosing oneness rather than divisiveness, compassion rather than domination, inclusion rather than exclusion, and fairness rather than injustice.

Although she is usually the interviewer, not the interviewee, Oprah has written and said a great deal that illuminates her values and beliefs. Here is a selection of quotes from her about her journeys and discoveries that reflect some facets of this genuinely intriguing human being.

"I learned to read at age three and soon discovered there was a whole world to conquer that went beyond our farm in Mississippi.[1] Books showed me there were possibilities in life, that there were actually people like me living in a world I could not only aspire to but attain. Reading gave me hope. For me, it was the open door."[2]

"For every one of us that succeeds, it's because there's somebody there to show you the way out. The light doesn't necessarily have to be in your family; for me it was teachers and school."[3]

"If you grow up a bully and that works, that's what you do. If you're the class clown and that works, that's what you do. I was always the smartest kid in class and that worked for me—by third grade I had it figured out. So, I was the one who would read the assignment early and turn the paper in ahead of time. That makes everyone else hate you, but that's what worked for me."[4]

"If I wasn't doing this, I'd be teaching fourth grade. I'd be the same person I always wanted to be, the greatest fourth-grade teacher, and win the Teacher of the Year award. But I'll settle for twenty-three Emmys and the opportunity to speak to millions of people each day and, hopefully, teach some of them."[5]

"As I peeled away the layers of my life, I realized that all my craziness, all my pain and difficulties, stemmed from me not valuing myself. And what I now know is that every single bit of pain I have experienced in my life was a result of me worrying about what another person was going to think of me."[6]

"I understand that many people are victimized, and some people certainly more horribly than I have been. But you have to be responsible for claiming your own victories, you really do. If you live in the past and allow the past to define who you are, then you never grow."[7]

"I am a woman in progress. I'm just trying, like everyone else. I try to take every conflict, every experience, and learn from it. All I know is that I can't be anybody else. And it's taken me a long time to realize that."[8]

"To me, one of the most important things about being a good manager is to rule with a heart. You have to know the business, but you also have to know what's at the heart of the business, and that's the people. People matter."[9]

"I don't invest in anything that I don't understand—it makes more sense to buy TV stations than oil wells."[10]

"I'm trying to create more balance, spend more time with my boyfriend, and concentrate on the things that are important. Because all the money in the world doesn't mean a thing if you don't have time to enjoy it."[11]

"I go into the closet in my makeup room and I just close the door. Here, standing among the shoes, I'll just close my eyes and pause for a minute to re-center myself. Because after I tape two shows, I know that there will be six people outside my office wanting to see me about one thing or another."[12]

"Before it was just a view [of Lake Michigan from my Chicago apartment]. And from season to season I would never see daylight. I'd come in to work at 5:30 in the morning when it was dark, and leave at 7:00 or 8:00 when it was dark. I went from garage to garage. This morning, I actually took time to enjoy the sun rising over the lake while I was drinking my cup of coffee. I actually allowed myself to see the sun reflected off the water and make it look like glass."[13]

"I've realized it's very simple things that make me happy, but that I have to be open to happiness. I have to want to be happy rather than just busy. And once I am more willing to be happy, it becomes easier for me to feel the happiness."[14]

"People have this fear of success. They're afraid if they get it, they can't keep it. I don't have a fear of it at all. Everything you do in life indicates how your life goes. I don't want to go all spiritual on you, but I just have always had this sense of connection. I was always a very eloquent child, and when I was twelve years old, I was paid five hundred dollars to speak at a church. I was visiting my dad and I remember coming home that night and telling him that was what I wanted to do for a living—to be paid to talk. I told my daddy then and there that I planned to be very famous."[15]

"For me, greatness isn't determined by fame. I don't know if you want to be famous. I don't know if you want to go to the bathroom and have people say, 'Is that you in there?' 'What is she doing?' That is the price of fame—and then reading about it in the tabloids. I don't know if you want that for yourselves, but I do believe that what you want is a sense of greatness. What Dr. King says, greatness is determined by service."[16]

"I'd like to set the record straight and let people know I really am not defined by dollars. I would do what I'm doing even if I weren't getting paid. And I was doing this when I was getting paid much, much less. At my first job in broadcasting, my salary was one hundred dollars a week. But I was just as excited about making that amount of money and doing what I love to do as I am now."[17]

"The external part of my life—where I live and what I drive, and what kind of panty hose I wear and can afford, and that kind of stuff—none of that stuff in the end means anything. The thing I'm most proud of is that I have acquired a lot of things, but not one of those things defines me…it feels like something outside of myself. It doesn't feel like me. It doesn't feel like who I am."[18]

"I remember when I was four, watching my Grandma boil clothes in a huge iron pot. I was crying and Grandma asked, 'What the matter with you, girl?' 'Big Mammy,' I sobbed, 'I'm going to die someday.' 'Honey,' she said, 'God doesn't mess with His children. You gotta do a lot of work in your life and not be afraid. The strong have got to take care of the others.'

"I soon came to realize that my grandma was loosely translating from the Epistle to the Romans in the New Testament—'We that are strong ought to bear the infirmities of the weak.' Despite my age, I somehow grasped the concept. I knew I was going to help people, that I had a higher calling, so to speak."[19]

"What I now feel is reenergized by a vision of empowerment in the ability to use television in a way that I know can be even more profound. To use the connection that I have established over the years with the viewers in such a way that lets them think about themselves differently, be moved to their own personal greatness."[20]

"I have church with myself: I have church walking down the street. I believe in the God force that lives inside all of us, and once you tap into that, you can do anything."[21]

"Because I'm so connected to the bigger picture of what God is, I realize I'm just a particle in the God chain. I see God as the ocean, and I'm a cup of water from the ocean."[22]

"Everything that happens to you happens for a reason—everything you do in your life comes back to you. I call it 'Divine Reciprocity.' That's why I try to be kind to people—more for my sake than theirs."[23]

"What I try to do is get God on the whisper. He always whispers first. Try to get the whisper before the earthquake comes because the whisper is always followed by a little louder voice, then you get a brick, I say, and then sometimes a brick wall, and then the earthquake comes. Try to get it on the whisper."[24]

"I believe we are all given the power to use our lives as instruments. What we think is what manifests in reality for all of us. If all of us would only strive for excellence in our own backyards, we would bring that excellence to the rest of the world. Yes, we would."[25]

1. "Oprah Donates $100,000 to Harold Washington Library," *Jet,* Oct. 7, 1991, p. 18.
2. Alan Ebert, "Oprah Winfrey Talks Openly About Oprah," *Good Housekeeping,* Sept. 1991, p. 62.
3. Stedman Graham, *You Can Make It Happen Every Day* (New York: Simon & Schuster, 1988), p. 136.
4. Marcia Ann Gillespie, "Winfrey Takes All," *Ms.,* Nov. 1988, p. 54.
5. Oprah Winfrey, Interview, America Online, Oct. 3, 1995.
6. Laura B. Randolph, "Oprah Opens Up About Her Weight, Her Wedding, and Why She Withheld the Book," *Ebony,* Oct. 1993, p. 131.
7. Lyn Torrnabene, "Here's Oprah," *Woman's Day,* Oct. 1, 1996, p. 59.
8. Miriam Kanner, "Oprah at 40: What She's Learned the Hard Way," *Ladies' Home Journal,* Feb. 1994, p. 96.
9. Gretchen Reynolds, "A Year to Remember: Oprah Grows Up." *TV Guide,* Jan. 7, 1995, p. 15.
10. "Oprah Winfrey, Media Magnate," *Esquire,* Dec. 1989, p. 114.
11. Linden Gross, "Oprah Winfrey, Wonder Woman," *Ladies' Home Journal,* Dec. 1988, p. 40.

12. Melina Gerosa, "Oprah: Fit for Life," *Ladies' Home Journal*, Feb. 1996, p. 108.

13. Joanna Powell, "I Was Trying to Fill Something Deeper," *Good Housekeeping*, Oct. 1996, p. 80.

14. Pearl Cleage, "Walking in the Light," *Essence*, June 1991, p. 48.

15. Judy Markey, "Brassy, Sassy Oprah Winfrey," *Cosmopolitan*, Sep. 1986, p. 96.

16. Oprah Winfrey, Graduation Address, Wesleyan University, Middletown, Connecticut, May 1998.

17. Susan Taylor, "An Intimate Talk with Oprah," *Essence*, Aug. 1987, p. 57.

18. J. Randy Taraborrelli, "The Change That Has Made Oprah So Happy," *Redbook*, May 1997, p. 94.

19. Leslie Rubinstein, "Oprah! Thriving on Faith," *McCall's*, Aug. 1987, p. 140.

20. Broadcast and Cable magazine, Jan. 24, 2005, quoted in P. J. Bednarski, "All About Oprah Inc."

21. "Upfront Goes to Zip-A-Dee-Doo-Dah Lunch with Oprah," Chicago, Nov. 1985, p. 16.

22. Melina Gerosa, "What Makes Oprah Run," *Ladies' Home Journal*, Nov. 1994, p. 200.

23. Chris Anderson, "Meet Oprah Winfrey," *Good Housekeeping*, Aug. 1986, p. 52.

24. Oprah Winfrey, Commencement Address, Wellesley College, Wellesley, Massachusetts, May 30, 1997.

25. Julia Cameron, "Simply Oprah," *Cosmopolitan*, Feb. 1989, p. 215.

Serena Williams   Venus Williams

Venus and **Serena Williams** are sisters and world-champion tennis players. The Women's Tennis Association (WTA) currently ranks Serena as World No. 2 and Venus as World No. 3. Both were ranked World No. 1 multiple times in the past. Serena has won two Olympic gold medals, Venus three. Serena is the reigning Australian Open and Wimbledon singles champion, and has won twenty-three Grand Slam titles. Venus is the reigning Australian Open, Wimbledon, and US Open doubles champion, and has won nineteen Grand Slam titles. The sisters have competed against each other twenty-one times in professional women's tennis, with the running score 10–11 to Serena. Serena supports numerous charities, including the fight against breast cancer, for which she received Avon's Celebrity Role Model Award in 2003. Venus took on the issue of gender inequality in professional tennis, meeting in 2005 with officials from the French Open and Wimbledon to argue against their practice of awarding less prize money to female tennis players than to males. After their refusal to change the policy, Venus led a campaign, sponsored by WTA and UNESCO, to promote gender equality in sports. In 2007, both tournaments bowed to the pressure and agreed to award equal prize money to all competitors in all rounds. www.serenawilliams.com, www.venuswilliams.com

CHAPTER FORTY-TWO

10 Rules for Living, Loving, and Winning
Venus and Serena Williams

As we travel all around the world to play in tennis tournaments, people ask us certain questions no matter where we go: *How have we become so successful? How do we deal with all of the criticism we receive? And how do we stay so close to each other even though we compete on the tennis court?*

From what our parents taught us while we were growing up and from our experiences in the world of sports, we've developed values and ways of conducting ourselves that have allowed us to excel professionally and lead happy personal lives. We wanted to share these ideas in the hope that we can help others achieve their big dreams just as we have achieved ours. These Sister Rules are our code for living, loving, learning, and playing with the right crowd. Make these rules your own as you go for your goals!

1. Beware of dream stealers.
Sister Rule #1: I don't just daydream—I build a dream team. And I don't let others steal my vision.

2. Why school is cool.
Sister Rule #2: Want to get ahead? Book smarts get you life smarts.

3. Respect yourself.

Sister Rule #3: Trophies don't tell whether I'm a winner. I win by doing right by me.

4. Hang with an incredible crew.

Sister Rule #4: Friendship is like tennis—it's all about the back and forth.

5. Be true—do you.

Sister Rule #5: What others think of me is none of my business. My life is my business—period.

6. Don't rush a crush.

Sister Rule #6: Boyfriends and girlfriends come and go, but friendships last forever.

7. Love the skin you're in.

Sister Rule #7: Mirror, mirror, on the wall, beauty lives inside us all.

8. All about the money, honey.

Sister Rule #8: Bling-bling isn't everything. When it comes to cash, it's better to stash than flash.

9. Step back, setbacks!

Sister Rule #9: Challenges? Bring 'em on! I keep my eyes on the ball and my head in the game of life.

10. It's better to give.

Sister Rule #10: You don't have to be rich or famous to share your blessings.

J. K. Rowling, the pen name of Jo Murray, is the author of the seven-book *Harry Potter* series, the last four of which set records as the fastest-selling books in history. The final book, *Harry Potter and the Deathly Hallows,* sold eleven million copies on the first day of its release in the United Kingdom and United States. The series has been translated into sixty-five languages and turned into movies. The Harry Potter phenom took the author from "the dole" to multimillionaire status in five years. Rowling supports a range of causes from ending poverty and social injustice to multiple sclerosis research.

The Fringe Benefits of Failure, and the Importance of Imagination

J. K. Rowling

The following is the commencement speech J. K. Rowling gave at Harvard University in 2008.

Delivering a commencement address is a great responsibility; or so I thought until I cast my mind back to my own graduation. The commencement speaker that day was the distinguished British philosopher Baroness Mary Warnock. Reflecting on her speech has helped me enormously in writing this one, because it turns out that I can't remember a single word she said. This liberating discovery enables me to proceed without any fear that I might inadvertently influence you to abandon promising careers in business, law, or politics for the giddy delights of becoming a gay wizard.

You see? If all you remember in years to come is the "gay wizard" joke, I've still come out ahead of Baroness Mary Warnock. Achievable goals: the first step towards personal improvement.

Actually, I have wracked my mind and heart for what I ought to say to you today. I have asked myself what I wish I had known at my own graduation, and what important lessons I have learned in the twenty-one years that has expired between that day and this.

I have come up with two answers. On this wonderful day when we are gathered together to celebrate your academic success, I have decided to talk to you about the benefits of failure. And as you stand on the threshold of what is sometimes called "real life," I want to extol the crucial importance of imagination.

These might seem quixotic or paradoxical choices, but please bear with me.

Looking back at the twenty-one-year-old that I was at graduation is a slightly uncomfortable experience for the forty-two-year-old that she has become. Half my lifetime ago, I was striking an uneasy balance between the ambition I had for myself, and what those closest to me expected of me.

I was convinced that the only thing I wanted to do, ever, was to write novels. However, my parents, both of whom came from impoverished backgrounds and neither of whom had been to college, took the view that my overactive imagination was an amusing personal quirk that could never pay a mortgage, or secure a pension.

They had hoped that I would take a vocational degree; I wanted to study English literature. A compromise was reached that in retrospect satisfied nobody, and I went up to study modern languages. Hardly had my parents' car rounded the corner at the end of the road than I ditched German and scuttled off down the classics corridor.

I cannot remember telling my parents that I was studying classics; they might well have found out for the first time on graduation day. Of all subjects on this planet, I think they would have been hard put to name one less useful than Greek mythology when it came to securing the keys to an executive bathroom.

I would like to make it clear, in parentheses, that I do not blame my parents for their point of view. There is an expiry date on blaming your parents for steering you in the wrong direction; the moment you are old enough to take the wheel, responsibility lies with you. What is more, I cannot criticize my parents for hoping that I would never experience poverty. They had been poor themselves, and I have since been poor, and I quite agree with them that it is not an ennobling experience. Poverty entails fear and stress, and sometimes depression; it means a thousand petty humiliations and hardships. Climbing out of poverty by your own efforts, that is indeed something on which to pride yourself, but poverty itself is romanticized only by fools.

What I feared most for myself at your age was not poverty, but failure.

At your age, in spite of a distinct lack of motivation at university, where I had spent far too long in the coffee bar writing stories, and far too little time at lectures, I had a knack for passing examinations, and that, for years, had been the measure of success in my life and that of my peers.

I am not dull enough to suppose that because you are young, gifted, and well-educated, you have never known hardship or heartbreak. Talent and intelligence never yet inoculated anyone against the caprice of the Fates, and I do not for a moment suppose that everyone here has enjoyed an existence of unruffled privilege and contentment.

However, the fact that you are graduating from Harvard suggests that you are not very well acquainted with failure. You might be driven by a fear of failure quite as much as a desire for success. Indeed, your conception of failure might not be too far from the average person's idea of success, so high have you already flown academically.

Ultimately, we all have to decide for ourselves what constitutes failure, but the world is quite eager to give you a set of criteria if you let it. So I think it fair to say that by any conventional measure, a mere seven years after my graduation day, I had failed on an epic scale. An exceptionally short-lived marriage had imploded, and I was jobless, a lone parent, and as poor as it is possible to be in modern Britain, without being homeless. The fears my parents had had for me, and that I had had for myself, had both come to pass, and by every usual standard, I was the biggest failure I knew.

Now, I am not going to stand here and tell you that failure is fun. That period of my life was a dark one, and I had no idea that there was going to be what the press has since represented as a kind of fairy tale resolution. I had no idea how far the tunnel extended, and for a long time, any light at the end of it was a hope rather than a reality.

So why do I talk about the benefits of failure? Simply because failure meant a stripping away of the inessential. I stopped pretending to myself that I was anything other than what I was, and began to direct all my energy into finishing the only work that mattered to me. Had I really succeeded at anything else, I might never have found the determination to succeed in the one arena I believed I truly belonged. I was set free, because my greatest fear had already been realized, and I was still alive, and I still had a daughter whom I adored, and I had an old typewriter and a big idea. And so rock bottom became the solid foundation on which I rebuilt my life.

You might never fail on the scale I did, but some failure in life is inevitable. It is impossible to live without failing at something, unless you live so cautiously that you might as well not have lived at all—in which case, you fail by default.

Failure gave me an inner security that I had never attained by passing examinations. Failure taught me things about myself that I could have learned no other way. I discovered that I had a strong will, and more discipline than I had suspected; I also found out that I had friends whose value was truly above rubies.

The knowledge that you have emerged wiser and stronger from setbacks means that you are, ever after, secure in your ability to survive. You will never truly know yourself, or the strength of your relationships, until both have been tested by adversity. Such knowledge is a true gift, for all that it is painfully won, and it has been worth more to me than any qualification I ever earned.

Given a time machine or a Time Turner, I would tell my twenty-one-year-old self that personal happiness lies in knowing that life is not a checklist of acquisition or achievement. Your qualifications, your CV, are not your life, though you will meet many people of my age and older who confuse the two. Life is difficult, and complicated, and beyond anyone's total control, and the humility to know that will enable you to survive its vicissitudes.

You might think that I chose my second theme, the importance of imagination, because of the part it played in rebuilding my life, but that is not wholly so. Though I will defend the value of bedtime stories to my last gasp, I have learned to value imagination in a much broader sense. Imagination is not only the uniquely human capacity to envision that which is not, and therefore the fount of all invention and innovation. In its arguably most transformative and revelatory capacity, it is the power that enables us to empathize with humans whose experiences we have never shared.

One of the greatest formative experiences of my life preceded Harry Potter, though it informed much of what I subsequently wrote in those books. This revelation came in the form of one of my earliest day jobs. Though I was sloping off to write stories during my lunch hours, I paid the rent in my early twenties by working in the research department at Amnesty International's headquarters in London.

There in my little office I read hastily scribbled letters smuggled out of totalitarian regimes by men and women who were risking imprisonment to inform the outside world of what was happening to them. I saw photographs of those who had disappeared without trace, sent to Amnesty by their desperate families and friends. I read the testimony of torture victims and saw pictures of their injuries. I opened handwritten, eyewitness accounts of summary trials and executions, of kidnappings and rapes.

Many of my coworkers were ex–political prisoners, people who had been displaced from their homes, or fled into exile, because they had the temerity to think independently of their government. Visitors to our office included those who had come to give information, or to try and find out what had happened to those they had been forced to leave behind.

I shall never forget the African torture victim, a young man no older than I was at the time, who had become mentally ill after all he had endured in his homeland. He trembled uncontrollably as he spoke into a video camera about the brutality inflicted upon him. He was a foot taller than I was, and seemed as fragile as a child. I was given the job of escorting him to the Underground Station afterwards, and this man whose life had been shattered by cruelty took my hand with exquisite courtesy, and wished me future happiness.

And as long as I live I shall remember walking along an empty corridor and suddenly hearing, from behind a closed door, a scream of pain and horror such as I have never heard since. The door opened, and the researcher poked out her head and told me to run and make a hot drink for the young man sitting with her. She had just given him the news that in retaliation for his own outspokenness against his country's regime, his mother had been seized and executed.

Every day of my working week in my early twenties I was reminded how incredibly fortunate I was, to live in a country with a democratically elected government, where legal representation and a public trial were the rights of everyone.

Every day, I saw more evidence about the evils humankind will inflict on their fellow humans, to gain or maintain power. I began to have nightmares, literal nightmares, about some of the things I saw, heard, and read.

And yet I also learned more about human goodness at Amnesty International than I had ever known before.

Amnesty mobilizes thousands of people who have never been tortured or imprisoned for their beliefs to act on behalf of those who have. The power of human empathy, leading to collective action, saves lives, and frees prisoners. Ordinary people, whose personal well-being and security are assured, join together in huge numbers to save people they do not know, and will never meet. My small participation in that process was one of the most humbling and inspiring experiences of my life.

Unlike any other creature on this planet, humans can learn and understand, without having experienced. They can think themselves into other people's minds, imagine themselves into other people's places.

Of course, this is a power, like my brand of fictional magic, that is morally neutral. One might use such an ability to manipulate, or control, just as much as to understand or sympathize.

And many prefer not to exercise their imaginations at all. They choose to remain comfortably within the bounds of their own experience, never troubling to wonder how it would feel to have been born other than they are. They can refuse to hear screams or to peer inside cages; they can close their minds and hearts to any suffering that does not touch them personally; they can refuse to know.

I might be tempted to envy people who can live that way, except that I do not think they have any fewer nightmares than I do. Choosing to live in narrow spaces can lead to a form of mental agoraphobia, and that brings its own terrors. I think the willfully unimaginative see more monsters. They are often more afraid.

What is more, those who choose not to empathize may enable real monsters. For without ever committing an act of outright evil ourselves, we collude with it, through our own apathy.

One of the many things I learned at the end of that Classics corridor down which I ventured at the age of eighteen, in search of something I could not then define, was this, written by the Greek author Plutarch: *What we achieve inwardly will change outer reality.*

That is an astonishing statement and yet proven a thousand times every day of our lives. It expresses, in part, our inescapable connection with the outside world, the fact that we touch other people's lives simply by existing.

But how much more are you, Harvard graduates of 2008, likely to touch other people's lives? Your intelligence, your capacity for hard work, the education you have earned and received, give you unique status, and unique responsibilities. Even your nationality sets you apart. The great majority of you belong to the world's only remaining superpower. The way you vote, the way you live, the way you protest, the pressure you bring to bear on your government, has an impact way beyond your borders. That is your privilege, and your burden.

If you choose to use your status and influence to raise your voice on behalf of those who have no voice; if you choose to identify not only with the powerful, but with the powerless; if you retain the ability to imagine yourself into the lives of those who do not have your advantages, then it will not only be your proud families who celebrate your existence, but thousands and millions of people whose reality you have helped transform for the better. We do not need magic to change the world, we carry all the power we need inside ourselves already: we have the power to imagine better.

I am nearly finished. I have one last hope for you, which is something that I already had at twenty-one. The friends with whom I sat on graduation day have been my friends for life. They are my children's godparents, the people to whom I've been able to turn in times of trouble, friends who have been kind enough not to sue me when I've used their names for Death Eaters. At our graduation we were bound by enormous affection, by our shared experience of a time that could never come again, and, of course, by the knowledge that we held certain photographic evidence that would be exceptionally valuable if any of us ran for prime minister.

So today, I can wish you nothing better than similar friendships. And tomorrow, I hope that even if you remember not a single word of mine, you remember those of Seneca, another of those old Romans I met when I fled down the Classics corridor, in retreat from career ladders, in search of ancient wisdom:

As is a tale, so is life: not how long it is, but how good it is, is what matters.

I wish you all very good lives.

Thank you very much.